SCIENCE PROBLEM-SOLVING CURRICULUM LIBRARY

Hands-On PHYSICAL SCIENCE ACTIVITIES

For Grades K–8

Marvin N. Tolman

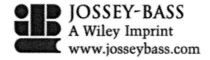

JOSSEY-BASS
A Wiley Imprint
www.josseybass.com

Published by Jossey-Bass
A Wiley Imprint
989 Market Street, San Francisco, CA 94103-1741   www.josseybass.com

Computer illustrations by Michelle Sullivan and David Bentley.

Jossey-Bass books and products are available through most bookstores. To contact Jossey-Bass directly call our Customer Care Department within the U.S. at (800) 956-7739, outside the U.S. at (317) 572-3986 or fax (317) 572-4002.

Jossey-Bass also publishes its books in a variety of electronic formats. Some content that appears in print may not be available in electronic books.

Library of Congress Cataloging-in-Publication Data

Tolman, Marvin N.
    Hands-on physical science activities : for grades K–8 /
Marvin N. Tolman.
        p.   cm.—(Science problem-solving curriculum library)
    Includes bibliographical references
    ISBN 0-13-230178-4
    1. Physics—Study and teaching (Elementary)   2. Physics—
Study and teaching (Secondary) 3. Physics—Study and teaching
—Activity programs. I. Title. II. Series.
QC30.T57   1995   95-34586
372.3'5—dc20

FIRST EDITION
        10 9 8 7 6 5 4 3 2

ABOUT THE AUTHOR

Dr. Marvin N. Tolman

Trained as an educator at Utah State University, Marv Tolman began his career as a teaching principal in rural southeastern Utah. The next eleven years were spent teaching grades one through six in schools of San Juan and Utah Counties, and earning graduate degrees.

Currently professor of elementary education, Dr. Tolman has been teaching graduate and undergraduate courses at Brigham Young University since 1975. Subject areas of his courses include math methods, science methods, and, formerly, computer literacy for teachers. He has served as a consultant to school districts, taught workshops in many parts of the United States, and published numerous articles in professional journals. Dr. Tolman is one of two authors of *What Research Says to the Teacher: The Computer and Education* (co-author Dr. Ruel Allred), published in 1984 by the National Education Association, and is a co-author of *Computers in Education*, published by Allyn & Bacon, 1996 (3rd edition). Dr. Tolman also wrote *Discovering Elementary Science: Method, Content, and Problem-Solving Activities* (co-author Dr. Garry R. Hardy), 1995, Allyn & Bacon. With Dr. James O. Morton, Dr. Tolman wrote the three-book series of elementary science activities called the *Science Curriculum Activities Library*, 1986, Parker Publishing Company.

Dr. Tolman now lives with his wife Judy in Spanish Fork, Utah, where they have reared five children.

ABOUT THE LIBRARY

The *Science Problem-Solving Curriculum Library* evolved from an earlier series by the same author, with Dr. James O. Morton as co-author: *The Science Curriculum Activities Library*. The majority of the activities herein were also in the earlier publication, and the successful activity format has been retained. The activities have been updated and in many cases clarified. Illustrations have been upgraded, and several new activities have been added. A significant feature of this series is the addition of a section called "For Problem Solvers" to most of the activities. This section provides ideas for further investigation and related activities for students who are motivated to extend their study beyond the activity as outlined in the procedural steps. It is hoped that most students will pursue at least some of these extensions and benefit from them.

The *Science Problem-Solving Curriculum Library* provides teachers with hundreds of science activities that give students hands-on experience related to many science topics. To be used in conjunction with whatever texts and references you have, the *Library* includes three books, each providing activities that explore a different field. The books are individually titled:

- *Hands-On Life Science Activities for Grades K–8*
- *Hands-On Physical Science Activities for Grades K–8*
- *Hands-On Earth Science Activities for Grades K–8*

More than ever before, children of today grow up in a world impacted by science and technology. A basic understanding of nature and an appreciation for the world around them are gifts too valuable to deny these precious young people who will be the problem solvers of tomorrow. In addition, a strong science program with a discovery/inquiry approach can enrich the development of mathematics, reading, social studies, and other areas of the curriculum. The activities in the *Library* develop these skills. Most activities call for thoughtful responses, with questions that encourage analyzing, synthesizing, and inferring instead of simply answering yes or no.

Development of thinking and reasoning skills, in addition to learning basic content information, are the main goals of the activities outlined herein. Learning how to learn, and how to apply the various tools of learning, are more useful in a person's life than is the acquisition of large numbers of scientific facts. Students are encouraged to explore, invent, and create as they develop skills with the processes of science. The learning of scientific facts is a byproduct of this effort, and increased insight and retention associated with facts learned are virtually assured.

HOW TO USE THIS BOOK

This book consists of over 180 easy-to-use, hands-on activities in the following areas of physical science:

- Nature of Matter
- Energy
- Light
- Sound
- Simple Machines
- Magnetism
- Static Electricity
- Current Electricity

Teacher Qualifications

Two important qualities of the elementary teacher as a scientist are (1) commitment to helping students acquire learning skills and (2) recognition of the value of science and its implications in the life and learning of the child.

You do not need to be a scientist to conduct an effective and exciting science program at the elementary level. Interest, creativity, enthusiasm, and willingness to get involved and try something new are the qualifications the teacher of elementary science needs most. If you haven't yet really tried teaching hands-on science, you will find it to be a lot like eating peanuts—you can't eat just one. Try it. The excitement and enthusiasm you see in your students will bring you back to it again and again.

Early Grades

Many of these concrete activities are easily adaptable for children in the early grades. Although the activity instructions ("Procedures") are written for the student who can read and follow the steps, that does not preclude teachers of the lower grades from using the activities with their children. With verbal instructions and slight modifications, many of these activities can be used with kindergarten, first-grade, and second-grade students. In some activities, steps that involve procedures that go beyond the level of the child can simply be omitted and yet offer the child an experience that plants the seed for a concept that will germinate and grow later on. For example, young children can experience the concept "Machines make work easier" by feeling it and seeing it happen. These children can be encouraged to report in terms of "easier" and "harder" instead of by mathematical comparisons.

Teachers of the early grades will probably choose to bypass many of the "For Problem Solvers" sections. That's okay. The "For Problem Solvers" sections are provided for those who are especially motivated and want to go beyond. Use the basic activities for which procedural steps are written and enjoy worthwhile learning experiences together with your young students.

Capitalize on Interest

These materials are both nongraded and nonsequential. Areas of greatest interest and need can be emphasized. As you gain experience with using the activities, your skill in guiding students toward appropriate discoveries and insights will increase.

Organizing for an Activity-centered Approach

Current trends encourage teachers to use an activity-based program, supplemented by the use of textbooks and many other reference materials. The activities herein encourage hands-on discovery, which enhances the development of valuable learning skills through direct experience.

One of the advantages of this approach is the elimination of the need for all students to have the same book at the same time, freeing a substantial portion of the textbook money for purchasing a variety of materials and references, including other textbooks, trade books, audio and video tapes, videodiscs, models, and other visuals. References should be acquired that lend themselves developmentally to a variety of approaches, subject matter emphases, and levels of reading difficulty.

Grabbers

The sequence of activities within the sections of this book is flexible and may be adjusted according to interest, availability of materials, time of year, or other factors. Most of the activities in each section can be used independently as *grabbers*, to capture student interest. Used this way, they can help to achieve several specific objectives:

- To assist in identifying student interests and selecting topics for study.

- To provide a wide variety of interesting and exciting hands-on activities from many areas of science. As students investigate activities that are of particular interest, they will likely be motivated to try additional related activities in the same section of the book.

- To introduce teachers and students to the discovery/inquiry approach.
- To be used for those occasions when only a short period of time is available and a high-interest independent activity is needed.

Unique Features

The following points should be kept in mind while using this book:

1. Most of these activities can be used with several grade levels, with little adaptation.

2. The student is the central figure when using the discovery/inquiry approach to hands-on learning.

3. The main goals are problem solving and the development of critical-thinking skills. The learning of content is a spin-off, but it is possibly learned with greater insight and meaning than if it were the main objective.

4. It attempts to prepare teachers for inquiry-based instruction and sharpen their guidance and questioning techniques.

5. Most materials needed for the activities are readily available in the school or at home.

6. Activities are intended to be open and flexible and to encourage the extension of skills through the use of as many outside resources as possible: (a) The use of parents, aides, and resource people of all kinds is recommended throughout; (b) the library, media center, and other school resources, as well as classroom reading centers related to the areas of study are essential in the effective teaching and learning of science; and (c) educational television and videos can greatly enrich the science program.

7. With the exception of the activities labeled "teacher demonstration" or "whole-class activity," students are encouraged to work individually, in pairs, or in small groups. In most cases the teacher gathers and organizes the materials, arranges the learning setting, and serves as a resource person. In many instances, the materials listed and the procedural steps are all students will need in order to perform the activities.

8. Information is given in "To the Teacher" at the beginning of each section and in "Teacher Information" at the end of each activity to help you develop your content background and your questioning and guidance skills, in cases where such help is needed. For teachers who desire additional background information on elementary science topics, the following book written by the same author is recommended: *Discovering Elementary Science: Method, Content, and Problem-Solving Activities* (co-author Dr. Garry R. Hardy), 1995, Allyn & Bacon.

9. Full-page activity sheets are offered when needed throughout the book. These sheets can easily be reproduced and kept on hand for student use.

At the end of the book are a bibliography, sources of free and inexpensive materials, and a list of science supply houses, as well as sources for video tapes, videodiscs, and computer software. This information can save you time in locating additional resources and materials.

Format of Activities

Each activity in this book includes the following information:

- *Activity Number*: Activities are numbered sequentially within each section for easy reference. Each activity has a two-part number to identify the section and the sequence of the activity within the section.

- *Activity Title*: The title of each activity is in the form of a question that can be answered by completing the activity. Each question requires more than a simple yes or no answer.

- *Special Instructions*: Some activities are intended to be used as teacher demonstrations or whole-group activities, or they require close supervision for safety reasons, so these special instructions are noted.

- *Take home and do with family and friends.* Many activities could be used by the student at home, providing enjoyment and learning for others in the family. Such experiences can work wonders in the life of the child, as he or she teaches others what has been learned at school. The result is often a greater depth of learning on the part of the child, as well as a boost to the self-esteem and self-confidence. An activity is marked as "Take home and do with family and friends" if it meets all of the following criteria:

  (1) It uses only materials that are common around the home.

  (2) It has a high chance of arousing interest on the part of the child.

  (3) It is safe for a child to do independently, i. e., it uses no flame, hot plate, or very hot water.

  Of course, other activities could be used at the discretion of parents.

- *Materials*: Each activity lists the materials needed. The materials are easily acquired. In some cases special instructions or sources are suggested.

- *Procedure*: The procedural steps are written to the student, in easy-to-understand language.

- *For Problem Solvers:* Most activities include this section, which suggest additional investigations or activities for students who are motivated to extend their study beyond the activity specified in the procedural steps.

- *Teacher Information*: Suggested teaching tips and background information are given. This information supplements that provided in "To the Teacher" at the beginning of each section.

Use of Metric Measures

Most linear measures used are given in metric units followed by units in the English system in parentheses. This is done to encourage use of the metric system. Other measures, such as capacity, are given in standard units.

Grade Level

The activities in this book are intended to be nongraded. Many activities in each section can be easily adapted for use with young children, while other activities provide challenge for the more talented in the intermediate grades.

Final Note

Discovering the excitement of science and developing new techniques for critical thinking and problem solving should be the major goals of elementary science. The discovery/inquiry approach also must emphasize verbal responses and discussion. *It is important that students experience many hands-on activities* in their learning of science *and that they talk about what they do*. Each child should have many opportunities to describe observations and to explain what they do and why. With the exception of recording observations, these activities usually do not require extensive writing, but that, too, is a skill that can be enriched through interest and involvement in science.

There is an ancient Chinese saying: "A journey of a thousand miles begins with a single step." May the ideas and activities in this book help to provide that first step.

Marvin N. Tolman

ACKNOWLEDGMENTS

Mentioning the names of all individuals who contributed to the *Science Problem-Solving Curriculum Library* would require an additional volume. The author is greatly indebted to the following:

- Teachers and students of all levels.

- School districts throughout the United States who cooperated by supporting and evaluating ideas and methods used in this book.

- Dr. James O. Morton, my mentor and my dear friend.

- Dr. Garry R. Hardy, my teaching partner for the past many years, for his constant encouragement and creative ideas.

- Finally, my angel Judy, for without her love, support, encouragement, patience, and acceptance, these books could never have been completed.

CONTENTS

Section 1
NATURE OF MATTER 1

Section 2
ENERGY 43

Section 3
LIGHT 83

Section 4
SOUND 139

Section 5
SIMPLE MACHINES 185

Section 6
MAGNETISM 245

Section 7
STATIC ELECTRICITY 271

Section 8
CURRENT ELECTRICITY 291

LISTING OF ACTIVITIES BY TOPIC

NATURE OF MATTER

Topic	Activities						
Acids and Bases	1.24						
Atoms and Molecules	1.13	1.14	1.15	1.16			
Buoyancy	1.5	1.6					
Crystals	1.23						
Elasticity	1.21						
Elements, Compounds	1.11						
Evaporation and Condensation	1.2	1.3					
Mixtures and Solutions	1.8	1.9	1.11	1.13	1.14		
Physical and Chemical Changes	1.1	1.8	1.10	1.11	1.12	1.20	
Polyethylene	1.22						
Solids, Liquids, and Gases	1.1	1.2	1.3	1.5	1.6	1.7	1.10
	1.18	1.19	1.20	2.10	2.11	2.12	2.17
Surface Tension	1.4						
Viscosity	1.17						

ENERGY

Topic	Activities						
Center of Gravity	2.19	2.20					
Centrifugal Force	2.22						
Conservation of Energy	2.23						
Gravity	2.16	2.17	2.19	2.20			
Heat	2.7 2.18	2.8	2.9	2.10	2.11	2.12	2.13
Inertia	2.21	2.22					
Kinetic Energy and Potential Energy	2.1	2.4	2.5	2.6			
Magnetism	2.15						
Solar Energy	2.7	2.8					
Sound	2.14						
Sources of Energy (tracing them)	2.4	2.5	2.6				
Work	2.2	2.3	2.15				

LIGHT

Topic	Activities						
Color	3.5	3.25	3.26	3.27	3.28	3.29	3.30
Lenses	3.12	3.13	3.14	3.15	3.16		
Reflection	3.17 3.24	3.18	3.19	3.20	3.21	3.22	3.23
Refraction	3.6 3.29	3.7 3.30	3.8	3.9	3.10	3.11	3.14
Shadows	3.1	3.2	3.3				
Sources	3.18						
Travels in Straight Lines	3.4	3.12					

SOUND

Topic	Activities						
Amplifying Sound	4.7	4.24	4.25	4.26	4.27		
Controlling Sound	4.8	4.22	4.26	4.27			
How Sound Travels	4.4	4.14	4.16	4.17	4.18	4.19	4.20
	4.23	4.27					
Human Voice	4.6	4.15					
Music							
Stringed Instruments	4.4	4.5	4.29				
Wind Instruments	4.11	4.12	4.13	4.29			
Percussion Instruments	4.9	4.10	4.24	4.29			
Recognition of Sounds	4.2	4.3	4.27				
Speed of Sound	4.21						
What Sound Is	4.1	4.4	4.5	4.6	4.7	4.14	4.24
	4.25						

MACHINES

Topic	Activities			
Friction	5.1	5.2	5.3	5.4
Identifying Machines	5.24			
Mechanical Advantage	5.8	5.9		
Simple Machines				
Block and Tackle	5.19			
Inclined Plane	5.20			
First-Class Lever	5.5	5.6	5.7	5.8
Second-Class Lever	5.10	5.11		
Third-Class Lever	5.12	5.13		
Pulley	5.16	5.17	5.18	5.19
Screw	5.22			
Wedge	5.21			
Wheel-and-Axle	5.14	5.15	5.23	

MAGNETISM

Topic	Activities					
Attraction and Repulsion	6.9	6.10	6.13			
Compasses	6.10	6.11	6.12	6.13		
Lodestones	6.1	6.4				
Magnetic Fields	6.13	6.15	6.16	6.17		
Magnetic and Nonmagnetic Materials	6.5	6.6				
Making Magnets	6.14					
What Magnets Are Like	6.2	6.3	6.4	6.7	6.8	6.13

STATIC ELECTRICITY

Topic	Activities						
Attraction and Repulsion	7.1	7.2	7.3	7.10	7.11		
Electrostatic Charge	7.2	7.4	7.5	7.6	7.7	7.8	7.9
	7.11	7.13					
Induction	7.1	7.4	7.5	7.6	7.7	7.8	7.9
	7.13						
Lightning	7.12						

CURRENT ELECTRICITY

Topic	Activities					
Batteries	8.17	8.18	8.19			
Circuit—What It Is	8.2					
Complete and Incomplete Circuits	8.3	8.5				
Conductors and Insulators	8.1					
Electromagnets	8.11	8.12	8.13	8.14	8.15	8.22
Relationship Between Magnetism and Electricity	8.9	8.10				
Electricity Can Produce Magnetism	8.9	8.10	8.16			
Magnetism Can Produce Electricity	8.20					
Resistance	8.8					
Series and Parallel Circuits	8.6	8.7				
Short Circuits	8.4					
Sunlight to Electricity	8.21					

NATURE OF MATTER

TO THE TEACHER

Everything around us is matter of one form or another. The air we breathe, the food we eat, the books we read, our bodies—all of these things are made of various types of chemicals and substances. The topic of this section is very broad and is related to many other science topics. No attempt has been made to be comprehensive in coverage, but only to expose students to a few of the basic properties and relationships of matter. Activities have been selected that involve materials and supplies common to the school or the home in preference to those requiring sophisticated equipment.

It is recommended that after a study of the nature of matter, you seek opportunities to apply the general concepts learned while studying other science topics. For example, in a study of weather, air, or water, the principles of evaporation and condensation are essential. The effect of temperature change on expansion and contraction is another idea common to weather, air, water, and the topic of this section. In a study of plants, animals, or the human body, the nature of matter has many applications.

Regarding the Early Grades

With verbal instructions and slight modifications, many of these activities can be used with kindergarten, first-grade, and second-grade students. With some activities, steps that involve procedures that go beyond the level of the child can simply be omitted and yet offer the child an experience that plants the seed for a concept that will germinate and grow later on.

Teachers of the early grades will probably choose to bypass many of the "For Problem Solvers" sections. That's okay. These sections are provided for those who are especially motivated and want to go beyond the investigation provided by the activity outlined. Use the outlined activities and enjoy worthwhile learning experiences together with your young students. Also consider, however, that many of the "For Problem Solvers" sections can be used appropriately with young children as group activities or as demonstrations, still giving students the advantage of an exposure to the experience, and laying groundwork for connections that will be made later on.

Activity 1.1
WHAT HAPPENS TO WATER WHEN YOU ADD SALT?

Materials Needed

- Hard-boiled egg
- Raw egg
- Large cup
- Salt
- Measuring spoon

Procedure

1. One of these eggs is raw and the other hard-boiled. Can you tell which is the hard-boiled egg?

2. Put both eggs in the cup and fill the cup with water.

3. Add salt to the cup, a tablespoon at a time, stirring until the salt dissolves, until something happens to the eggs.

4. What happened?

5. Why do you think salt makes this difference? Share your ideas with other students, and learn from one another.

For Problem Solvers: Did the two eggs respond to the salt water at the same time, or did one of them require more salt than the other? If they were different, which one responded first? Do some research and find out why.

Try spinning a raw egg and a boiled egg. Do they spin equally well? If not, which one spins best, and why?

Teacher Information

When the eggs are put in the untreated water, they will both sink to the bottom of the glass. As salt is added to the water, the eggs will rise to the top. This is because salt increases the density of the water. The eggs are more dense than is tap water, but less dense than salt water.

Floating an egg in brine solution is the method some people use to tell when the brine is just right for pickling.

It is hoped that your problem solvers noticed that the raw egg rises before the boiled egg does. For these students the activity shows not only that salt water is more dense, and therefore more buoyant, but that boiled eggs are more dense than raw eggs are. The challenge for these young researchers is to find out why. Hard-boiled eggs also spin better than raw ones.

Have students spin a raw egg, stop it, and let it go, and it will begin to spin again. Because of inertia, the inside of the egg continues to move after the outside of the egg stops. Sometimes you can hear or feel the inside of a raw egg if you shake it. The boiled egg is solid, so the spinning action isn't affected by movement of materials inside the egg.

INTEGRATING: Math, reading, language arts

SKILLS: Observing, inferring, measuring, communicating, comparing and contrasting, researching

Activity 1.2
HOW DRY CAN YOU WRING A WET SPONGE?

 Take home and do with family and friends.

Materials Needed

- Meter stick (or yardstick)
- Sponge
- Paper and pencil
- String
- Water

Procedure

1. Wet the sponge, then wring all the water you can out of it.

2. Tie the sponge to one end of the meter stick.

3. Tie a string near the middle of the meter stick, then suspend it by tying it to something overhead. Slide the string on the meter stick to cause it to hang level as in Figure 1.2-1.

Figure 1.2-1

Balanced Meter Stick

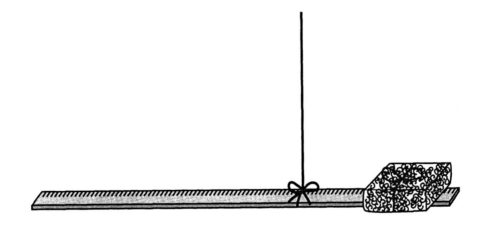

4. Record the time and draw a picture of the setup as it appeared when you prepared it.

5. Every 15 minutes for two hours, record the time and draw a picture of the setup.

6. What happened to the meter stick during the two hours? Explain why you think this happened. How can you find out if you were right?

For Problem Solvers: How much water is in a sponge after you wring it out as dry as you can? Can you measure it? Clue: How much does the sponge weigh?

After you figure that out, find out how much water is in your bath towel after you dry yourself following a shower. If you live in a humid area, find out if there is more water in a "dry" towel within a few hours after the towel comes out of the dryer than there was right after the towel was dried. Clue: Think about the activities you did with the sponge.

Teacher Information

The sponge cannot be wrung completely dry. As it sits for the two-hour period, much if not all of the remaining moisture will evaporate. As the water evaporates, the sponge becomes lighter and the system will no longer be balanced. The process of drawing the position of the setup several times will make students aware of the change as it is taking place. Students will probably want to feel the sponge. This should be avoided until the end of the investigation because of the risk of sliding the string on the stick and nullifying the results.

Students who do the "For Problem Solvers" section will need access to a gram balance or other sensitive weighing device, in order to determine the amount of water that is in the wrung-out sponge. With the bath towel activity, they will probably be able to detect a before/after difference with their bathroom scales at home. To get an accurate measurement they will need greater precision—perhaps back to the gram balance. They might be amazed to find out how much water is on their body when they get out of the shower or bathtub. To measure the water absorbed from the air by a towel, they will again need the gram balance.

INTEGRATING: Math

SKILLS: Observing, comparing and contrasting, measuring, using space-time relationships

Activity 1.3
WHAT IS CONDENSATION?

(Teacher-supervised activity)

Materials Needed

- Saucepan
- Water
- Pie tin (preferably cold)
- Hot plate

Procedure

1. Put about 1 cm (1/2 in.) of water in the saucepan.
2. Heat the water until it boils.
3. Hold the pie tin over the boiling water.
4. Observe the pie tin carefully. What do you see forming on the bottom of the pie tin? Explain why you think this happens.

For Problem Solvers: Have you noticed that your bathroom mirror is clean and shiny before you get in the shower or bathtub, but that it gets foggy as the hot water runs? Where does the water come from that gets on the mirror? Try to explain how it happens.

Notice the outside of the windows of cars and houses on a cool summer morning. Often you will find moisture on them. Where did the moisture come from? Investigate and find out how this happened. If you live in a cold climate, you will sometimes find frost on the windows. Where does it come from?

Teacher Information

As water is heated, the rate of evaporation increases. The pie tin held over the escaping water vapor cools the vapor and causes it to condense into liquid form, as shown by the drops of water forming on the bottom. This process will be speeded up if the pie tin is cooled first.

Similar evidence of condensation can be observed by placing a pitcher (or other container) of ice water out on a table. Water vapor in the air is cooled by the pitcher, and drops of water form on its surface.

SKILLS: Observing, inferring

Activity 1.4
WHAT IS THE SHAPE OF A DROP OF WATER?

 Take home and do with family and friends.

Materials Needed

- Waxed paper
- Water
- Eye dropper
- Pencil

Procedure

1. Draw some water into the dropper.

2. Put several drops on the waxed paper, keeping each separate from the others. Hold the dropper about 1 cm (1/2 in.) above the waxed paper as you squeeze lightly on the bulb.

3. Examine the drops of water. What is their shape? How do they compare in size?

4. Put the point of your pencil into a drop of water, observing carefully to see how the water responds. What did the drop of water do at the surface? Do the water molecules seem to be more attracted to the pencil lead or to each other?

5. Push one of the drops around with your pencil point, observing its behavior.

6. Push two drops together—then three or four. What did they do as they came near each other?

7. What can you say about the attraction of water molecules for each other? For the pencil lead? For the waxed paper?

8. If you could put a drop of water out in space where there is no gravity, what do you think it would look like? What shape would it have?

For Problem Solvers: Place a drop of water on various surfaces and examine each drop with a hand lens. Try it on a sheet of plastic, a sheet of paper, and aluminum foil. Try it on a paper towel. What is the shape of the drop of water? What differences do you see?

Place a drop of water on a penny. Now what is its shape? How many more drops do you think you could put on the penny? Write your estimate, then try it and test your estimate.

Teacher Information

Water molecules attract one another. The attraction of like molecules for one another is called *cohesion*. Within the liquid the force of this attraction is balanced, as each molecule is attracted by other molecules all the way around. The molecules on the surface are pulled downward and sideways but not up. This creates a skinlike effect called *surface tension*. The roundness of the drops on the waxed paper is an indication of surface tension. When several drops are put together they flatten out more, because of the increased effect of gravity.

Because of surface tension, a drop of water in the absence of gravity would take on the shape of a perfect sphere. However, a drop of water out in space would evaporate almost instantly.

The surface tension of water forms a bond strong enough to support the weight of a razor blade or paper clip laid carefully on the water. When detergent is added to the water, the surface tension is broken and the floating object will sink.

Many other substances have surface tension. It has been suggested that better ball bearings could be formed in space than in factories on earth because a drop of molten steel would naturally form a perfect sphere.

SKILLS: Observing, inferring, predicting, communicating

Activity 1.5
HOW DOES A HYDROMETER WORK?

 Take home and do with family and friends.

Materials Needed

- Lipstick tube cap (or small test tube)
- Several small nails (or screws)
- Tape (or gummed label)
- Plastic tumbler
- Water
- Salt
- Variety of liquids
- Marker
- Paper and pencil

Procedure

1. Fill the tumbler about two-thirds full of water.
2. Place 8 or 10 weights (small nails or screws) in the lipstick cap.
3. Put the gummed label or a piece of tape lengthwise on the lipstick cap.
4. Place the lipstick cap, open end up, in the glass of water. Add or remove weights until the cap floats vertically with the water level about halfway up the cap.

Figure 1.5-1

Hydrometer Floating Vertically in Water

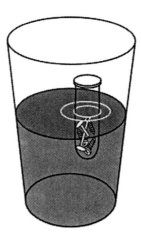

5. Mark the water level on the cap.

6. Your cap can now be used as a hydrometer. Hydrometers are used for measuring density of liquids, comparing them with the density of water. If the density of the liquid is greater than that of water, the cap will float higher than it floats in water. If the density of the liquid is less than that of water, the cap will sink deeper.

7. Dissolve about 1/4 cup of salt in your glass of water. Without changing the number of weights in the cap, put it in the salt water. Does your hydrometer float deeper than it did in plain water or does it float higher? What does this tell you about the density of salt water?

8. Test other liquids, such as milk, vinegar, and rubbing alcohol.

9. As you test various liquids, make a list of those you think have a greater density than water and those that have a lesser density.

For Problem Solvers: Get several plastic tumblers and fill them about one-half full, each with a different liquid, such as water, salt water, cooking oil, and rubbing alcohol. Line up the containers in order of least dense to most dense, according to your prediction. Use your hydrometer to compare the liquids, then arrange the liquids in order, with the liquid of least density on the left and the liquid of greatest density on the right. Did you predict them correctly?

Gather a variety of small objects that are made of plastic, wood, metal, etc. Place these items in the liquids, one at a time. Try to find at least one item that will float on each liquid but not on the next liquid to the left.

Teacher Information

Any object that floats displaces an amount of liquid equal to its own weight (Archimedes' principle). If the specific gravity (density) of the liquid is greater, the object floats higher, as it has to displace less liquid to equal its own weight. If the hydrometer floats deeper, it is in a liquid of lower density.

Hydrometers are used to test such liquids as antifreeze and battery acid, following the Archimedes' principle.

SKILLS: Observing, inferring, classifying, measuring, predicting, communicating, comparing and contrasting

Activity 1.6
HOW CAN THE DEPTH OF A BATHYSCAPH BE CONTROLLED?

Materials Needed

- Deep pan (or bucket) of water
- Small glass jar with tight-fitting lid
- Latex cement (such as Shoe Goo)
- Plastic tubing

Procedure

1. Make two holes in the lid. One should be just large enough to insert the tube through it and the other can be much smaller.

2. Insert one end of the tubing through the larger hole in the lid and put latex cement on the lid around the tubing to seal it from leakage of water or air. Allow the cement at least an hour to dry.

3. Fill the jar about half full of water and put the lid on tight.

4. Place the jar in the bucket of water.

5. Hold the lid-end of the jar under water. Put the end of the tube in your mouth and adjust the amount of water in the jar by blowing or drawing on the end of the tube until the jar floats just beneath the surface of the water.

6. Now draw on the tube very slightly to allow a little more water to enter the jar. What happened to the jar?

7. Blow and draw on the tube to change the amount of water in the jar. What happens to the jar?

8. How could this idea be used in a bathyscaph designed to study the ocean at different depths?

Teacher Information

A vessel in water can be caused to float at different depths by altering the density of the vessel. Density can be increased by displacing a chamber of air (or a portion of it) with water, or decreased by displacing the water with air. This is one way the depth of an underwater vessel can be adjusted.

SKILLS: Observing, inferring, predicting, communicating, identifying and controlling variables

Activity 1.7
WHAT ARE SOLIDS, LIQUIDS, AND GASES?

Materials Needed

- Charcoal briquette or small piece of coal
- Hammer
- Block of wood
- Ice cube
- Dish
- Paper towel
- Paper and pencil

Procedure

1. Put the ice cube in the dish and place the block of wood and the dish on a table.

2. Place the paper towel over the block of wood and the charcoal on the paper towel. The purpose of the wood is to provide a pounding block.

Figure 1.7-1

Dish with Ice, Wood, Paper Towel, and Briquette

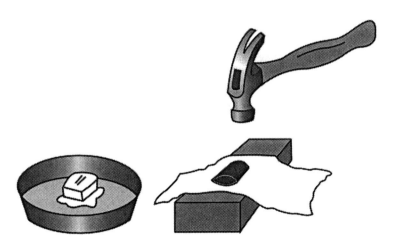

3. Examine and describe the charcoal and the ice cube. How are they alike? How are they different? Tell whether you think each is a solid, liquid, or gas.

4. Crush the piece of charcoal with the hammer. Be sure it is on the paper towel and the wood block when you do. Pound lightly with the hammer so the pieces don't scatter.

13

For additional safety, you can put the briquette in a plastic bag (such as a sandwich bag) before pounding.

5. Examine the charcoal again. In what ways is it the same as it was before? How is it different? Is it a solid, liquid, or gas?

6. Let the ice cube remain in the dish. Examine and describe it after a few minutes, after an hour, and after a day. Each time, decide whether it is a solid, a liquid, or a gas.

7. After the last observation, again compare the charcoal with the ice cube. How did they respond differently when they were left undisturbed? Why do you think this happened?

8. Make a list of solids, a list of liquids, and a list of gases.

For Problem Solvers: If ice cubes are placed in room-temperature conditions, they will become liquid before evaporating as a gas. Sometimes, however, ice cubes slowly evaporate as they stand in the ice tray, without even being removed from the freezer. Meat will also eventually dehydrate if left too long in the freezer. See if you can identify any substance that naturally changes from solid to gas, at room temperature, without becoming a liquid.

Do some research and find out how many substances you can identify that exist in nature in all three states—solid, liquid, and gas. How many more can you find that exist in nature as both a solid and a liquid?

Teacher Information

All matter is either solid, liquid, or gas. Charcoal remains a solid even when powdered. Water has the unusual property of being easily changed to any of the three states. The solid and liquid states are easily observed. Point out that when water becomes a gas it is invisible. In many substances, including wood and charcoal, certain elements combine with oxygen, when burned, and produce a gaseous substance, except for a small amount of ash left behind in solid form. As gases form during burning, visible solid and liquid particles are often suspended in the gases. We call this smoke.

Those who choose to accept the "For Problem Solvers" challenge will truly be challenged. Moth balls change from solid to gas at room temperature without becoming liquid. Perhaps these little sharpies will find other substances as well. The only common material that exists in nature in all three states is water.

SKILLS: Observing, predicting, comparing and contrasting, using space-time relationships

Activity 1.8
HOW CAN YOU GET SALT OUT OF PEPPER?

 Take home and do with family and friends.

Materials Needed

- Plastic bag
- 1/2 cup salt
- 1 teaspoon pepper

Procedure

1. Mix the salt and the pepper together in the bag.
2. Now your challenge is to get the pepper out of the salt. How might you do it?
3. Test your ideas.

Teacher Information

This activity is intended to help children learn to conduct and evaluate problem-solving procedures. There is no "right" answer but some procedures may be more effective or efficient than others. For example, picking the pepper out is slow and tedious. Dissolving the salt in water and straining the solution through a cloth is more efficient. Encourage the children to think of and try as many ways as possible. This could introduce a discussion of the way science and technology have combined to find easier and more efficient ways to do things.

SKILLS: Observing, inferring

Activity 1.9
WHAT ARE MIXTURES AND SOLUTIONS?

Materials Needed

- Two glass jars
- Spoons (or stirrers)
- Sugar
- Water
- Marbles or small rocks
- Paper clips
- Toothpicks
- Bits of paper
- Paper and pencil

Procedure

1. Fill each jar about half full of water.
2. Put the marbles, paper clips, toothpicks, and bits of paper in one jar and a spoonful of sugar in the other jar.
3. Stir both jars and observe what happens to the materials in the water.
4. Compare the results in the two jars. One is a mixture and the other is a solution.
5. Try other substances in water, such as sand, powdered milk, or powdered chocolate. Make a list of those you think produce mixtures and those that produce solutions. Explain the differences you observe.

For Problem Solvers: Try to identify mixtures and solutions that are already in your environment. What about the soil in a flower bed at home or at school? What about the air? Make a list of all the mixtures you can find in nature and another list of all the solutions you can find. Notice different food products in your cupboards at home or on grocery-store shelves. Add these to your lists.

Teacher Information

A mixture consists of two or more substances that retain their separate identities when mixed together. Solutions result when the substance placed in a liquid seems to become part of the liquid. A solution is really a special kind of mixture—one in which the particles are all molecular in size.

Materials listed can easily be substituted or supplemented with other soluble and nonsoluble materials.

SKILLS: Observing, inferring, classifying, comparing and contrasting

Activity 1.10
IS THE DISSOLVING OF SOLIDS A PHYSICAL CHANGE OR A CHEMICAL CHANGE?

Materials Needed

- Tumbler
- Sugar (or salt)
- Paper and pencil
- Water
- Stirrer

Procedure

1. Put about two teaspoons of sugar and a small amount of water in a tumbler and stir until the sugar is completely dissolved.

2. Put the tumbler where it can remain undisturbed while the water evaporates.

3. Check the tumbler twice each day. If you notice anything different about it, record your observations.

4. When the water has completely evaporated, record your observations of the tumbler. Do you think the dissolving of the sugar in the water was a physical change or a chemical change? Why do you think as you do? Support your answer with your observations.

For Problem Solvers: Take a small piece of paper and tear it up into the smallest bits you can. Was that a physical change or a chemical change? Place a drop of lemon juice on a piece of paper, and let it dry. Is a physical change or a chemical change taking place? Hold the paper near a light bulb until it begins to look different where the drop of juice was. Is this a physical change or a chemical change? Identify other physical changes and chemical changes that occur in your world. What about a cake as it bakes? What about the soles of your shoes, as they slowly wear away?

Teacher Information

A physical change usually alters only the state of matter, such as from a solid to a liquid or from a liquid to a gas, or the shape, texture, etc. Physical changes are frequently reversible. For example, water can be obtained by condensing it out of the air or by melting an ice cube. Chemical changes involve changes in molecular structure and are not reversible. As the water in this activity evaporates, crystals of sugar appear. They will be massed together and will not look the same, but a taste will reveal that it is sugar.

You might also burn a bit of sugar for students to compare. After the burned substance has cooled, let someone taste it and determine whether the sugar underwent a physical change or a chemical change. It will no longer taste like sugar, except to the extent that unburned sugar crystals remain. The burning process produces a chemical change. The sugar has been oxidized through heat, leaving a carbon residue.

INTEGRATING: Math

SKILLS: Observing, inferring, classifying, measuring, comparing and contrasting

Activity 1.11
WHAT IS RUST?

Materials Needed

- Two small identical jars
- Two small identical dishes
- Paper and pencil
- Steel wool
- Water

Procedure

1. Put a small wad of steel wool into one of the jars. Push it clear to the bottom. Pack it just tightly enough that it will stay at the bottom of the jar when the jar is turned upside down.

2. Put about 2 cm (3/4 in.) of water in each of the two dishes. Be sure you put the same amount in each one.

3. Turn the two jars upside down and stand one in each of the dishes. One jar should have steel wool in the bottom and one should be empty.

Figure 1.11-1

**Two Dishes with Inverted Jars
One Has Steel Wool**

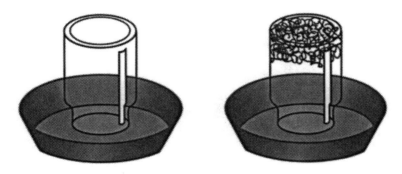

4. Examine the jars each day for one week and record your observations, noting such things as water level and appearance of the steel wool.

5. At the end of one week, study the recorded day-by-day observations and explain the noted changes.

For Problem Solvers: Notice the color of the rust that forms on the steel wool. Try to find items that are made of steel or iron and that have been used for a long time and examine them for spots of rust. See if you can find the same thing on items that are made of plastic. Find out what stainless steel is, then find some items that are made of stainless steel. Can you find rust on them? Look up stainless steel in your encyclopedia and try to find out how stainless steel is different and why it is used.

Teacher Information

As steel wool is exposed to moist air over a period of time, the moisture serves as a medium to bring oxygen molecules in the air in close contact with molecules of iron in the steel wool. Oxygen molecules and iron molecules combine to make iron oxide. This process uses up some of the oxygen in the air inside the jar, reducing the amount of gas (air) in the jar. This, in turn, reduces the air pressure inside the jar, thus the atmospheric pressure outside the jar is greater than the pressure inside the jar, and water is forced into the jar. Student observations should include the rising water level inside the jar containing steel wool as well as the rust color forming on the steel wool.

INTEGRATING: Math, reading

SKILLS: Observing, inferring, comparing and contrasting, measuring

Activity 1.12
HOW CAN CHEMICAL CHANGES HELP YOU WRITE A SECRET MESSAGE?

 Take home and do with family and friends.

Materials Needed

- Small jar
- Milk (only a few drops)
- Toothpick
- White paper
- Lamp with light bulb

Procedure

1. Dip the toothpick into the milk and use it as a pen to write a message on the paper. Let the milk dry.

2. What happens to your message as the milk dries?

3. Hold the paper close to a burning light bulb. What happens as the paper absorbs heat from the light bulb? What can you say about this?

For Problem Solvers: Did you do the "For Problem Solvers" part of Activity 1.10? If so, you should be able to think of another liquid to use for writing secret messages. Try it, then see if you can think of still more materials that will work.

Teacher Information

As the milk dries, the residue blends in with the white paper and becomes invisible. When heat is applied, a chemical reaction takes place in the milk residue, turning it dark and making it easily visible against the white paper.

Students could try the same activity using lemon juice instead of milk as their "ink."

SKILLS: Observing, inferring, predicting, comparing and contrasting

Activity 1.13
HOW DOES TEMPERATURE AFFECT THE SPEED OF MOLECULES?

Materials Needed

- Two tumblers
- Food coloring
- Paper and pencil
- Two eye droppers
- Hot and cold water

Procedure

1. Put very cold water in one tumbler and hot water in the other. Fill each about half full.

2. Draw four or five drops of food coloring into each of the two eye droppers. Put as near the same amount in each as possible.

3. Hold a dropper over each tumbler and squeeze to empty the contents of both at exactly the same time.

4. Compare the movement of the color in the two containers. In which tumbler did the color spread more rapidly?

5. If you have time, try different colors and different water temperatures. Record your observations.

For Problem Solvers: Try the same experiment, but using color as the variable. Put water of the same temperature in both containers. See if one color of food coloring diffuses through the water any faster than another color. Find a stopwatch and time them to find out exactly how long it takes to fully diffuse, so that the water is equal in color throughout.

Next, test water at different temperatures, timing the diffusion at each temperature. Does temperature make a big difference, a small difference, or none at all?

Compare diffusion time of various liquids. Do you think the food coloring will diffuse through milk at the same rate as water, if the two liquids are the same temperature? Try it. What other liquids could you compare?

Teacher Information

As temperatures increase, molecules move faster. The food coloring will diffuse noticeably more rapidly in the hot water than in the cold water. In this experiment, water temperature is the variable. Your "problem solvers" will try the same experiment with color as the variable.

For instance, use two tumblers of cold water and put red in one and green (or blue) in the other. They are also encouraged to use a stopwatch and a thermometer and record the actual time required for maximum diffusion (equal color throughout, as judged by the students).

INTEGRATING: Math

SKILLS: Observing, inferring, measuring, predicting, communicating, comparing and contrasting, using space-time relationships, formulating hypotheses, identifying and controlling variables, experimenting

Activity 1.14
HOW DOES TEMPERATURE AFFECT SOLUBILITY?

Materials Needed

- Two tumblers (equal size)
- Cold water
- Hot water (or a heat source)
- Two spoons (or other stirring instruments)
- Measuring spoons
- Sugar
- Marker

Procedure

1. Be sure the tumblers are equal size.
2. Make a mark on each tumbler about a fourth of the way down from the top. The mark should be at exactly the same point on each tumbler.
3. Using cold water for one tumbler and hot water (very hot) for the other, fill each exactly to the mark.
4. Using a measuring spoon (teaspoon is about right) put one level spoonful of sugar in each tumbler.
5. Stir the water in each tumbler until the sugar has completely dissolved in the water.
6. Add another level spoonful of sugar and again stir until completely dissolved.
7. Continue doing this, counting the spoonsful of sugar added to each tumbler. Stop adding sugar when you can no longer make it completely dissolve in the water.
8. Which dissolved more sugar, the cold water or the hot water? How much more? Why do you think this was so?

For Problem Solvers: Get some sugar cubes and see if they dissolve at the same rate as loose sugar. Compare them in hot and cold water. Time the dissolving rate with a stopwatch. Measure the temperature of the hot water and the cold water. Considering the dissolving rate for both of these, predict the dissolving rate if the water is halfway between these two temperatures. Try it.

Do you think stirring has an effect on dissolving rate? See what you can do to find out.

Do you think salt dissolves at the same rate as sugar? Do you think water temperature has the same effect on the dissolving rate of salt as it has on sugar? Devise an experiment to find out, and carry out your experiment.

Teacher Information

Hot water molecules move more rapidly than cold water molecules do. The dissolving sugar molecules are therefore dispersed more completely throughout the liquid and a greater amount of sugar is dissolved in the hot water.

Your "problem solvers" will compare the dissolving rate of sugar cubes with the dissolving rate of loose sugar. They will also investigate the effect of stirring on the dissolving rate of sugar. If their interest holds, they will find out if salt dissolves at the same rate as sugar. Your young scientists might think of other variables to test as well.

INTEGRATING: Math

SKILLS: Observing, inferring, measuring, predicting, communicating, comparing and contrasting, using space-time relationships, formulating hypotheses, identifying and controlling variables, experimenting

Activity 1.15
HOW CAN PERFUME GET INTO A SEALED BALLOON?

Materials Needed

- Two balloons
- Two small bowls
- Perfume
- Water
- String

Procedure

1. Put one-half cup of water in each of the two bowls.

2. Mix several drops of perfume into the water of one bowl.

3. Blow up both balloons and tie them. Use a string with a bow knot so they can be untied later.

4. Place one balloon in each bowl. Press them into the bowl to create an air-tight seal.

5. Leave the materials undisturbed for at least two hours.

6. After at least two hours, take the balloons to another room where the perfume in the bowl cannot be smelled.

7. Untie the balloon that was on the nonperfume bowl. Let the air out slowly and smell it.

8. Untie the balloon that was on the perfume bowl. Let the air out slowly and smell it.

9. What did you notice about the air in the balloons? What can you say about this?

For Problem Solvers: Do you think the perfume getting into the balloon would be affected by how tightly the balloon is blown up? Test this question by using three balloons. Be sure the balloons are identical, except that one will be blown up more and one less than before.

How about also testing the permeability of different plastic wraps? Put your perfume water in drinking cups or drinking glasses, and seal the plastic wrap over the tops of the containers; then see if you can smell the perfume through the plastic. Compare different brands of plastic wrap. Before you begin, make your predictions. Will they be the same? Do you think permeability of plastic wraps matters with foods that are stored in the refrigerator? Why?

Teacher Information

Molecules in the perfume are small enough to permeate the balloon. When the air is let out of the balloon after a two-hour period, the smell of perfume in the air of the balloon should be evident.

Foods sometimes take on odors from each other while wrapped and in the refrigerator. Your "problem solvers" will find out why.

INTEGRATING: Math

SKILLS: Observing, inferring, classifying, measuring, predicting, communicating, comparing and contrasting, using space-time relationships, formulating hypotheses, identifying and controlling variables, experimenting

Activity 1.16
HOW CAN YOU CAUSE MOLECULES TO MOVE THROUGH SOLIDS?

Materials Needed

- Balloon
- String
- Marker
- Paper and pencil

Procedure

1. Blow up a balloon and tie it.
2. Measure the size of the balloon by wrapping the string around it at the largest point and marking the string. Record the length of string required to go around the balloon.
3. Place the balloon where it will not be disturbed and where the temperature will remain quite constant.
4. For three days, measure the balloon twice a day with the same string and mark the string to indicate the length required to go around the balloon. Each time you measure, record the length of string required.
5. At the end of three days, describe your observations. Try to explain any changes you noted.

For Problem Solvers: Find some balloons of different brands and different quality and repeat this activity. Set up an experiment to compare the different types of balloons. Be sure to use balloons of the same size and shape, to blow them up to the same size, and to tie them in the same way.

Teacher Information

You might check to see that the balloon is tied tightly so air cannot leak through the opening. You can do this by submerging it in water to check for air bubbles. As the balloon sits, air molecules actually permeate the balloon walls and it will lose air slowly even though air is not escaping by any observable means. For the duration of this activity the air temperature should remain as constant as possible. If air temperature changes, the balloon will expand or contract (in warmer and cooler air, respectively), which will nullify the results.

INTEGRATING: Math

SKILLS: Observing, inferring, classifying, measuring, predicting, communicating, comparing and contrasting, using space-time relationships, formulating hypotheses, identifying and controlling variables, experimenting

Activity 1.17
WHAT IS VISCOSITY?

Materials Needed

- Four tall olive jars with lids (or other tall, skinny jars)
- Four marbles (different colors)
- Corn syrup
- Mineral oil
- Vegetable oil
- Water
- Paper and pencil

Procedure

1. Be sure all four jars are the same size.
2. Place a marble in each jar.
3. Fill each jar with one of the liquids and put the lid on it. There should be no air under the lid.
4. When all lids are tightly in place, get someone to help you turn all four jars upside down at once. Observe the marbles.
5. Record which marble sank to the bottom first, second, third, and fourth. Repeat and compare the results with your first trial.
6. Test other liquids and compare with these.
7. Discuss your findings with your friends or your teacher.

For Problem Solvers: Read about viscosity in a dictionary. Find an encyclopedia article that tells about the viscosity of oil and read the article. Talk to a mechanic and find out why oil is made at different viscosities for automobile engines. Why does it matter, and what are the advantages of light oil (low viscosity) and of heavy oil (high viscosity)? Some engine oils are even multiple-viscosity. What does that mean, and why do they make them that way?

Teacher Information

Other liquids can be substituted for those listed above, but they should vary in viscosity (thickness). The marbles will sink more slowly in liquids with greater viscosity. Viscosity is *resistance to flow*. If olive jars or other tall, thin jars are not available, baby-food jars can be used. Try to get the larger size, for height. Test tubes work very well, if they are available. They must have stoppers, of course.

The activity can even be done in open bowls. Put the liquids in separate bowls and a spoon in each bowl. Students should take a spoonful of the liquid and pour it back into the same bowl, observing how fast it pours out of the spoon. This doesn't have quite the interest or accuracy of the marble activity, but it will work.

As a practical application of this concept, your "problem solvers" will find out why automobile engines use oils of various viscosities. One factor is temperature. As is true of honey, oils become thinner (less viscous) as they become warmer. Heavier oil is generally preferred for hot weather and thinner oil for cold weather. Modern oils are also made in multiple viscosities; they have properties that cause them to behave as a heavier oil in hotter temperatures and as a lighter oil in colder temperatures.

INTEGRATING: Reading, math

SKILLS: Observing, inferring, classifying, measuring, predicting, communicating, comparing and contrasting, using space-time relationships, formulating hypotheses, identifying and controlling variables, experimenting, researching

Activity 1.18
HOW CAN A BLOWN-OUT CANDLE RELIGHT ITSELF?

(Teacher-supervised activity)

Materials Needed

- Two candles
- Metal pan
- Match

Procedure

1. For this activity, keep the candles over the pan and be sure you have a supervisor with you.
2. Light both candles.
3. Hold the two candles horizontally with one flame about an inch above the other.

Figure 1.18-1

Two Candles, One above the Other, Both Burning

4. Holding both candles steady, blow out the lower flame and observe for a few seconds.
5. What happened? Can you explain why?

For Problem Solvers: Observe the flame of a burning candle very carefully. Where is the flame resting? Does it seem to be sitting right on the wick, and burning the wick, or is it above the wick? What do you think is burning?

See what you can find out about flames. What part of a flame is the hottest? What causes the colors you see in the flame? Find answers to these questions and to other questions you think of.

Teacher Information

Wax, in solid form, does not burn. Heat changes wax to a vapor, which burns when combined with oxygen in the air. When a candle flame is blown out, hot gases continue to rise for a short time. These gases can ignite and act as a wick if another flame is close by and in their path. The flame will burn down the gases and relight the lower candle.

INTEGRATING: Reading, language arts, math

SKILLS: Observing, inferring, measuring, predicting, communicating, using space-time relationships, formulating hypotheses, identifying and controlling variables, experimenting, researching

Activity 1.19
HOW CAN YOU REMOVE THE FLAME FROM A CANDLE WITHOUT PUTTING IT OUT?

Materials Needed

- Glass jar with lid
- Birthday candle
- Tablespoon
- 30 cm (1 ft.) of pliable wire
- Baking soda
- Vinegar
- Match

Procedure

1. Put two tablespoons of vinegar and one tablespoon of baking soda in the bottom of the jar. Bubbles will form.
2. Set the lid upside down on the jar, to cover the jar without sealing it.
3. Let the jar sit until the bubbling has nearly stopped.
4. While you are waiting for the bubbles to stop, form a holder for the candle from the wire.
5. Place the candle in your wire holder and light the candle.
6. Remove the cover from the jar and slowly lower the candle into the jar until the top of the wick is about an inch below the rim of the jar, then bring the candle back up.
7. Try it again. Explain what happens.

Figure 1.19-1

Candle Lowered by Wire into Jar

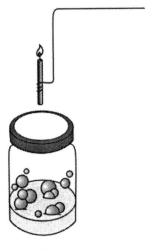

33

Teacher Information

CAUTION: Careful suprvision is required due to the involvement of fire. Combining vinegar and baking soda forms carbon dioxide, which is heavier than air and therefore drives the air out of the jar, leaving the jar filled with carbon dioxide. As the flame is lowered below the rim of the jar, it is starved for oxygen and the candle actually burns out. Gases continue to rise from the candle for a short time, however, and the flame sits on top of the layer of carbon dioxide, burning the rising gases in the presence of oxygen.

SKILLS: Observing, inferring, measuring, predicting, communicating

Activity 1.20
HOW CAN YOU MAKE A FIRE EXTINGUISHER?

(Teacher-supervised activity)

Materials Needed

- Large soda bottle (or quart jar)
- Vinegar
- Baking soda
- Candle
- Match
- Sink or pan
- Tablespoon
- Measuring cup

Procedure

1. Stand the candle in the sink or pan. Be sure there are no flammable materials nearby. Light the candle.

2. Put one tablespoon of baking soda into the bottle.

3. Measure about 3–4 ounces of vinegar with the measuring cup and pour it into the bottle.

4. As bubbles form, hold the bottle over the candle flame and tip it as though you were pouring water from the bottle onto the flame, but do not tip it far enough to pour out the vinegar.

5. What happened to the flame? Explain why you think this happened.

For Problem Solvers: Carbon dioxide is heavier than air. Why does that help it to be effective in putting out fires? See what you can learn about fire fighting, and what chemicals are commonly used for putting out fires.

Teacher Information

CAUTION: This activity must be carefully supervised due to the involvement of fire.

Baking soda is sodium bicarbonate. Vinegar contains acetic acid. When the two mix, carbon dioxide (CO_2) is formed. Carbon dioxide is heavier than air, so when the bottle is tipped, the CO_2 pours out. You don't see it pour because carbon dioxide is colorless. As it pours over the flame, the CO_2 deprives the flame of oxygen and the flame is extinguished. Carbon dioxide is commonly used in some fire extinguishers.

Carbon dioxide is one of the more common gases. Humans and other animals produce it and breathe it into the air. Plants absorb it and, in turn, make oxygen. Carbon dioxide is put into soft drinks to give them bubbles, or fizz. Dry ice is carbon dioxide, frozen to make it solid. If dry ice is available, have students repeat this activity, using a small piece of dry ice in the place of vinegar and baking soda. **CAUTION: Any use of dry ice must be carefully supervised, as it can burn the skin. It should never be put in the mouth. Also, dry ice must not be placed in a sealed bottle (or any other sealed container), because it can build up enough pressure to explode the bottle.**

INTEGRATING: Reading, math

SKILLS: Observing, inferring, measuring, predicting, communicating, identifying and controlling variables, experimenting, researching

Activity 1.21
HOW CAN YOU MAKE A BALL BOUNCE BY ITSELF?

(Teacher-supervised activity)

Materials Needed

- Old tennis ball
- Scissors

Procedure

1. With the scissors, cut the tennis ball in half to make two dish-shaped halves. You will need to start the cut by punching a hole with the point of the scissors or with a knife.

2. Trim around the edge of one of the halves until its diameter is about 5 cm (2 in.).

3. Turn the ball dish inside out and set it on the floor or on a table. Observe for several seconds.

4. What happened? Explain why you think it behaved this way. What might you do to make it happen faster or more slowly?

For Problem Solvers: Get your friends to help you ask around for and locate several tennis balls that are old and not needed any more. Experiment with the amount that you trim off for this activity. Try to create the ball that will bounce the highest. See if you can control the delay time (from the time you set it down until it flips up) by how much of the ball you trim off.

Teacher Information

After a brief observation, the "dish" should jump. Rubber molecules act like tiny springs, giving rubber the tendency to spring back to its original shape when distorted. This property gives rubber its bounce. With the inverted "dish," the restoring action of the rubber first has to overcome the resistance of the backward bend. When it reaches a certain point, though, the movement is very quick. The edges strike the surface with considerable force and the ball flips into the air.

As students ponder the last question in step 4, you might need to encourage them to try trimming a little more off the edges of the dish or taking the other half of the ball and trimming off less than they did with the first one. Trimming less will delay the action and trimming more will speed it up. Your "problem solvers" are encouraged to investigate with these factors.

INTEGRATING: Math

SKILLS: Observing, inferring, classifying, measuring, predicting, communicating, using space-time relationships, formulating hypotheses, identifying and controlling variables, experimenting, researching

Activity 1.22
WHAT IS POLYETHYLENE?

Materials Needed

- One polyethylene bag with tie
- One nonpolyethylene plastic bag with tie
- Sharpened pencil
- Water
- Sink or large pan

Procedure

1. Check to be sure one of the bags is polyethylene. It will be indicated on the container.
2. Fill both bags with water and put ties around the tops. Keep them over a sink or large pan.
3. Stab the pencil through the nonpolyethylene bag and observe what happens.
4. Stab the pencil through the polyethylene bag. Compare the results with what happened in step 3.
5. What can you say about this?

Teacher Information

Polyethylene has the strange property of shrinking together when it is torn. When the bag is punctured, the polyethylene shrinks and stops (or reduces) the flow of water. This property is a factor in puncture-resistant tires.

SKILLS: Observing, inferring, classifying, measuring, predicting, communicating, comparing and contrasting, using space-time relationships, formulating hypotheses, identifying and controlling variables, experimenting

Activity 1.23
HOW CAN YOU MAKE LARGE SUGAR CRYSTALS FROM TINY ONES?

(Teacher-supervised activity)

Materials Needed

- Drinking glass or jar
- Water
- Cotton string or thread
- Pencil
- Sugar
- Pan
- Heat source
- Stirrer or wooden spoon

Procedure

1. Put a cup of water in the pan and heat it until it boils.

2. When the water begins to boil, turn off the heat and add about 1.5 cups of sugar and stir.

3. If all the sugar dissolves, add a bit more and stir. Keep doing this until no more sugar will dissolve in the water.

4. Let the water cool, then pour it into a drinking glass.

5. Tie a piece of cotton thread or string to a pencil and lay the pencil across the glass, allowing the string to extend to the bottom of the glass.

6. Place the drinking glass on a shelf where it can remain undisturbed for several days.

7. Examine the glass, particularly the string, each day and write down your observations. DO NOT TOUCH THE GLASS.

8. When you observe no more changes, try to explain what happened during the days the glass remained on the shelf.

For Problem Solvers: Use the same procedure to experiment with other substances you can find. Include salt and powdered alum among the materials you try. Examine your crystals with a hand lens and with a microscope if you have one. Observe and compare very carefully and share your observations with others.

Teacher Information

As sugar dissolves in water the crystals break down into molecules so small they can't be seen even with a powerful microscope. A molecule of sugar is the smallest particle of sugar that can exist. If it were any smaller, it would no longer be sugar.

In this activity sugar crystals are dissolved into molecules, forming a supersaturated solution (containing more sugar in solution than could be dissolved at room temperature). Then, as the solution cools, crystals begin coming out of solution and collecting around the string. As this happens, large sugar crystals are formed. You could call it rock candy.

"Problem solvers" will also try forming crystals from other substances, such as salt and/or powdered alum, following the same procedure.

SKILLS: Observing, inferring, classifying, measuring, predicting, communicating, comparing and contrasting, using space-time relationships, formulating hypotheses, identifying and controlling variables, experimenting

Activity 1.24
WHAT DOES LITMUS PAPER TELL US ABOUT SUBSTANCES?

Materials Needed

- Red litmus paper
- Blue litmus paper
- Glass containing a small amount of vinegar water (about half vinegar and half water)
- Glass containing a small amount of baking soda mixed in water
- Glass containing a small amount of tap water
- Paper and pencil

Procedure

1. Write "Vinegar Water," "Baking Soda Water," and "Water" across the top of your paper.
2. Write "Blue Litmus Paper," Red Litmus Paper," and "Acid, Base, or Neutral" down the left side of your paper.
3. Dip one end of a strip of blue litmus paper into the vinegar water.
4. Did it change colors? If so, what color is it now?
5. Write the color in the space for vinegar water and blue litmus paper.
6. Dip one end of a strip of red litmus paper into the vinegar water.
7. What happened this time?
8. Write the color in the space for vinegar water and red litmus paper. If the litmus paper stayed the same color, write "no change."
9. Repeat steps 3 through 8 for the baking soda water.
10. Repeat steps 3 through 8 again for the water.
11. If a substance turns blue litmus paper red we say the substance is an acid. If the substance turns red litmus paper blue we say the substance is a base. If the substance does not change the color of either litmus paper we say the substance is neutral.
12. Fill in the bottom line of your chart, identifying each of the three substances as either acid, base, or neutral.
13. Compare your information with others. Did they get the same results?

	VINEGAR WATER	BAK. SODA WATER	WATER
BLUE LP	_____	_____	_____
RED LP	_____	_____	_____
A, B, or N	_____	_____	_____

For Problem Solvers: Stronger acids turn blue litmus paper darker red, and stronger bases turn red litmus paper darker blue. Find other substances to test with litmus paper. Some of the materials you could test are milk, tea, coffee, window cleaner, bathtub cleaner, and mouthwash. You will think of others as you go. Identify which of the materials you tested are strong acids, which are weak acids, which are strong bases, and which are weak bases.

Test a variety of brands of soft drinks. Before you test them, predict whether they will be acid, base, or neutral. If you think they will be acid or base, predict which drinks will be the strongest. After testing them, list them in the order of their strength, as shown by the litmus test.

Find as many sources of water as you can find in your area. These might include tap water, rain water, pond water, swamp water, river water, and others. Use the litmus paper test on each one, and list them in order according to your litmus test results.

Teacher Information

This activity will provide an introduction to the terms "acids" and "bases" and to the use of litmus paper as an indicator for determining which is which. It will also become a practical and useful experience for your problem solvers who decide to extend the activity into various drinks and into water from various sources. If acid rain is sometimes a problem in your area, you might also want to have your students collect samples of rain water during each storm and keep record of the acid levels from each. Do the same with snow; melt it down and test it.

As a long-term project, consider having your students determine whether the acidity of rainwater changes throughout the year in your area.

In the absence of litmus paper, or in addition to it, try red cabbage juice. You can either boil the cabbage, then strain the juice to remove the solids, or put red cabbage and water in a blender, again straining the juice. To use it as an acid-base indicator, take a small amount of juice, such as in a spoon, and add a drop or two of the liquid being tested. Compare the color changes to the changes in litmus paper.

INTEGRATING: Math, social studies

SKILLS: Observing, inferring, classifying, measuring, predicting, communicating, comparing and contrasting, experimenting

Section Two

ENERGY

TO THE TEACHER

We use many forms of energy every day, yet we never see it. The sun's energy literally powers the earth, but it is so common we take it for granted. It is just there. Energy comes in many forms, none of which looks like "energy." It is disguised as a match stick, a lump of coal, a gallon of gasoline, or a glass of orange juice; it is never just energy. In a broad sense, energy is so much a part of us and our surroundings that it would be impossible to deal with it as a topic separate from other topics treated in this book. The sun's energy keeps us warm and gives us light. Part of the sun's energy is converted by plants into food for animals. Cattle convert some of that energy from plant form to muscle, which we eat (beefsteak, hamburger, and so forth). Energy is consumed by people in both plant and animal form. We, in turn, convert it into human flesh and bones. The sun's energy is a vital ingredient of our own bodies and of a great deal of our surroundings.

In a narrower sense, energy is sometimes defined as the capacity for performing work (*Webster's New Collegiate Dictionary*). It exists in two forms, potential energy and kinetic energy. *Potential energy* is the ability to do work. Work is defined as force acting through a distance. Specifically, Work = Force × Distance. *Kinetic energy* is the energy of motion. A rubber band stretched out has potential energy. When it is released, its potential energy is converted to kinetic energy. A stick of dynamite has potential energy. When a small electrical charge or the right amount of heat is applied, the potential energy is converted to kinetic energy with great force.

The potential energy in dynamite is chemical energy. The potential energy in the rubber band, or in a set mousetrap, or in a raised hammer is mechanical energy.

The energy we consume in the form of meat, fruit, and vegetables isn't all used to build body cells. We use some of it to walk and talk. We even use some of this energy as we think.

Most sections of this book deal directly or indirectly with forms of energy. This section recognizes these but emphasizes additional topics, such as heat, gravity, and the relationship between energy and work.

Activities that appear complex can usually be used in the lower grades by deemphasizing terminology and mathematical applications. With simplified explanations of the concepts, children can participate in the activities and benefit from exposure to these principles.

Regarding the Early Grades

With verbal instructions and slight modifications, many of these activities can be used with kindergarten, first-grade, and second-grade students. In some activities, steps that involve procedures that go beyond the level of the child can simply be omitted and yet offer the child an experience that plants the seed for a concept that will germinate and grow later on.

Teachers of the early grades will probably choose to bypass many of the "For Problem Solvers" sections. That's okay. These sections are provided for those who are especially motivated and want to go beyond the investigation provided by the activity outlined. Use the outlined activities and enjoy worthwhile learning experiences together with your young students. Also consider, however, that many of the "For Problem Solvers" sections can be used appropriately with young children as group activities or as demonstrations, still giving students the advantage of an exposure to the experience and laying groundwork for connections that will be made later on.

Activity 2.1
HOW DO POTENTIAL ENERGY AND KINETIC ENERGY COMPARE?

(For older children or teacher demonstration)

Materials Needed

- Mousetrap
- Ball
- String
- Pencil eraser

Procedure

1. Set the mousetrap. What kind of energy does it have?

2. Drop the pencil eraser on the release lever. What kind of energy is present at the moment the trap springs shut?

3. Drop the ball and let it bounce a few times. Describe one full bounce, from the top of the bounce to the bottom and back to the top, in terms of the presence of kinetic and potential energy.

4. Tie the eraser to the string. Hold the end of the string and swing the eraser like a pendulum. Describe one full swing, back and forth, in terms of the presence of kinetic and potential energy.

For Problem Solvers: Think through the actions involved in a baseball game. List as many examples of potential energy as you can, and list as many examples of kinetic energy as you can. What about the pitcher standing in a relaxed position with ball in hand? The moment when the pitcher is wound up and ready to release the ball? The moment the ball connects with the bat? When the ball is zooming toward left field and the left-fielder is jumping to catch it? Add all of the actions you can think of, and list them as examples of either potential energy or kinetic energy.

Teacher Information

This activity requires the student to distinguish between kinetic and potential energy. When the mousetrap is set, the presence of the loaded spring gives it potential energy. At the moment the spring is released, the potential energy is converted to kinetic energy, or moving energy. Great care should be taken to assure that fingers are not injured by the mousetrap.

As the ball is held above the floor, it has potential energy. The ball is released and the potential energy is converted to kinetic energy as the ball falls toward the floor. When the ball strikes the floor, it is compressed and the kinetic energy is converted to potential energy. The potential energy in the compressed rubber propels the ball into the air, again converting the potential energy to kinetic energy. Some of the energy escapes in the form of heat as the ball meets resistance with the air and the floor. Thus, the height of the cycle decreases as the ball bounces.

The swinging pendulum passes through a cycle similar to that of the bouncing ball. All energy contained in the system is potential energy at the instant the pendulum is all the way to the top on either side of the cycle. At the moment the pendulum is at the bottom, moving neither upward nor downward, all of the energy is kinetic.

If the pendulum is at rest, it has neither potential nor kinetic energy. When in a position that gravity can cause movement when released, it has potential energy.

Your baseball stars and fans will enjoy dissecting a baseball game in terms of what they have learned about potential energy and kinetic energy and identifying the changes from one form of energy to the other.

INTEGRATING: Math

SKILLS: Observing, inferring, classifying, measuring, predicting, communicating, comparing and contrasting, using space-time relationships, formulating hypotheses, identifying and controlling variables, experimenting

Activity 2.2
HOW MUCH HORSEPOWER DO YOU HAVE?

(For upper grades)

Materials Needed

- Stairs
- Stopwatch
- Paper and pencil

  Note: The formula for computing horsepower was proposed by James Watt, who found that a horse could do 550 foot-pounds of work in one second. This formula is still used in determining the horsepower of automobile engines. The formula is

  $$Horsepower \ = \ \frac{Foot\text{-}pounds}{Seconds \times 550}$$

Procedure

1. Measure 10 feet (vertical distance) up the stairs or ladder.
2. Have someone time you as you climb that distance as fast as you can.
3. Compute your "horsepower" by using the above formula. For "foot-pounds," multiply your weight by 10 (number of vertical feet climbed).
4. A small motorbike has about 30–50 horsepower. A medium-sized car has about 100–300 horsepower. How many horsepower do you have?

Teacher Information

Using the formula should not be too difficult for students of the upper elementary grades. The following example assumes the student's weight to be 100 pounds and the time required to climb 10 vertical feet to be 3 seconds:

$$Horsepower \ = \ \frac{100 \times 10}{3 \times 550} \ = \ \frac{1000 \ foot\text{-}pounds}{1650} \ = \ 0.61$$

INTEGRATING: Math

SKILLS: Observing, inferring, measuring, predicting, communicating, using space-time relationships, formulating hypotheses, identifying and controlling variables, experimenting

Activity 2.3
HOW IS WORK MEASURED?

Materials Needed

- One-pound weight
- Foot ruler

Procedure

1. Stand the ruler on the table or the floor.

2. Raise the one-pound weight to the top of the ruler. The amount of work you did to raise one pound a distance of one foot is called one foot-pound.

3. Raise the one-pound weight six inches. How much work did you do? How much potential energy does the weight have at that point?

4. Raise the weight two feet. How much work did you do this time? How much potential energy does the weight have?

5. Set the weight on the table. How much potential energy does it have now?

6. Slide the weight to the edge of the table. How much potential energy does it have at that position?

7. Try to determine the amount of potential energy of various objects from different positions and the amount of work required to move those objects certain distances.

8. Climb a flight of stairs. How much work did you do to get to the top? What is your potential energy, assuming the possibility of falling or jumping to the bottom?

For Problem Solvers: Find a ten-pound weight. Lift the weight over your head. Measure the distance from the floor to the highest point you lifted the weight. Measure the height, in feet, and multiply that number by 10. That's the number of foot-pounds of work you did in lifting the weight one time. How much work can you do with the same weight in one minute? Do the same exercise every other day for two weeks. Make a graph showing the amount of work you do with the weight each time. It's okay to practice between your measured sessions if you want to. See how much you can improve in two weeks. Maybe your friends would like to join you and see how much they can improve, too.

Teacher Information

The foot-pound is a standard unit for measuring work or potential energy. Mechanics use a torque wrench to measure the degree of stress on a bolt as it is turned to hold the head or some other part of an engine. The torque wrench indicates the stress in foot-pounds, which is a measure of the work done to turn the bolt. (The metric system equivalent to foot-pounds is Newton-meters, or joules, not at all in common usage in the United States.)

A durable plastic or cloth bag filled with one pound of sand, beans, or other material would be an excellent weight for this activity. If a hard object is used, newspaper or other material could be placed on the table or floor to muffle the sound when the weight is dropped and to protect the surface from possible damage.

INTEGRATING: Math

SKILLS: Observing, inferring, measuring, predicting, communicating, using space-time relationships, identifying and controlling variables, experimenting

Activity 2.4
HOW MUCH ENERGY IS STORED IN A BOW?

(Teacher-supervised activity to be done outdoors)

Materials Needed

- Toy bow
- Toy arrow tipped with suction cup
- Spring scale
- Foot ruler
- Measuring tape

Procedure

1. Do this activity outdoors. Find an isolated area.
2. Put the arrow on the bow. Hold the bow and arrow at a comfortable height and point the arrow straight ahead in a direction away from people.
3. Draw the bowstring back six inches and let it go.
4. Measure the distance the arrow traveled.
5. Attach the spring scale to the bowstring and pull the string back six inches. How many ounces or pounds of force were required to pull the string back six inches?
6. Predict the amount of force required to pull the string back one foot. Measure it with the spring scale.
7. Predict the distance the arrow will travel with the string pulled back one foot.
8. Shoot the arrow with the string pulled back one foot. Be sure the bow is held at the same height as before and still aimed straight ahead.
9. Measure the distance and compare with your predictions.
10. Predict the force required to pull the string back 1.5 feet and the distance the arrow will travel. Try it and test your predictions.

For Problem Solvers: Try a similar test with your own throwing ability. Find a one-kilogram (2.5-pound) weight. With your arm fully outstretched, pull your arm back 10 cm (4 in.), and from that point see how far you can throw the weight. For this exercise, hold your body still and make your arm do the work. Have a friend measure the distance your arm moves. Try it again with a 20-cm (8-in.) throwing range, then 30 cm (12-in.), etc. Find your optimum throwing position (the position at which you can throw the farthest).

Where did the energy come from that shot the arrow? What about the energy that threw the weight? Trace the energy to its original source.

Teacher Information

Even though the arrow used in this activity is tipped with a suction cup for safety, close supervision is very important. Injury can still result if a child is hit in the face with the arrow. Young children can do the activity with less measuring and still predict the distances the arrow will travel. A ruler (or stick) could be marked at appropriate points to indicate the distance from the string to the bow. Children can indicate their predictions for distance the arrow will travel by placing a marker on the ground.

INTEGRATING: Math, physical education

SKILLS: Observing, inferring, classifying, measuring, predicting, communicating, comparing and contrasting, using space-time relationships, formulating hypotheses, identifying and controlling variables, experimenting

Activity 2.5
HOW CAN YOU POWER A RACER WITH A RUBBER BAND?

 Take home and do with family and friends.

Materials Needed

- Thread spool
- Cotton swab (or sandwich skewer)
- Washer
- Paper clip

Procedure

1. Thread the rubber band through the spool.
2. Put the paper clip through one end of the rubber band to prevent the rubber band from slipping back through the hole in the spool.
3. Thread the other end of the rubber band through the washer.
4. Insert the cotton swab through the rubber band, next to the washer.
5. Position the cotton swab so that one end is farther than the other from the rubber band.
6. Turn the cotton swab around and around to wind up the rubber band.
7. Set your racer on the floor and let it go!
8. Have races with others who made a similar racer.
9. What provides the energy for your racer? Is it really the rubber band? Think about it and discuss your ideas with others.

Figure 2.5-1

Spool Racer

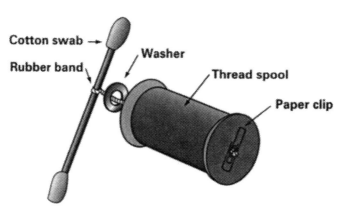

52

For Problem Solvers: Find a shorter rubber band. Predict whether your racer will do better with the shorter rubber band, or not as well. Try a longer rubber band, but be sure to predict again before you test it. Find the best rubber band for the racer.

Could you make a similar racer with other cylinders? How about a small soup can? A larger can? A two-liter plastic bottle? Other things? Get creative—what else can you design that would be powered by a rubber band?

Teacher Information

This is a good opportunity for students to work with a familiar object as a source of energy and to trace energy sources. It's also a good opportunity for children to explore creatively and to share their ideas. As they work together they will learn of the benefits of cooperative efforts.

Students should recognize that the rubber band has no energy until energy is put into it by the winding action. The winding energy is fed into the rubber band by muscles of the human body. The muscles acquire their energy, directly or indirectly, from food made by plants—out of nutrients from the ground and the energy of the sun.

INTEGRATING: Math

SKILLS: Observing, inferring, measuring, predicting, communicating, comparing and contrasting, identifying and controlling variables, experimenting

Activity 2.6
HOW CAN WIND ENERGY BE USED TO TURN SOMETHING?

Materials Needed

- Square poster paper (about 15 cm [6 in.] square)
- Pencil with eraser
- Straight pin
- Scissors
- Ruler
- Stapler

Procedure

1. Draw two lines on the card from corner to corner. The lines should cross at the center.
2. Make a pencil mark at the center of the card, where the lines cross (see Figure 2.6-1).
3. You now have a center point and four lines that connect the center point to the corners of the card.
4. Make a pencil mark on each of the four lines, 2.5 cm (1 in.) from the center point.
5. Make four cuts in the card with the scissors. Cut along each line, from the corner toward the center point, to the mark you made on the line.
6. You now have eight points. Fold every other point into the center of the card.
7. Staple the folded points at the center. This is your windmill.
8. Push the straight pin through the center of the windmill and into the eraser of the pencil (see Figure 2.6-2). Blow on the pinwheel to see that it spins freely.
9. When the wind blows, take your pinwheel outdoors. Share it with others.

Figure 2.6-1

Card Prepared for the Pinwheel

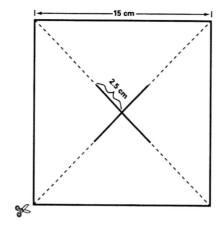

54

Figure 2.6-2

Pinwheel

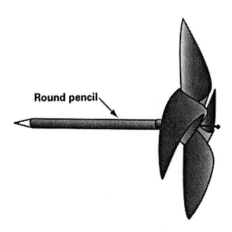

For Problem Solvers: Find two plastic or paper drinking cups. One of these can be very small. Push the pencil through the larger cup, so the cup becomes a stand for the pinwheel. Tape one end of the string to the pencil, near the end opposite the pinwheel, and fasten the other end of the string to the small cup (see Figure 2.6-3). Blow on the pinwheel and the string should wind around the pencil, lifting the cup. Now let's call it a *windmill*.

Next, your challenge is to think of other ways to move things with wind power. You might make a different design of windmill or a completely different device. Discuss your ideas with others and learn together.

By the way, where does wind energy come from? Trace its source.

Figure 2.6-3

Windmill Ready to Raise a Load

Teacher Information

In this activity students use wind as a source of energy. Discuss the notion that even wind energy comes from the sun. Challenge students to explain that.

As students create objects that use wind as a source of energy to move something, they develop their creative skills and their problem-solving skills. If your problem solvers get bogged down in trying to think of ideas, you might want to encourage them to first research ways that wind power has been used and is now used. As they learn about ways wind power has been used historically, perhaps new and creative ideas will come to them. Encourage students also to discuss their ideas with one another. Talking about an idea often stimulates new thoughts for the person who is doing the explaining.

INTEGRATING: Reading, language arts, math, social studies

SKILLS: Observing, inferring, measuring, predicting, communicating, identifying and controlling variables, experimenting, researching

Activity 2.7
HOW CAN YOU GET THE MOST HEAT ENERGY FROM THE SUN?

Materials Needed

- Three identical jars
- Paper and pencil
- Black paper
- Aluminum foil
- Tape
- Three thermometers
- Sand

Procedure

1. Fill the three jars with sand.

2. Cover one jar with black paper, including the top, and tape the paper in place.

3. Cover the second jar with aluminum foil, including the top, and tape the foil in place.

4. Leave the third jar uncovered.

5. Record the temperature shown on the thermometers. Be sure all three indicate the same temperature.

6. Insert one thermometer into the sand in each jar. With the two covered jars, puncture a hole in the top covering and insert the thermometer through the hole.

7. Place all three jars in sunlight. All should receive the same direct sunlight.

8. Check and record the temperature of the three thermometers every 15 minutes for about two hours.

9. How do the temperatures compare? What can you say about the effect of a black surface and a shiny surface on absorption of energy from the sun?

10. Remove the jars from the sunlight and continue to record the temperatures of the three thermometers for two more hours.

11. How do the temperature changes compare? What cah you say about the effect of a black surface and a shiny surface on heat loss?

For Problem Solvers: Here are more ways to compare the effect of color on heat absorption. Place a thermometer on a paper plate and lay a sheet of black paper over it. Prepare a second plate using a thermometer and white paper, then a third using aluminum foil. On a warm, sunny day, place all three plates in direct sunlight. Check and record the temperatures on the thermometers after one-half hour, then again after one hour.

If you live in a cold climate, place papers of various colors on a snow bank, in the sunlight. Use a black paper, a white paper, and a piece of aluminum foil of the same size. Use other colors also if you'd like to. Line them up, so they all have direct sunlight. After an hour, check the snow under the papers to find out how much has melted. Check them again after two hours.

Share your results with your class.

Teacher Information

The uncovered jar of sand will provide a control to help students observe the effect of both the black and the shiny surface. The temperature of the jar with the black surface will likely increase noticeably faster than that of the other two. The foil will reflect heat and the temperature increase of the sand covered by it will be very slow.

Astronauts wear reflective clothing to help protect them from the direct rays of the sun.

INTEGRATING: Math

SKILLS: Observing, inferring, classifying, measuring, predicting, communicating, comparing and contrasting, using space-time relationships, formulating hypotheses, identifying and controlling variables, experimenting

Activity 2.8
WHAT OTHER TYPE OF ENERGY ACCOMPANIES LIGHT FROM THE SUN?

(Teacher-supervised activity)

Materials Needed

- Two magnifying glasses
- One sheet of paper
- Glass bowl

Procedure

1. Ask your teacher where you should do this experiment. You will need to be in bright sunlight with no wind.

2. Put the paper in the bowl.

3. Hold the magnifying glass between the paper and the sun so a beam of light focuses on the paper.

4. Notice that as you move the magnifying glass closer to and farther from the paper, the point of light changes in size. Notice also that it gets brighter as it gets smaller.

5. Adjust the distance between the paper and the magnifying glass to make the point of light very small and bright.

6. Pull the magnifying glass back about 1 cm (1/2 in.) and watch the paper.

7. Do you see anything happening to the paper? If so what, and why do you think it is happening? What kind of energy is causing this to happen?

8. What do you think might happen if you used two magnifying glasses focused on the same spot on the paper? Try it.

Figure 2.8-1

Magnifying Glass with Sheet of Paper in Glass Bowl

59

Teacher Information

As light rays from the sun are concentrated by a magnifying glass, so are the infrared, or heat, rays. The magnifying glass can concentrate bright sunlight to such a degree that it will scorch the paper or even possibly ignite it. As illustrated in Figure 2.8-2, the focal distance for heat (infrared) rays is slightly longer than the focal distance for light. For this reason, step 5 suggests moving the lens back slightly after the focal point is found. You will need to adjust the distance from lens to paper slightly to find the focal point for heat—the point at which the greatest possible concentration of heat is focused on the paper.

Figure 2.8-2

Focal Distance for Heat and Light

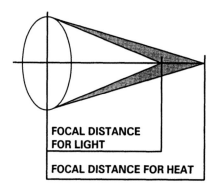

FOCAL DISTANCE FOR LIGHT

FOCAL DISTANCE FOR HEAT

SKILLS: Observing, inferring, classifying, measuring, predicting, communicating, using space-time relationships, formulating hypotheses, identifying and controlling variables, experimenting

Activity 2.9
HOW DO MOLECULES BEHAVE WHEN HEATED?

(Teacher demonstration)

Materials Needed

- Chalk or masking tape

Procedure

1. Have several students stand in a group.

2. Mark a border on the floor around the group with chalk or tape. Leave a few inches between the group and the border all the way around.

3. Ask students to move around slowly. Everyone should move constantly, but no one should move fast and there should be no pushing and shoving. They are to try to stay within the border marked on the floor.

4. Now instruct those in the group to move a bit faster. They are still to try to stay within the border.

5. Continue speeding up the movement of the group until they can no longer remain within the line marked on the floor.

6. Discuss what happened as those in the group increased their speed. Ask how this relates to the movement of molecules as temperature is increased.

Teacher Information

As a substance increases in temperature, molecules move faster but do not increase in size. In their rapid movement they bump into each other more frequently and require more space, just as did the group of students. If the members of the group were all running at top speed, they would have required much more space.

INTEGRATING: Physical education

SKILLS: Observing, inferring, comparing and contrasting

Activity 2.10
WHAT HAPPENS TO SOLIDS AS THEY ARE HEATED AND COOLED?

(Teacher-supervised activity)

Materials Needed

- Wire, about 1 m (1 yd.) long
- Large nail or small bolt
- Candle
- Match

Procedure

1. Wrap one end of the wire around the nail and anchor the other end to a support. Adjust the wire so the nail swings freely but barely misses the table or floor.
2. Light the candle and heat the wire.
3. Observe the nail. What happened?
4. Remove the candle and allow the wire to cool.
5. Observe the nail. What happened?
6. What can you say about the effect of heat on solids?

For Problem Solvers: Did you ever notice how hard it is to remove the ring from a jar of fruit? Try running hot water over the lid, then remove it. What do you think makes the difference?

Why are sidewalks made with joints every few feet? See what you can learn about expansion joints. See if you can find expansion joints as you drive across overpasses or bridges on the highway. Why are these joints built into the bridge? Try to find expansion joints in large buildings.

If you know an automobile mechanic, ask him or her why wheel bearings are sometimes installed on axles when they are very hot.

Teacher Information

CAUTION: This activity uses open flame, necessitating close supervision.

As the wire is heated by the candle, it will expand and the nail, which was swinging freely above the surface, will drag. As it cools, the wire will contract and the nail will swing freely again. Other solids expand and contract similarly when heated and cooled.

SKILLS: Observing, inferring, predicting, communicating, comparing and contrasting, using space-time relationships, formulating hypotheses, identifying and controlling variables

Activity 2.11
WHAT HAPPENS TO LIQUIDS AS THEY ARE HEATED AND COOLED?

Materials Needed

- Narrow-necked jar with a one-hole rubber stopper
- Balloon stick (available from craft or party-supply stores)
- Marker, rubber band, or masking tape
- Water

Procedure

1. Fill the jar completely with cold water.
2. Insert the plastic tubing through the rubber stopper.
3. Place the stopper in the jar. As you press the stopper into place, there should be no air space beneath the stopper, and water should be forced part way (not more than halfway) up the tube above the stopper.
4. Mark the tube at the water level with a marker, or by putting a rubber band or tape around it.
5. Place the jar in a window in direct sunlight.
6. Check the water level in the tube every few minutes for at least two hours.
7. What happened to the water level as the water warmed in the sunlight?
8. Remove the jar from the sunlight and place it in a cool place.
9. Again check the water level in the tube every few minutes.
10. What happened to the water level as the water cooled?
11. What can you say about the effect of temperature change on liquids?

For Problem Solvers: If a motorist goes to the filling station on a hot day and fills the fuel tank clear to the brim, then parks the vehicle in the sun for two or three hours, sometimes the tank will overflow and spill fuel onto the ground. Think about the above activity and see if you can explain why the tank overflows. The manager at your local filling station would probably be glad to discuss it with you if you have any questions or if you'd just like to find out if your explanation is correct. Any experienced truck driver could also discuss it with you.

Teacher Information

The ideal tube for this activity is a balloon stick, available at party supply outlets.

As the jar of water warms in the sunlight, the water will expand and the water level will rise in the tube, demonstrating that as the temperature of a liquid increases the liquid expands. As the water cools it will contract, and the level of the water in the tube will drop.

If food coloring is available, have students add a few drops to the water. This makes the water level in the tube easier to see, and the change is more evident.

This device can become a thermometer if you have students attach a card to the tube and mark the card at different temperatures, by taking temperature readings from a commercial thermometer. Water evaporation in the tube will eventually destroy the accuracy of it as a thermometer and it will need to be recalibrated.

Filling stations store gasoline in large tanks beneath the ground. Thus, the fuel is cool. If a motorist fills the tank, then parks the vehicle in the sun for a time, the fuel will expand from the heat and will sometimes overflow onto the ground.

INTEGRATING: Math, social studies

SKILLS: Observing, inferring, classifying, measuring, predicting, communicating, comparing and contrasting, using space-time relationships, formulating hypotheses, identifying and controlling variables, researching

Activity 2.12
WHAT HAPPENS TO GASES AS THEY ARE HEATED AND COOLED?

Materials Needed

- Narrow-necked jar with one-hole stopper
- Balloon stick (available from craft or party-supply stores)
- Water

Procedure

1. Put a small amount of water in the bottom of the jar.
2. Insert the plastic tube through the stopper.
3. Place the stopper in the jar. The lower end of the tube must be in the water.
4. Notice the water level in the tube.
5. Place the jar in a window in direct sunlight.
6. Check the water level in the tube every three or four minutes for at least one-half hour.
7. What happened to the water level as the air warmed in the sunlight? Why?
8. Remove the jar from the sunlight and place it in a cool place.
9. Again check the water level in the tube every few minutes.
10. What happened to the water level as the air cooled? Why?
11. What can you say about the effect of temperature change on gases?

For Problem Solvers: Blow up a balloon and measure the distance around it with a string. Mark the string to show the length required to reach around the balloon. Place the balloon over a heat vent or in front of a heater for a few minutes. Use the same string to measure the distance around the balloon again. Is there a difference? Can you explain why?

Learn what you can about hot-air balloons. Why do they rise into the air? Why do they come down again? Do balloon pilots usually fly their ships in the cool air of morning or in the heat of the afternoon? Why?

Teacher Information

This activity is very similar to Activity 2.11, but this time the changes in water level in the tube are caused by expansion and contraction of air within the jar instead of expansion and contraction of liquid. As the air in the jar warms in the sunlight, it will expand, forcing water up the tube and very likely spilling it out the top of the tube, demonstrating that as the temperature of a gas increases, the gas expands. As the air cools, it will contract and the level of the water in the tube will drop.

If food coloring is available, add a few drops to the water to make the water level in the tube more visible. This is a type of thermometer.

INTEGRATING: Math

SKILLS: Observing, inferring, measuring, predicting, communicating, comparing and contrasting, using space-time relationships, formulating hypotheses, identifying and controlling variables, experimenting

Activity 2.13
HOW DOES A NAIL CHANGE AS IT IS DRIVEN INTO A BOARD?

(Teacher-supervised activity)

Materials Needed

- Hammer
- Nail, at least 5 cm (2 in.) long
- Board, at least 4 cm (1 1/2 in.) thick
- Pounding surface

Procedure

1. Place the board on a good pounding surface such as another board, a stack of newspapers, or concrete.
2. Pound the nail at least 2.5 cm (1 in.) into the board. Do not pound it all the way in.
3. As soon as you stop pounding, feel the nail. What difference do you notice in the nail?
4. Pull the nail out of the board with the hammer.
5. As soon as you get the nail out of the board, feel it again.
6. What difference do you notice in the nail by feeling it? What can you say about this?

For Problem Solvers: Rub your hands together, hard and fast. Do you feel a temperature change? How is this similar to what you experienced with the nail in the above activity?

Teacher Information

As the nail is pounded into the board, some of the energy from the hammer is changed to heat energy due to friction between the nail and the board. As the nail is removed from the board, friction again changes some of the energy to heat. If the nail is pulled out quickly, the heat might be even more noticeable than when it was pounded in.

SKILLS: Observing, inferring, comparing and contrasting

Activity 2.14
HOW CAN THE ENERGY OF SOUND CAUSE SOMETHING TO MOVE?

Materials Needed

- Two guitars

Procedure

1. Be sure the two guitars are tuned alike.

2. Stand the two guitars face to face, about 5–10 cm (2–4 in.) apart.

3. Strum the strings of one guitar. After two or three seconds, silence the strings of the guitar you strummed by putting your hand on them.

4. Listen carefully to the other guitar.

5. What do you hear? How did it happen?

Teacher Information

This activity shows that sound can actually do work. It can make something move. Energy is transferred from one guitar to the other by sound waves, and the strings of the second guitar vibrate. The two guitars should be tuned alike so the vibrating frequency is the same for the two sets of strings.

INTEGRATING: Music

SKILLS: Observing, inferring

68

Activity 2.15
HOW CAN MAGNETISM DO WORK?

Materials Needed

- Magnet
- Steel ball

Procedure

1. Place the magnet on the table.
2. Place the steel ball on the table about 2–3 cm (1 in.) from the end of the magnet.
3. Let go of the steel ball.
4. What happened?
5. What is work, and how was work done in step 3?

For Problem Solvers: Find a variety of magnets. Predict which ones are strongest and weakest, and lay them out in order from strongest to weakest, according to your predictions. Then continue with the above activity, comparing the strength of these magnets. Which one seems to attract the steel ball from the farthest distance?

Were your predictions accurate? Compare size with strength. Are larger magnets always stronger than smaller magnets?

Teacher Information

Work was defined in this section's "To the Teacher" as moving something (a force acting through a distance). The magnet should cause the steel ball to roll toward it. If this did not happen, try putting the steel ball a bit closer to the magnet or find a stronger magnet.

A paper clip can be used in the place of the steel ball if necessary.

INTEGRATING: Math

SKILLS: Observing, inferring, classifying, measuring, predicting, communicating, formulating hypotheses, experimenting

Activity 2.16
HOW DOES GRAVITY AFFECT HEAVY AND LIGHT OBJECTS?

 Take home and do with family and friends.

Materials Needed

- Large book
- Small book
- Wadded paper
- Pencil
- Eraser
- Paper clip
- Paper

Procedure

1. Take the large book in one hand and the small book in the other. Hold the two books at exactly the same height.

2. Drop both books at the same time, but before you drop them, predict which one will fall faster. Have someone watch to see which book hits the floor first.

3. Repeat the book drop three times to be sure of your results.

4. Which book falls faster, the large one or the small one?

5. Compare the pencil and the paper in the same way. First predict which you think will fall faster.

6. Compare the various objects, two at a time. In each case predict which will fall faster, then drop them together three times to test your prediction.

7. Of all the materials you tried, which falls fastest? Most slowly?

8. Explain how the force of gravity compares with objects that are large, small, heavy, and light, according to your findings. How do the falling speeds compare?

9. Compare the falling speed of the wadded paper with that of a flat sheet of paper dropped horizontally.

10. Compare the falling speeds of two flat sheets of paper, one dropped vertically and the other horizontally.

11. Compare the falling speed of the wad of paper with that of a flat sheet of paper dropped vertically.

12. Discuss your observations with your group.

For Problem Solvers: Go to encyclopedias and other resources and do some research about gravity. Can you find out what really causes gravity? How large does an object have to be in order for it to have a gravitational attraction for other things? How much do scientists know about gravity?

Teacher Information

The force of gravity pulls all objects to the earth at the same rate, regardless of the size or weight of the object. Air resistance can slow the rate of fall, so the flat paper held in horizontal position will fall more slowly. Except for the factor of air resistance, however, the rate of fall is equal. A rock and a feather will fall at the same speed if placed in a vacuum chamber.

Scientists are still trying to figure out exactly what gravity is. They have learned a great deal about it. They know that all objects have a gravitational attraction for all other objects, though the force is too weak to really notice unless the objects are huge, as with planets and stars.

INTEGRATING: Reading, math

SKILLS: Observing, inferring, predicting, communicating, comparing and contrasting, experimenting, researching

Activity 2.17
WHAT HAPPENS WHEN YOU BURN A CANDLE AT BOTH ENDS?

(Teacher demonstration)

Materials Needed

- Candle
- Match
- Toothpicks
- Water glasses

Procedure

1. Prepare a candle so the wick may be lighted at both ends.

2. Insert round toothpicks into the candle and balance it on the water glasses as shown in the illustration. It doesn't have to balance perfectly.

3. Predict what will happen if you light both ends of the candle.

4. Light both ends of the candle. Observe for several minutes. What happened?

5. Think about it, and explain what happened the best you can. Share your ideas with others in your group.

Figure 2.17-1

Candle Burning at Both Ends, Balanced Between Glasses

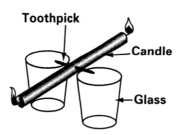

Teacher Information

CAUTION: Activities with fire or heat should be done only under close adult supervision or as a teacher demonstration.

When the candle is lighted at both ends, the end tilting downward will burn wax away more rapidly and become lighter. When it tilts up, the other end will be down, and it will burn wax away more rapidly. As this process continues to reverse, the candle will rock back and forth, often quite vigorously.

SKILLS: Observing, inferring, predicting, communicating, formulating hypotheses

Activity 2.18
WHAT IS CENTER OF GRAVITY?

 Take home and do with family and friends.

Materials Needed

- Meter stick (or yardstick)
- String
- Chair
- Various books

Procedure

1. Balance the meter stick on the back of the chair. It will balance at its "center of gravity," which should be at or very near the 50-cm (18-in.) mark. The part of the chair where the meter stick rests is the *fulcrum*.

2. Get two identical books and tie a string around each one.

3. Make a loop in the other end of each string and slide the loops over opposite ends of the meter stick. Leaving the books supported at the ends of the meter stick, where is the center of gravity (where the fulcrum has to be to balance the books)?

4. Replace one of the books with a smaller book. With the books still suspended at the ends of the meter stick, where is the center of gravity?

5. Replace the other book with a larger one. Where is the center of gravity now?

6. What can you say about the center of gravity when a large object is balanced with a small object? Consider the teeter-totter as you explain your answer.

For Problem Solvers: Do you know what a mobile is? Build one, then explain why it is important to know about center of gravity when constructing mobiles. If you do not know what a mobile is, ask your teacher, a parent, or a friend to help you get started.

Teacher Information

This activity is closely related to the activities on first-class levers in the section, "Simple Machines." Center of gravity is the balance point of an object. The center of gravity of spherical objects is at the center, assuming, of course, that the mass is equally distributed throughout the object.

Mobiles are fascinating to construct and provide excellent application of the concept of center of gravity. Encourage students to make a mobile, as suggested in the "For Problem Solvers" section.

INTEGRATING: Math

SKILLS: Observing, inferring, identifying and controlling variables

Activity 2.19
WHERE IS YOUR CENTER OF GRAVITY?

 Take home and do with family and friends.

Materials Needed

- Pencil or other small object

Procedure

1. Put your pencil on the floor.
2. Standing near the pencil, pick it up without bending your legs or moving your feet.
3. Stand against the wall, with your heels touching the wall.
4. Drop your pencil on the floor near your feet.
5. Bend over and pick up your pencil without moving your feet or bending your legs. You must also not lean against anything or hold onto anything for support.
6. What happened? Why?
7. Repeat steps 1 and 2. Notice your movements as you pick up the pencil. Explain what happened in step 5 in terms of the effect of the center of gravity.

For Problem Solvers: Try this activity with family members and friends. Try replacing the pencil with a coin or with a dollar bill. Can you find anyone who can pick up the object without breaking the rules?

Teacher Information

Any time we are on our feet, whether we are walking, running, standing, or bending over, we are constantly adjusting to the center of gravity in order to remain "balanced." The body makes these adjustments so automatically that we don't think about them.

The "For Problem Solvers" section invites students to try this activity with family members. Replacing the pencil with a dollar bill and offering it to the person who can pick it up without breaking the rules will increase interest and effort substantially. The money is as safe as if it were behind lock and key.

INTEGRATING: Physical education, dance

SKILLS: Observing, inferring, communicating

Activity 2.20
HOW CAN YOU BALANCE SEVERAL NAILS ON ONE NAIL?

 Take home and do with family and friends.

Materials Needed

- Wood base with nail hole in center
- Several flat-headed nails

Procedure

1. This is an activity you can use to trick your family and friends. After they give up, you can show them how smart you are.

2. Stand one nail (we'll call it #1) in the hole in the board.

3. Lay a second nail (#2) on the table.

4. Place the remaining nails on the table with their heads over nail #2, in alternating directions.

5. Lay the last nail on top of nail #2, where the nail-heads overlap.

6. Pick up nail #2 and the last carefully by the ends. If you have set it up correctly, the criss-crossed nails will come, too.

7. Carefully balance the whole system on nail #1.

Figure 2.20-1

Balancing Nails

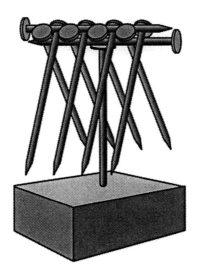

For Problem Solvers: In Activities 2.18 and 2.19 you learned about center of gravity. What is the role of center of gravity with the nail-balancer? Why don't the overhanging nails tip the system over?

Did you ever see a tightrope walker? They usually carry a low-bending pole. Can you see a similarity with the nail-balancer? Do some research about tightrope walkers and learn what you can about the way they use center of gravity to their advantage.

Teacher Information

First you might want to just give the materials to students with verbal instructions to stand one nail in the wood base and balance all of the other nails on the one that's standing. Let them struggle with it for a while. The instructions and illustration above will help students when you're ready for them to have it.

Although nails are stretching out in two directions, the fourteen nails will balance on the first nail, because the center of gravity is at the center of the system of nails. The overhanging nails actually hold the system in balance, instead of tipping it over as one might expect at first glance. Tightrope walkers use low-bending poles to help them balance for the same reason.

This is a great activity for students to do at home. Encourage them to let their victims struggle; don't be in a hurry to show them how to do it.

SKILLS: Observing, inferring, communicating, researching

Activity 2.21
WHAT IS INERTIA?

Materials Needed

- Two chairs
- Broom
- Four lengths of cotton thread about 45 cm (1.5 ft.) each
- Two rocks (or other weights) about 1 kg (2 lbs.) each

Procedure

1. Lay the broom across the backs of two chairs (or other supports).
2. Tie two pieces of thread to the broom handle, several inches apart.
3. Tie one of the rocks to each of the threads attached to the broom handle. The rocks should hang down several inches from the broom handle.
4. Tie one of the other two threads to each of the rocks. These threads should hang freely from the rocks.
5. Hold tightly to one of the lower threads and pull down slowly but firmly until a thread breaks.
6. Hold tightly to the other lower thread and jerk quickly, breaking a thread.
7. Which thread broke when you pulled slowly—the upper thread or the lower thread? Which one broke when you jerked? Explain.
8. Get some new thread and repeat the activity to verify your results.

For Problem Solvers: Pick a spot (target) on the floor or the sidewalk. Walk to the target and stop with your feet exactly on it. Now run to the target and stop with your feet exactly on it. Next, run as fast as you can, and try to stop with your feet exactly on it, without slowing down before you get there. What effect is inertia having on your effort to stop?

Think about seat belts. Why is it important to use them when riding in a motor vehicle? What does inertia have to do with the need for seat belts?

Why do Earth and the other planets remain in orbit around the sun, instead of being pulled into the sun by gravity? What do you think inertia has to do with this?

Teacher Information

As a lower thread is pulled slowly, the force of the pull is equal on both the upper and lower thread. In addition, the upper thread is supporting the weight of the rock (pull of gravity). Thus, the upper thread will usually break if the two threads are identical.

Newton's first law of motion states that an object at rest tends to remain at rest and an object in motion tends to remain in motion in the same direction and at the same speed unless it is acted upon by an outside force. This is sometimes referred to as the law of *inertia*. Inertia is the resistance to change in motion. The rock, in this case, is an object at rest. As the lower thread is given a quick jerk in step 6, the resistance, or inertia, of the rock protects the upper thread from receiving the full impact of the downward force. Thus, greater force is applied to the lower thread than to the upper thread, and the lower thread will break.

SKILLS: Observing, inferring, communicating, comparing and contrasting

Activity 2.22
WHAT IS CENTRIFUGAL FORCE?

Materials Needed

- Small tube, about 10 cm (4 in.) long
- String, about 1 m (1 yd.) long
- Two pencil erasers (or other small weights)

Procedure

1. Thread the string through the tube.
2. Tie one pencil eraser to each end of the string.
3. Hold the tube upright and move it around in a circular motion so the top weight swings around and around.

Figure 2.22-1

Tube, String, and Erasers—One Swinging

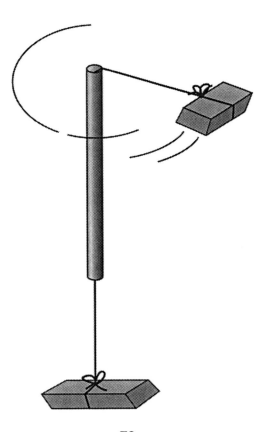

4. Swing the weight around faster. Do not swing it near anyone. The tendency of the upper weight to move outward when rotating is commonly called *centrifugal force*.

5. Change the speed of rotation, faster and slower, and observe the lower weight.

6. What happens to the lower weight as you increase and decrease the speed of rotation? What can you say about the speed of rotation and its effect on centrifugal force?

Teacher Information

The tube used in this activity could be a cardboard tube. It could even be the barrel of a ball-point pen. If a small, sturdy tube is not available, use a wooden bead out of someone's toy box. The bead needs to be large enough to hold firmly in the hand without interfering with the movement of the string passing through it.

Centrifugal force is the force that tends to impel an object outward from a center of rotation. Newton's first law of motion states that an object at rest tends to remain at rest and an object in motion tends to remain in motion at the same speed and in the same direction unless it is acted upon by an outside force. The tendency of the object to continue moving in a straight line and at the same speed is called *inertia*. If the object is held back by another force, it cannot do that, thus the circular motion. The force that holds it back is called *centripetal force*, defined as the force that tends to pull an object toward the center of rotation. Thus, what we call centrifugal force is really an interaction between inertia and centripetal force.

SKILLS: Observing, inferring, comparing and contrasting

Activity 2.23
HOW WELL DO YOU CONSERVE ENERGY AT HOME?

Materials Needed

- Pencil and paper

Procedure

1. Are you careful about how much energy you use? Use the following energy checklist at home to see how well you and others who live there are conserving energy. Perhaps you would like to add other items to the list.

   a. Is cold water or warm water used when washing clothes, instead of hot water?

   b. Are draperies used to increase efficiency of heating and air conditioning by opening them when sunlight needs to be let in and closing them at times when they are needed as insulation?

   c. Are air conditioners and furnaces used sparingly?

   d. Are heating and cooling systems serviced regularly to assure safe and efficient operation?

   e. Are filters in the heating and cooling systems regularly serviced (cleaned or changed)?

   f. Are heating and cooling vents free from obstruction?

   g. If there is a fireplace, is the damper on the chimney closed when the fireplace is not in use?

   h. Are lights used only when needed?

   i. Are electrical appliances turned off when they are not in use?

   j. Are refrigerator doors closed promptly after use?

   k. Are refrigerator door gaskets tight, so they seal properly?

   l. Are windows and doors tight, and do they prevent draft? Is caulking and weather stripping around doors and windows in good condition?

2. After completing the home energy checklist, compare notes with others and discuss things that need to be done in the homes to help conserve energy.

For Problem Solvers: Decide which parts of the energy checklist also apply at school. Using this list of things to check, or another list that you write, find out how well energy is being conserved at school. You might have some suggestions for improvement. You could do this activity as a group if you prefer. Consider writing a letter to the school principal, custodian, or to the school district office, outlining your findings and suggestions. In most cases, the principal and custodian would probably be the best people to notify of your concerns.

Teacher Information

This activity should help your students to be more energy conscious. If it seems appropriate, suggestions from the class could be sent out to the homes, listing only general ideas, and not pointing out individual problems that might be offensive.

If the energy survey at school produces fruitful recommendations, invite the media to feature the class with a short story spotlighting the efforts of the students. Do this only if it does not create embarrassment for others involved.

INTEGRATING: Language arts, math, social studies

SKILLS: Observing, inferring, classifying, measuring, predicting, communicating, using space-time relationships, formulating hypotheses, identifying and controlling variables, experimenting, researching

Section Three

LIGHT

TO THE TEACHER

Like many other scientific phenomena, light is so common that we take it for granted. Yet without it we could not live. Plants use light from the sun to produce oxygen, which is vital to all animal life, including humans. Without plants we would have no food. Light from the sun also heats the earth, and without heat there could be no life at all.

The question of what light really is has evaded scientists for centuries. Yet it is as fascinating as it is elusive, and continues to be the object of many studies. We know a great deal about light because of these studies. For instance, we know that light is a form of energy that travels freely through space. We also know that in addition to the sources of natural light (the sun and the stars), light can be created in various ways. When light comes from sources that people control, it is called artificial light. We use artificial light every day in the form of fluorescent lights and incandescent lights. The laser produces a form of light that has found widespread use in industry, medicine, and communications.

Activities included in this section encourage investigation into some of the ways in which light behaves. As students participate in these activities, the teacher should encourage them to ponder the relationship of this topic to the study of the eyes and to art.

The scope of the activities in this section is limited to a few very basic concepts about light. Students investigate shadows, color, reflection, and refraction, and they are introduced to prisms and lenses. Many of these concrete activities are easily adaptable for children in the early grades. For the student whose interests extend beyond these basic investigations, many resources are available—trade books, encyclopedias, science reference books, and suppliers of scientific equipment.

Regarding the Early Grades

With verbal instructions and slight modifications, many of these activities can be used with kindergarten, first-grade, and second-grade students. In some activities, steps that involve procedures that go beyond the level of the child can simply be omitted and yet offer the child an experience that plants the seed for a concept that will germinate and grow later on.

Teachers of the early grades will probably choose to bypass many of the "For Problem Solvers" sections. That's okay. These sections are provided for those who are especially motivated and want to go beyond the investigation provided by the activity outlined. Use the outlined activities, and enjoy worthwhile learning experiences together with your young students. Also consider, however, that many of the "For Problem Solvers" sections can be used appropriately with young children as group activities or as demonstrations, still giving students the advantage of an exposure to the experience, and laying groundwork for connections that will be made later on.

Activity 3.1
WHAT CAN YOU MAKE WITH A SHADOW?

 Take home and do with family and friends.

Materials Needed

- Projector or flashlight
- Wall or screen

Procedure

1. Using a blank wall or a piece of paper or cardboard as a screen, see if you can make the animal shapes shown in Figure 3.1-1 with shadows.

2. Create some other shapes of your own.

3. What happens to the shadow figures as you move your hands closer to or farther from the light?

4. Where is the darkest part of the shadow? Explain why it is darker there.

Figure 3.1-1

Shadow Pictures

For Problem Solvers: Find a white bed sheet, a projector, and some way to hang the sheet up so you can shine light on it from the projector. Get some friends to help you create a shadow play from behind the screen. Some members of your group can create the images while the rest are watching them from the front of the screen.

Here's a challenge for you. One member of your group gets behind the screen and makes a shadow on the screen with his or her body. Another member of the group tries to make the same body shape by looking at the shadow. Someone else moves the screen and checks to see if the two body shapes are about the same.

Find some three-dimensional geometric shapes, such as a cube, a cylinder, a rod, a sphere, and so on. Have one person make shadows with these and another person try to guess which object(s) are being used to make the shadow. Try the same thing with any other object, such as a pencil, a thumb tack, an eraser, or whatever you can find.

Teacher Information

This activity is intended mostly for enjoyment and creativity. In reference to step 4, however, the student should notice that the shadow is darkest toward the middle. The outer edges of the figure are not shaded from the entire light bulb, as illustrated in Figure 3.1-2, and are therefore not as dark as the portion that is completely shaded.

The last part of "For Problem Solvers" works very nicely as a group activity using the overhead projector. Stand a book or other visual barrier at the back of the projector plate so students can't see the items being placed on the projector plate. Turn the projector light off while placing the item on the plate, then turn the light on and project the shadow on the screen.

As another group activity, divide the class into two groups. Have Group A stand behind the bed-sheet screen. Have one person at a time from Group A stand in the light behind the screen and Group B try to guess who it is, based on the appearance of the shadow on the screen.

Figure 3.1-2

Light Creating a Shadow, Darkened in the Middle

SKILLS: Observing, inferring, comparing and contrasting

Activity 3.2
HOW DOES CLOSENESS TO LIGHT AFFECT SHADOW SIZE?

Materials Needed

- Projector or flashlight
- Screen or blank wall

Procedure

1. Place the projector across the room from the screen or blank wall.
2. Turn the projector on and the room lights off.
3. Stand in the light, near the screen or wall, and look at your shadow.
4. Move slowly toward the projector, watching your shadow as you move.
5. What happened to your shadow as you moved toward the projector?
6. Why do you think this happened?

For Problem Solvers: Stand directly under a streetlight at night. Where is your shadow? At what time of day do you cast a shadow like that from sunlight? Predict what your shadow will look like if you take two steps forward. Try it. How far will it reach if you take two more steps forward? Watch how shadows of different objects change as cars drive by at night with their headlights on.

See what else you can learn about shadows. Try to find a double shadow. See if you can figure out what causes it.

Teacher Information

Light from the projector passes through the lens and spreads out as it travels through space, forming a cone-shaped path of light with the lens at the narrow end of the cone. As an object moves toward the light source (the lens), the object blocks out a greater and greater portion of the light. Since the shadow is the area not receiving direct rays of light, the shadow increases in size as more of the light is blocked.

Those who investigate shadows further, as suggested in the "For Problem Solvers" section, will find that shadows can be very fascinating. When an object casts two shadows, there must be two light sources. Students will enjoy finding them, noting the relationship between the position of the light source; the size, shape, and position of the object casting the shadow; and the size, shape, and position of the shadow.

Another related fun activity is to have students draw each other's shadow on the ground, then lie down on their own shadow and try to fit into it. Later in the day they come back and try to fit their shadow into the outline of the former shadow. Next, have them predict what their shadow will look like the next morning, and at various other times of the day. New insights will be born.

While student interest is high for shadows and their changing shapes, it would be an excellent time to introduce them to sundials. They can make a sundial with a pencil standing in the center of a paper plate, or with the tetherball pole or flagpole, or in many other ways.

INTEGRATING: Math

SKILLS: Observing, inferring, measuring, predicting, communicating, comparing and contrasting, using space-time relationships, formulating hypotheses, identifying and controlling variables, experimenting

Activity 3.3
HOW DOES YOUR SHADOW CHANGE?

Materials Needed

- Chart paper, butcher paper, or newsprint for each person (long enough to contain the child's shadow)
- Crayon or marker
- Partner
- Sunny day

Procedure

1. Lay the paper on the sidewalk.
2. Stand with your shadow on the paper.
3. Have your partner outline your shadow with the crayon.
4. Trade places and outline your partner's shadow on a different paper.
5. Lie down on your paper and see if your body fits the outline of your shadow.
6. Explain what happened.
7. Stand up to your partner's paper and try to make your shadow fit your partner's outline.
8. Talk about what happened.
9. Come back in one hour and see if your shadow still fits your outline.
10. Explain what happened.
11. With another color of crayon, draw your shadow the way you think it will look two hours later. Come back and check it out.
12. Discuss what happened.

For Problem Solvers: Do some research and learn what you can about shadow clocks and sundials. Can you use your shadow as a clock? Talk about it with your group and figure out a way to make a shadow clock with your shadow.

Which do you think would make the best shadow clock, your shadow or the shadow of the tetherball pole? Why? See if you can get permission to draw on the pavement with chalk and make lines for a shadow clock around the tetherball pole. Be sure to plan carefully and clear your plan with your teacher before you make any lines on the playground.

Teacher Information

In this activity students learn that shadows aren't always the same size and shape as the objects that cast the shadows. They will also learn that shadows change in size, shape, and direction as the day goes on and the sun moves across the sky.

Your problem solvers will learn something about how shadows can be used to indicate time of day. If they decide to try making a shadow clock on the playground, you need to insist that they plan carefully and make it neatly so it will be accurate and so that others will use it. If the playground is not paved, students can draw their lines for the shadow clock in the soil. If there is no tetherball pole on the school playground, a flagpole or any other pole can be used—even a corner of the school building.

INTEGRATING: Math, reading, language arts, social studies, art

SKILLS: Observing, inferring, measuring, predicting, communicating, comparing and contrasting, using space-time relationships, formulating hypotheses, identifying and controlling variables, researching

Activity 3.4
WHAT PATH DOES LIGHT FOLLOW?

Materials Needed

- Four 5 × 8 in. cards
- Clay
- Flashlight (or projector)
- Ruler
- Paper punch

Procedure

1. Punch a small hole in the center of each card.
2. Stand each card in a small ball of clay.
3. Space the cards about 30 cm (1 ft.) apart, with the center holes lined up.
4. Have someone hold the flashlight so that it shines into the hole of one of the end cards while you look through the hole of the card at the other end.
5. What do you see?
6. Now move one of the cards about one inch to the side and repeat step 4.
7. What happened? What does this tell you about the path light travels?

Figure 3.4-1

Flashlight Shining Through Cards

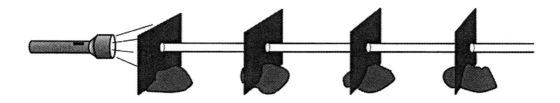

Teacher Information

This activity will help children realize that light travels in a straight path. Unless the cards are positioned with the holes in a straight line, the light does not pass through the holes in the cards.

SKILLS: Observing, inferring

91

Activity 3.5
HOW DOES COLOR AFFECT ENERGY ABSORBED FROM LIGHT?

Materials Needed

- Two equally calibrated thermometers
- Heat lamp (or a high-wattage bulb)
- One sheet of white paper and one sheet of black paper of the same thickness
- Paper and pencil

Procedure

1. Prop the thermometers in an upright position about 20 cm (8 in.) apart, facing in the same direction.
2. Record the temperatures of both thermometers.
3. Place the sheet of white paper in front of one thermometer and the black paper in front of the other.
4. Shine the heat lamp at the sheets of paper in such a way that it faces both equally. It should be about 40–50 cm (16–20 in.) away from the papers.
5. After the heat lamp has shone on the papers for about two minutes, check and record the temperatures of the two thermometers again.
6. Repeat for two more minutes and again record the temperatures.
7. Compare the changes in the first and last temperature readings of the two thermometers.
8. What can you say about the effect of color in this activity?

Figure 3.5-1

Heat Lamp, Sheets of Paper, and Thermometers

For Problem Solvers: In the above activity you compared heat absorption from white paper and black paper. Find several different colors of paper. Use only paper that is the same except for color. Construction paper will work well. From what you have already learned, predict which colors will absorb the most heat from the light bulb and which will reflect the most heat. Arrange the papers in order, according to your predictions. Design an investigation to find out if your predictions are accurate.

Were you right? Why is it important that you don't use construction paper for some colors, typing paper for some colors, and art paper for still other colors?

That raises another interesting question—does one *type* of paper absorb more heat than another? Now, to test that question, what will you do about color?

Teacher Information

Dark materials have a greater tendency to absorb heat than do lighter-colored materials. The thermometers behind the two sheets of paper will verify this tendency.

On a sunny day, direct sunlight could be used instead of the heat lamp. As an enrichment (or perhaps introductory) activity, invite students to go to the parking lot (on a warm day) and feel the surfaces of cars of various colors. Which colors tend to be warmest? This needs to be carefully supervised to avoid offending car owners.

Your "problem solvers" will enjoy the challenge of some real science, while they test the variables of color and types of paper with respect to heat absorption.

INTEGRATING: Math

SKILLS: Observing, inferring, classifying, measuring, predicting, communicating, comparing and contrasting, using space-time relationships, formulating hypotheses, identifying and controlling variables, experimenting

Activity 3.6
WHAT HAPPENED TO THE PENCIL?

 Take home and do with family and friends.

Materials Needed

- Clear tumbler or bowl
- Water
- Pencil (or spoon)

Procedure

1. Fill the tumbler or bowl about two thirds full of water.
2. Put the pencil into the water.
3. Look at the pencil from the top and from the side.
4. What appears to happen to the pencil at the water level? What ideas do you have about this effect?

Teacher Information

Light travels at different speeds through different substances, creating a bending effect on any light rays that enter a substance at an angle. This is called *refraction*. Light travels faster through air than it does through water. The bending of the light rays as they pass from air to water or from water to air results in an optical illusion as the object in the water appears to be broken at the surface of the water.

SKILLS: Observing, inferring

Activity 3.7
CAN YOU FIND THE COIN?

 Take home and do with family and friends.

Materials Needed

- Opaque bowl
- Water
- Coin (or button)

Procedure

1. Place the coin in the bowl.
2. Stand in such a position that the coin is just hidden from your view by the edge of the bowl.
3. Without shifting your position, have your partner slowly fill the bowl with water, being careful not to disturb the coin at the bottom of the bowl.
4. What happened to the coin as your partner poured water into the bowl?
5. What do you think could have caused this?

For Problem Solvers: Challenge your friends to a test of skills at spear fishing. Put some water in a dishpan or sink. Place a coin (that's the fish) at the bottom of the pan. Use a meter stick, a metal rod, or any other straight and narrow shaft as a spear. Place the tip of your spear on the edge of the pan, but not in the water. Aim at the fish, and quickly push the spear to the bottom of the pan, being sure to keep the spear at the same angle as when it was aimed.

Talk about eagles and bears, and their ability to strike at the right place when catching a fish. How do you think they learned to do that?

Teacher Information

Light travels in what appears to be a straight line in air, but when it passes from water to air, it is bent by refraction, because it travels more slowly through water than through air. As water is poured into the bowl, the light will bend and more of the bottom of the bowl will be exposed. The coin will appear.

Your students will enjoy the challenge of the "problem solver" activity. With trial and error they will improve their spearing accuracy. Perhaps eagles and bears also learn by trial and error.

Figure 3.7-1

Bowl and Coin Showing How Water Bends Light

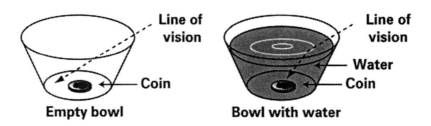

SKILLS: Observing, inferring, predicting, communicating, comparing and contrasting, identifying and controlling variables

Activity 3.8
HOW CAN A POSTAGE STAMP HIDE UNDER CLEAR GLASS?

 Take home and do with family and friends.

Materials Needed

- Empty short jar (such as peanut butter jar) with lid
- Water
- Postage stamp or sticker

Procedure

1. Put the stamp on the table.
2. Fill the jar with water and put the lid on.
3. Place the jar on the stamp.
4. Look at the stamp.
5. Explain your observations.

For Problem Solvers: Replace the jar with a plastic cup. Try this same activity with many different containers. They all need to be clear, of course, but try various shapes and sizes, using both glass and plastic. Do they all work the same? What are the differences? Can you tell why?

Teacher Information

As light passes from water to air the light bends (refracts) because it travels through these materials at different speeds. In this activity the refraction makes the stamp appear higher than it really is. When it is looked at from an angle, reflected light from the stamp doesn't reach the eyes, so the stamp seems to have disappeared. The lid on the jar prevents the observer from looking straight down on the stamp.

SKILLS: Observing, inferring, predicting, communicating

Activity 3.9
WHAT MAKES LIGHT BEND?

Materials Needed

- Aquarium three fourths full of water
- Flashlight or projector
- Milk
- Two chalkboard erasers that are chalky
- One sheet of paper
- Tape

Procedure

1. Pour milk into the aquarium, a little at a time, until the water has a *slightly* cloudy appearance. Easy does it—you might need only a spoonful.

2. Wrap and tape the paper around the flashlight like a tube, to concentrate the light into a narrow beam.

3. Turn the room lights off.

4. Aim the light at the water on an angle. Have someone clap the chalkboard erasers together over the aquarium to make the beam of light easier to see in the air.

5. Observe carefully the angle of the light beam as it extends from the flashlight to the water and as it continues through the water.

6. What happens to the light beam as it enters the water? What do you think causes the change?

Figure 3.9-1

Aquarium, Flashlight, and Two Chalkboard Erasers

98

Teacher Information

This experiment makes the phenomenon of refraction easily visible. With the chalk dust the light can be seen in the air, and the milk makes it easily observable in the water.

SKILLS: Observing, inferring, comparing and contrasting

Activity 3.10
HOW DOES WATER AFFECT THE WAY LIGHT TRAVELS?

Materials Needed

- Glass jar with lid
- Paper
- Markers
- Water

Procedure

1. Draw a simple diagram on the paper and color it with dark or bright colors.
2. Hang the paper on the wall or lean it against something on a table.
3. Fill the jar with water and put the lid on.
4. Hold the jar between your eyes and your diagram.
5. What do you see?
6. Keeping your eyes on the diagram, hold the jar at different distances from your eyes and from the diagram.
7. Explain your observations.

For Problem Solvers: Try this activity with bottles of different sizes and shapes. What differences do you find? Do you see any patterns? Does the design look the same regardless of the size or shape of the bottle? Does the same thing happen at the same distance regardless of the size of the bottle?

Teacher Information

The jar filled with water acts as a convex lens and reverses the image.

SKILLS: Observing, inferring, comparing and contrasting

Activity 3.11
HOW CAN YOU MAKE A GLASS DISAPPEAR?

Materials Needed

- Two large glass jars
- Two small glass jars or drinking glasses
- Water
- Cooking oil

Procedure

1. Place the two small jars inside the large jars.
2. Fill one pair of jars with water.
3. Can you see the small jar?
4. Fill the other pair of jars with cooking oil.
5. Can you see the small jar?
6. Explain your observations.

For Problem Solvers: Think of some other ways to do this activity. Use containers with different shapes. Try plastic containers instead of glass containers. Does it work out differently in water if you put food coloring in the water? Think of other ways to test refraction of light.

Teacher Information

As light passes from one transparent material to another (such as air, water, and glass), the light is bent at the boundary between the two materials. This happens because of the differing speeds at which the materials transmit light. Light moves at about the same speed through petroleum products (including cooking oil) as it does through glass. Therefore, as light passes between glass and oil it doesn't bend at the boundaries, leaving the boundaries invisible.

SKILLS: Observing, inferring, communicating, comparing and contrasting, identifying and controlling variables

Activity 3.12
HOW DOES A CAMERA SEE THE WORLD?

(Teacher demonstration)

Materials Needed

- Pinhole camera
- Candle
- Match

Procedure

1. Darken the room.
2. Light the candle.
3. Point the pinhole in the box toward the candle.
4. Look at the image on the tissue paper at the back of the box. What do you observe about the image of the candle flame?
5. What can you say about this?

Teacher Information

As the light from the candle passes through the pinhole, the image is inverted because light travels in a straight line (Figures 3.12-1, 3.12-2, and 3.12-3).

The human eye also receives images upside down on the retina, but the brain somehow turns them right side up again as we "see" them. **CAUTION: Close supervision of candle flame is needed. This should be a teacher-demonstration activity.**

Figure 3.12-1

Shoe Box with Pinhole and Tissue Paper

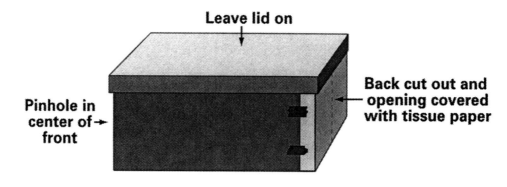

Figure 3.12-2
Diagram of Candlelight Going Through Pinhole Camera

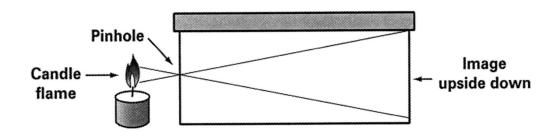

Figure 3.12-3
End View of Box

SKILLS: Observing, inferring

Activity 3.13
HOW DOES A LENS AFFECT THE WAY LIGHT TRAVELS?

(Teacher-supervised activity)

Materials Needed

- Candle
- Match
- White cardboard
- Magnifying glass
- Pan

Procedure

1. Prop the cardboard on a table.
2. Stand the candle in a pan or other nonflammable container about 60–90 cm (2–3 ft.) away from the cardboard.
3. Light the candle.
4. Hold the magnifying glass near the cardboard. Move it slowly toward the flame until a clear image of the flame appears on the cardboard.
5. Do you see anything strange about the flame? What effect do you think the magnifying glass has on what you see?

Figure 3.13-1

Candle, Lens, and Cardboard

Figure 3.13-2

Candle, Lens, and Cardboard, with Inverted Image

For Problem Solvers: Try to find a variety of lenses—different types and sizes. Try the candle-flame activity with each lens. If you notice differences in what happens, describe those differences. If you have many lenses, put them in groups according to the way they worked for you.

Teacher Information

The bending of light through refraction (see also Activities 3.6 and 3.7) results in an inverse image of the flame as it is projected onto the cardboard. The same thing happens with the eye. Images are projected onto the back of the eye upside down, but they are reversed to their true perspective as they are interpreted by the mind.

SKILLS: Observing, inferring

Activity 3.14
HOW CAN YOU MAKE A LENS FROM A DROP OF WATER?

 Take home and do with family and friends.

Materials Needed

- Small sheet of clear plastic or glass (or even plastic wrap)
- Eye dropper
- Water
- Book

Procedure

1. Place a drop of water on the sheet of plastic.
2. Lay the plastic over the page of a book and look at a letter or punctuation mark through the drop of water.
3. What does the drop of water do to the images on the paper?
4. Examine other things through the drop of water, such as a piece of cloth or the back of your hand, by laying the plastic on them.
5. Explain what happened and why.

For Problem Solvers: Get a piece of wire that you can bend easily and make a small loop in one end, just about the width of a drop of water. Place a drop of water in the loop. Hold the loop near a page of print. What happens? How is it different from what you saw with the water on plastic, in the above activity? Try making a wire loop just a little bit bigger, then make one a little bit smaller. Does it seem to make any difference? Shake some of the water out of the wire loop, leaving just enough to remain stretched across the loop. Look at the page of print again. What do you think makes the difference?

Teacher Information

Any transparent substance with a convex surface will cause light rays to bend and converge. Many vision-aiding devices are based on this principle, including eyeglasses, hand lenses, binoculars, microscopes, and telescopes. The drop of water isn't the best lens, because it must be handled carefully and the degree of surface curve is difficult to control, but it is a lens.

If you prefer, you can bypass the sheet of plastic and place the drop of water directly on a page of print. The plastic provides transportability for multiple uses.

SKILLS: Observing, inferring, comparing and contrasting

Activity 3.15
HOW ARE CONVEX AND CONCAVE LENSES DIFFERENT?

Materials Needed

- Convex lens
- Concave lens
- Small sheet of clear glass
- Flashlight or projector
- Sheet of paper
- Tape
- White surface

Procedure

1. Roll the paper into a tube around the end of the flashlight and tape it in place.
2. Shine the light on a white surface.
3. Hold each lens and the sheet of glass, one at a time, in the path of the light. What happened each time?

Figure 3.15-1

Flashlight with Paper Tube Around It

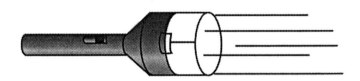

For Problem Solvers: Examine the surface of a book, a picture, your fingernail, and other objects using the two lenses. Explain the differences in the images you see. Examine the shapes of the lenses carefully. How are they alike? How are they different?

One of these lenses is called a concave lens and the other is called a convex lens. Do some research about lenses and see if you can find out why they have a different effect on images that are seen through them.

Teacher Information

When light passes between media of differing densities (such as air and glass or air and water) the light can be refracted, or bent. Convex lenses are thicker in the middle than on the edges and cause light rays to converge, or come together. Concave lenses are thicker on the edges than in the middle and cause light rays to diverge. A convex lens in the path of the light will concentrate the light on the white surface, causing it to appear brighter, while a concave lens will spread the beam of light over a larger surface. Convex lenses are used as magnifiers, while concave lenses are used to make things appear smaller.

Figure 3.15-2
Convex and Concave Lenses

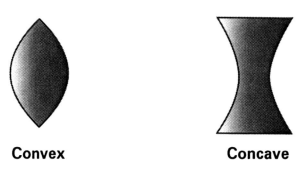

Convex   **Concave**

SKILLS: Observing, inferring, comparing and contrasting

Activity 3.16
HOW CAN YOU MEASURE THE MAGNIFYING POWER OF A LENS?

Materials Needed

- Hand lens
- Lined paper

Procedure

1. Lay the hand lens on the lined paper and count the number of lines from one edge of the lens to the other.
2. Pick up the lens and hold it in such a position that the lines on the paper come into focus.
3. How many lines do you see in the lens?
4. Compare the number of lines in step 1 with the number of lines in step 3.
5. From your information, what would you say is the magnifying power of your lens: Two power? Three power? Five power?

Teacher Information

If the lens itself spans six lines but only three lines can be seen through the lens when held in focus position, the lens is about two power. If only two of the six can be seen through the lens in focus position, the lens is about three power. It makes things look about three times as large as they are. This is not an accurate measurement of lens magnification, but it will provide a close estimate. If you are using a ten-power lens, you will need to use lines, or other equally spaced objects that are quite close together in order to get a workable count. The smaller and more powerful the lens, the closer the counted objects will need to be.

INTEGRATING: Math

SKILLS: Observing, measuring, predicting, communicating, comparing and contrasting

Activity 3.17
WHAT AFFECTS THE QUALITY OF REFLECTION?

Materials Needed

- Tin can
- Damp cloth
- Dry cloth
- Toothpaste
- Sandpaper

Procedure

1. Polish the bottom of the can by rubbing it with toothpaste, using a damp cloth. Shine it with a dry cloth.
2. Look at your reflection in the polished surface.
3. Scuff the polished surface lightly with the sandpaper.
4. Look at your reflection again.
5. Explain the difference in your reflection before and after the sandpaper treatment. What made the difference? Why do you think this happened?

For Problem Solvers: Find a variety of surfaces to shine the light on and compare reflections. Try a mirror, clear glass, textured glass, as is often used in bathroom windows, and other surfaces. Try a painted wall. You can see the reflection if you will tap two dusty chalkboard erasers together in the path of the light.

Teacher Information

A polished surface reflects light rays in a consistent pattern. A rough surface diffuses light rays (reflects them in all directions), preventing a clear focus.

Figure 3.17-1

Two Flashlights, Two Surfaces

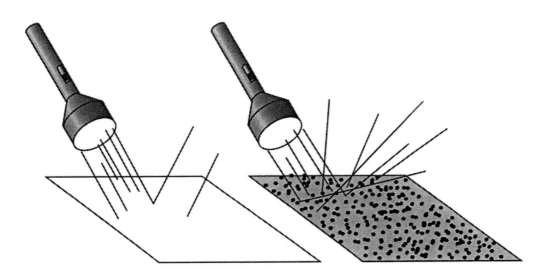

SKILLS: Observing, inferring, classifying, measuring, predicting, communicating, comparing and contrasting, identifying and controlling variables, experimenting

Activity 3.18
WHAT IS THE DIFFERENCE BETWEEN REFLECTED LIGHT AND SOURCE LIGHT?

Materials Needed

- Mirror

Procedure

1. Look briefly at the light in your room.
2. Now hold the mirror so that you can see the room lights in the mirror.
3. Which of these is the "source light" and which is "reflected light"?
4. If you were to cover the source light, what would happen to the reflected light?
5. If you cover the reflected light, what happens to the source light?
6. Light from your desk enables you to see the desk. Is it source light or reflected light?
7. Does the sun give off source light or reflected light? What about the moon? Explain.

Teacher Information

We receive light by two means—from sources that produce light and from objects that reflect light. There are relatively few sources of direct light (source light); everything else we see gives off reflected light. Light sources include light bulbs, fluorescent light tubes, burning matches and other fire, and the sun. Other objects can be seen only when there is light to be reflected from one or more of these sources.

SKILLS: Observing, inferring, comparing and contrasting

Activity 3.19
WHAT IS REFLECTED LIGHT?

Materials Needed

- Projector or flashlight
- Two chalkboard erasers
- Mirror
- Darkened room

Procedure

1. Arrange the projector and the mirror so that the light from the projector can be focused on the mirror.
2. With the room darkened, shine the projector light on the mirror at an angle.
3. Clap the chalkboard erasers together lightly in the beam of light and notice the angle of the light beam as it approaches and as it leaves the mirror. How do they compare?
4. Change the position of the projector so the light from the projector shines toward the mirror from different angles. Use chalk dust as needed to keep the light beam visible.
5. Each time you change the position of the projector, compare the angle of the light beam approaching the mirror to the angle of the reflected light beam.

Figure 3.19-1

Projector, Mirror, and Two Chalkboard Erasers

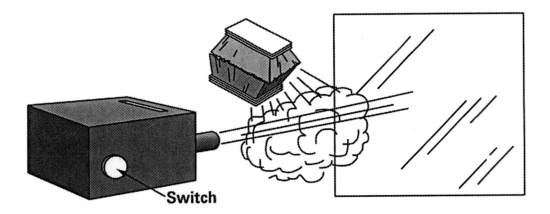

Teacher Information

When light is reflected from a mirror, it is always reflected at the same angle as the angle of the light from the source to the mirror. In other words, the angle of reflection is always equal to the angle of incidence (approaching angle).

SKILLS: Observing, inferring, comparing and contrasting, formulating hypotheses, identifying and controlling variables, experimenting

Activity 3.20
HOW IS LIGHT REFLECTION LIKE THE BOUNCE OF A BALL?

Materials Needed

- Rubber ball
- Darkened room
- Mirror
- Flashlight or projector

Procedure

1. Bounce the ball from the floor as straight as you can.

2. Now bounce the ball to your partner.

3. Try bouncing the ball at different angles. Notice the angle of the ball's path as it approaches the floor and compare it with the angle of its path as it leaves the floor. How do they compare?

4. Now place the mirror on the floor and "bounce" the light from the flashlight off the mirror, first shining the light straight down at the mirror, then at different angles.

5. Compare the angles of light approaching and leaving the mirror. How do they compare with the angles of the bouncing ball approaching and leaving the floor?

Figure 3.20-1

Bouncing Ball

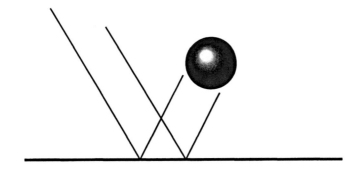

Figure 3.20-2

Bouncing Ball and Reflecting Light

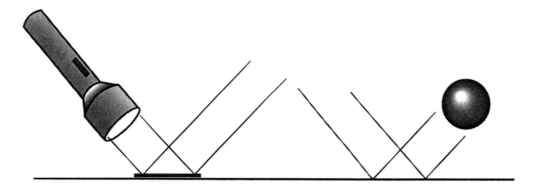

For Problem Solvers: Does a "crazy ball" follow the same path when it bounces as light does when it is reflected? Try it.

Teacher Information

The purpose of the activity of bouncing the ball is to provide a familiar model. The student should notice that the angle of incidence (angle of the ball's path as it approaches the floor) equals the angle of reflection (angle of the ball's path as it leaves the floor). To avoid the curve in the ball's path, created by the force of gravity, put a table next to a wall and roll the ball across the table to the wall.

INTEGRATING: Math

SKILLS: Observing, inferring, measuring, predicting, comparing and contrasting, formulating hypotheses, identifying and controlling variables

Activity 3.21
HOW MANY IMAGES CAN YOU SEE?

(Teacher-supervised activity)

Materials Needed

- Two mirrors, one with a peephole in the center
- Small object

Procedure

1. Hold the two mirrors a few centimeters (inches) apart with the reflecting surfaces facing each other (Figure 3.21-1).

2. Hold a small object between the mirrors and look at it through the peephole (Figure 3.21-2).

3. What do you see?

4. Hold the object in different positions and tilt the mirrors at different angles.

5. Explain what you see and why you think it happens.

Figure 3.21-1

Two Mirrors Facing Each Other, with a Peephole in One

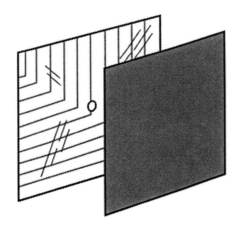

Figure 3.21-2

A Small Object Held Between the Mirrors

Teacher Information

To prepare the peephole mirror, use a knife to scrape away the silvering from the back of one mirror to form a small peephole about a centimeter (half inch) in diameter right in the center of the mirror.

As light is reflected from one mirror to the other, an infinite number of images can be seen if the mirrors are kept parallel to each other. As the mirrors are held at a slant with respect to each other, fewer images will be seen because the slant brings the image closer to the top of the mirror with each reflection.

SKILLS: Observing, inferring, comparing and contrasting

Activity 3.22
HOW WELL CAN YOU CONTROL THE REFLECTION OF LIGHT?

(Upper grades)

Materials Needed

- Projector or flashlight
- Several partners
- One mirror for each person
- Darkened room

Procedure

1. Arrange the people with mirrors in a pattern such that light can be reflected from one to the other.

2. From what you know about the reflected angles of light, see if the group can direct the light from the projector to one mirror and have it reflected from the first mirror to a second mirror. From the second to a third?

3. Determine who will reflect the light to whom in order to reflect the projector light all around the group.

4. Pick a spot (target) on the wall opposite the last person and light up the target with reflected light. Be sure the light from the projector reflects from all mirrors before lighting up the target.

5. With the light reflecting from all mirrors, compare the angle of reflection (the light leaving the mirror) with the angle of incidence (the light approaching the mirror) for each mirror. If necessary, have someone stand in the middle and clap two chalkboard erasers together lightly to make the beams more visible.

6. How does the angle of reflection compare with the angle of incidence?

Figure 3.22-1

Projector and Series of Mirrors

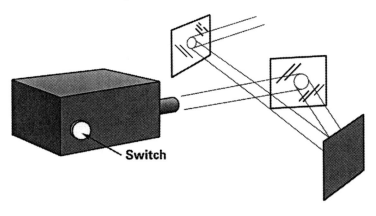

119

For Problem Solvers: With three friends, each of you with a mirror, play a game of "Reflection Relay." Select a target and position yourselves to reflect the light from a projector through all four mirrors and hit the target. Time yourselves and see if you can improve your time with each new target you select. Challenge another group, and have a contest. Perhaps the entire class would like to get involved.

Teacher Information

Students will enjoy the challenge of reflecting the light from mirror to mirror in various patterns. They should notice that the angle of reflection and the angle of incidence are always equal.

Students who choose to try the reflected relay suggested in "For Problem Solvers" will acquire new insights with light and reflections. As they practice, they will learn that they need to stay near the light source and near one another, because the light spreads out and gets dimmer with distance. They will also learn to position themselves such that they are reflecting the light to one another as directly as possible, again to maximize brightness.

INTEGRATING: Math

SKILLS: Observing, measuring, predicting, communicating, comparing and contrasting, identifying and controlling variables, experimenting

Activity 3.23
HOW DOES A PERISCOPE WORK?

(Teacher-supervised activity for upper grades)

 Take home and do with family and friends.

Materials Needed

- Two 1-quart milk cartons
- Two mirrors (same width as milk carton)
- Knife or scissors
- Tape

Procedure

1. Cut the tops off both milk cartons.
2. Cut an opening about 5 cm (2 in.) in diameter in one side of each carton, near the bottom.
3. Tape a mirror in the bottom of each carton, facing the opening at a 45-degree angle.
4. Tape the cartons together at the open ends to make a long tube.
5. Look into the mirror at one end of your periscope. What do you see?
6. Can you put your periscope together in such a way that you can look behind you? To your right?

Figure 3.23-1

Milk Carton Periscope

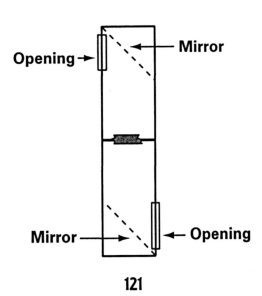

For Problem Solvers: Design your own periscope. What can you do to make it longer? Can you make it so that you can turn it around 360 degrees, so you can see in any direction without turning yourself around? Do you need more mirrors in your design? Can you find round tubing, or something else that will work better than milk cartons?

Teacher Information

The periscope activity is likely to attract a lot of interest and could be used as an enrichment activity. It is an application of the concept of angle of reflection students learn about in other activities of this unit. Students might enjoy expanding their periscopes to include three, four, or more milk cartons to make the periscope longer or to give it creative shapes, as suggested in "For Problem Solvers." Additional mirrors might be needed as students expand with creative ideas. Other tubes could be substituted for the milk cartons. This is a good time to be creative.

INTEGRATING: Math

SKILLS: Observing, measuring, predicting, communicating, identifying and controlling variables, experimenting

Activity 3.24
HOW CAN YOU POUR LIGHT?

(Enrichment activity)

 Take home and do with family and friends.

Materials Needed

- Tall, slim olive jar with lid
- Flashlight
- Nail
- Masking tape or plastic tape
- Newspaper or light cardboard
- Hammer
- Water
- Sink or dishpan

Procedure

1. With the hammer and nail, make two holes in the lid of the jar. The holes should be near the edge but opposite each other. One hole should be quite small. Work the nail in the other hole to enlarge it a bit.

2. Fill the jar about two thirds full of water and put the lid on (Figure 3.24-1).

Figure 3.24-1

Jar with Lid On, Showing Two Different-sized Holes

3. Put tape over the holes in the lid until you are ready to pour.

4. Lay the jar and flashlight end to end, with the face of the flashlight at the bottom of the jar.

5. Roll the newspaper around the jar and flashlight to enclose them in a light-tight tube. Tape the tube together so it will stay (Figure 3.24-2).

Figure 3.24-2

Flashlight and Jar Taped Together

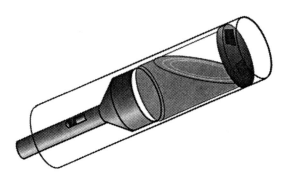

6. Slide the flashlight out of the tube, turn it on, and slide it back into the tube. Darken the room.

7. Hold the apparatus upright and remove the tape from the lid. With the large nail hole down, pour the water into the sink (Figure 3.24-3).

8. What happened to the beam of light as the water poured into the sink?

9. Do you have any idea what caused this?

10. Share your ideas together.

Figure 3.24-3

Same System with Water Pouring from Larger Hole

124

For Problem Solvers: Use your creativity with this activity. Try different containers for the water, and different light sources. Try putting some food coloring in the water. Does that provide the same effect as if you put a colored filter (colored acetate) over the flashlight?

Teacher Information

Although light travels in straight lines, it is reflected internally at the water's inner surface and follows the path of the stream of water. Because of the phenomenon of internal reflection, fiber optics can be used to direct light anywhere a wire can go, even into the veins and arteries of the human body.

SKILLS: Observing, inferring, communicating

Activity 3.25
WHAT COLOR IS WHITE?

(Upper grades)

 Take home and do with family and friends.

Materials Needed

- White posterboard
- Compass
- String 1 m (1 yd.) long
- Crayons
- Scissors

Procedure

1. With your compass, draw a circle 15 cm (6 in.) in diameter on the posterboard.
2. Cut out the circle with the scissors.
3. Draw three equal pie-shaped sections on the posterboard and color them red, green, and blue.
4. Make two small holes near the center of the circle.

Figure 3.25-1

Divided and Colored Circle with Two Holes Punched

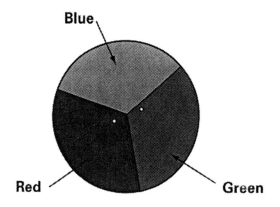

5. Thread the string through the holes (in one hole and out the other) and tie the ends of the string together, forming a loop that passes through the two holes of the disk.

6. Center the disk on the string loop and make the disk spin by alternately stretching and relaxing the string.

7. As the disk spins, watch the colored side.

8. What happens to the colors? Why do you think this happens?

For Problem Solvers: Try the same thing with more disks and different color combinations. Try using only two sections and coloring them with complementary colors, such as yellow and blue. Try several sections, alternating the same two colors back and forth and see if you get the same result as with two large sections. Each time you try a new design or color combination, make a prediction of what you will see as the disk spins—then try it, and test your prediction.

Teacher Information

As the primary colors spin, they should blend together to form a grayish white. If one of the colors seems to dominate, some of that color should be replaced with more of the other two colors. Blue might need a bit more than its share. Students will enjoy experimenting with various color combinations and testing their predictions of the resulting blends, as suggested in "For Problem Solvers."

The disk may spin better if its weight is increased by doubling the thickness of posterboard or pasting the disk onto cardboard or by gluing a button on the back of the disk. Another option is to mount the disk onto a sanding pad designed for a quarter-inch drill. The drill could then be used to spin the disk. If a drill is used, the disk must be secured well, as it could otherwise fly off and cause injury. This is less likely to happen if you use a drill with a variable-speed switch and avoid high speed.

INTEGRATING: Art

SKILLS: Observing, inferring, classifying, measuring, predicting, communicating, comparing and contrasting, identifying and controlling variables, experimenting

Activity 3.26
HOW CAN YOU SPIN DIFFERENT COLORS?

Materials Needed

- White posterboard
- Black fine-tipped marker
- Newspapers
- String 1 m (1 yd.) long
- Scissors
- Compass
- Pencil
- Ruler

Procedure

1. Use the compass to draw a circle on the posterboard 15 cm (6 in.) in diameter. Cut out the circle with the scissors (Figure 3.26-1).

Figure 3.26-1

Circle Drawn on Paper, Scissors

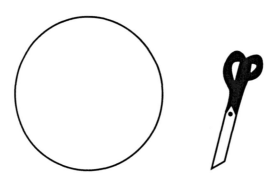

2. Put a layer of several thicknesses of newspaper on the table and place your white disk on the newspaper.

3. With the fine-tipped marker, make one of the patterns shown in Figure 3.26-2. Let it dry.

Figure 3.26-2

Disk Patterns

4. Make two small holes on opposite sides of the center point, each about 1 cm (3/8 in.) from the center point (Figure 3.26-3).

Figure 3.26-3

Center Point and Holes Marked on Patterns

Off center points   **Center point**

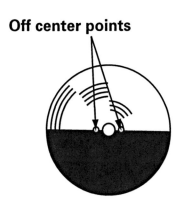 

5. Thread the string through the holes of the disk and tie the ends together.

6. Put one finger of each hand through the string, and wind up the disk on the string. Make the disk spin by successively pulling and relaxing the string.

7. As the disk spins, watch the painted side.

8. What do you see? Can you explain it?

For Problem Solvers: Create your own patterns for the disk. Yours might work out better than the ones shown here.

Teacher Information

When the retina receives repeated flashes of white light, they are interpreted by the brain as color. Such flashes of white light are produced by the spinning black-and-white disk. This phenomenon was discovered by Benham in the nineteenth century. If you have a phonograph turntable with adjustable speed, the effect can be studied by making a hole in the center of the disk and laying it on the turntable. Or attach the disk to a sanding pad for an electric drill, and turn the disk with the drill. Be sure the drill has a variable speed switch. **CAUTION: If it spins too fast, the disk could fly off and cause injury.**

INTEGRATING: Art

SKILLS: Observing, inferring, classifying, measuring, predicting, communicating, comparing and contrasting, identifying and controlling variables, experimenting

Activity 3.27
WHAT DO COLOR FILTERS DO TO COLORS?

(Group activity)

Materials Needed

- Red, blue, and green acetate, cut into strips about 5 cm (2 in.) × 15 cm (6 in.)
- Multi-colored construction paper (one piece of each color available, each numbered with heavy black marker)

Procedure

1. Each person in the group should have one strip of red acetate, one strip of green, and one strip of blue.
2. Each person should have a copy of the chart below.
3. Assign one person to be the paper holder.
4. Each person should hold the red acetate in front of his or her eyes.
5. The "paper holder" should hold up construction paper #1.
6. Without removing the acetate from the eyes, each person looks at construction paper #1 and *writes the color he or she sees*, without removing the acetate or trying to guess what color the paper really is.
7. The paper holder puts construction paper #1 out of sight.
8. The paper holder holds up construction paper #2, and each person again writes the color he or she sees.
9. Continue this procedure until all of the colors of construction paper have been used.
10. Repeat the entire process with participants using blue acetate.
11. Repeat the procedure again with green acetate.
12. Without looking at the paper, compare notes and predict what color each numbered paper really was.
13. Without acetate in front of eyes, the paper holder holds up construction paper #1.
14. Discuss with the group what each person wrote as the color he or she saw when looking at paper #1 through red acetate, blue acetate, and green acetate.
15. Repeat steps 12 and 13 with construction paper numbers 2 through 8.
16. Discuss the effect of each color of acetate, and compare information from the group. Did everyone see the same color each time?

COLOR OF ACETATE	1	2	3	4	5	6	7	8
Red	——	——	——	——	——	——	——	——
Blue	——	——	——	——	——	——	——	——
Green	——	——	——	——	——	——	——	——

Teacher Information

We see objects because of the light they reflect. If no red is present in the color that is reflected from the paper, and the acetate filters out everything but red, the person viewing the paper will probably see an unpleasant muddy color.

The strip of acetate can be turned into a pair of groovy goggles and add interest to the activity. Staple the acetate to a two-hole section from a plastic six-pack soda-pop carrier (see Figure 3.27-1). Rubber bands can then be attached to the ends of the goggles. The rubber bands can go over the ears or on around the back of the head to hold the goggles in place. Students might do other things to add interest and design to the goggles.

Other items around the room can be viewed with the goggles. If there is something of a fluorescent color—on the wall of the classroom or on someone's T-shirt, for instance, great aesthetic experiences will be had by all!

Figure 3.27-1

Six-pack Goggles

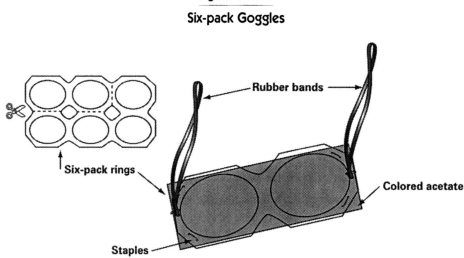

INTEGRATING: Art

SKILLS: Observing, inferring, classifying, measuring, predicting, communicating, comparing and contrasting

Activity 3.28
HOW DO DETECTIVES USE COLOR TO SOLVE CRIMES?

 Take home and do with family and friends.

Materials Needed

- Water-base markers
- Coffee filters (or other filter paper)
- Half-liter (pint) jars
- Paper clips
- Scissors
- Water

Procedure

1. Cut the filter paper into strips, about 2.5 cm (1 in.) wide.
2. Using one of the markers, place a dot about 2.5 cm (1 in.) from one end of one strip of filter paper.
3. Put a small amount of water in the jar.
4. Using an opened paper clip to hold the paper, and a pencil for support, suspend the strip of filter paper in the jar. Be sure the end of the filter paper is in the water and the colored dot is above the water.
5. Write your prediction of what will happen to the color as the water soaks up the filter paper.
6. Check the filter paper every few minutes for about 30 minutes.
7. Was your prediction accurate?
8. Discuss your observations. Try to explain what happened.

For Problem Solvers: Extend this activity to more than just water-base markers. Using water as the solvent, you can use a powdered drink mix (use only a small amount of water so it's highly concentrated), and food coloring. For permanent ink you can try rubbing alcohol or white vinegar as the solvent. Try various brands of markers—any you can find. Find out if all manufacturers use the same color combinations in making specific colors. Keep a record of your findings and share your information with others who are doing this activity, or who are interested in it.

If you had a friend who is allergic to a certain color of food dye, could you use this technique to find out if that color is in a particular package of powdered drink mix, or if it is used as a part of a combination of colors in another color of food dye?

How do you think police investigators might use this technique to help solve the mystery of a crime?

Teacher Information

This process is called "color chromatography." Many inks used in pens and markers have surprising combinations of coloring agents in them. (Among the markers you use, try to include the Bic Banana black.) This is also true of coloring agents used in powdered drink mixes and in food colorings. Colors that are soluble in water will dissolve into the water as the water soaks up the filter paper. How high the color will go up the paper will depend on how soluble that particular ingredient is and how well it binds, or sticks, to the filter paper.

Color chromatography is actually used by investigators in solving mysteries. For example, could the pen found on Joe Scribbler's body have been used in writing the suicide note?

INTEGRATING: Art, social studies

SKILLS: Observing, inferring, classifying, measuring, predicting, communicating, comparing and contrasting, using space-time relationships, formulating hypotheses, identifying and controlling variables, experimenting

Activity 3.29
WHAT DOES A PRISM DO TO LIGHT?

Materials Needed

- Prism
- Projector or flashlight
- Screen, white paper, or white wall

Procedure

1. Shine the projector light on the screen or other white surface.
2. What do you think will happen if you place the prism in the path of the beam of light?
3. Place the prism in the path of the beam of light. Were your predictions accurate?
4. What is white light?
5. Which color seems to bend the most as light passes through the prism? Which the least?

For Problem Solvers: Examine the colors very carefully that you get as the light shines from the projector through the prism and onto the white background. This is called a color spectrum. How many colors are there? Make a sketch of the color bands on paper and give each color a name. Then do the same thing again, using the flashlight instead of the projector. Do you get the same colors? Are they in the same order? Are they as bright? Try it again, using the sun as your light source. Try it with a light bulb.

Can you find still other light sources to project light through your prism? Are the colors and the sequence always the same? Did you try a colored light bulb? Try shining the light through colored plastic film before it reaches the prism. Does that change anything?

Share your findings with others who are doing this investigation.

Teacher Information

White light is a combination of many colors. Each color has its own wave length and is bent to a different degree as light passes through a prism, forming a continuous spectrum. Violet has the shortest waves and is bent the most. Red has the longest waves and is bent the least. Five other "pure" colors exist in the spectrum between violet and red. In order, these are indigo, blue, green, yellow, and orange. Sometimes blue and indigo are treated as one color.

Water droplets in the air can act as tiny prisms when conditions are right, thus creating a rainbow. Many jewelry stores sell leaded glass crystals cut in different shapes; these crystals act as prisms and produce beautiful rainbows.

INTEGRATING: Art

SKILLS: Observing, inferring, classifying, predicting, communicating, comparing and contrasting, formulating hypotheses, identifying and controlling variables, experimenting

Activity 3.30
HOW CAN YOU MAKE A PRISM WITH WATER?

 Take home and do with family and friends.

Materials Needed

- Sunny day
- Mirror
- Tray or pan
- Water
- White surface

Procedure

1. Place the tray on a table or on the floor in direct sunlight. Put about 2–3 cm (1 in.) of water in the tray.

2. Place a mirror in the tray and focus the reflected sunlight on the white surface. At least part of the mirror should be submerged in the water.

3. What do you see in the reflection on the white surface?

Figure 3.30-1

Mirror Leaning in a Pan, Mostly Submerged

For Problem Solvers: Do you have an empty aquarium? You need to put it in a place where sunlight is coming through a window and will shine directly on the aquarium. Put several inches of water in it and place a large mirror at the bottom, leaning against the side. With the sun shining into the mirror, look around the room for rainbows. Look directly into the aquarium and walk around it slowly, again looking for rainbows.

Teacher Information

As light passes through a transparent substance (water) at an angle, the light rays are bent. White light contains many other colors, each of which bends to a different degree. Thus, the reflected light on the wall shows a separation of those colors. The colors separate as light passes through a glass prism, and the same effect is produced in this activity with a water prism. This same phenomenon occurs in nature as water droplets in the air separate the colors in sunlight. We see it as a rainbow. Rainbows can sometimes be seen in fine sprays of water, such as that produced by some lawn sprinklers.

INTEGRATING: Art

SKILLS: Observing, inferring, classifying, predicting, communicating, formulating hypotheses, identifying and controlling variables, experimenting

SOUND

TO THE TEACHER

Sound is a very important part of our lives. It is one of the first stimuli to which newborn infants respond, and its presence or absence shapes and affects us throughout our entire lives. This section introduces sound, its causes and uses. A study of sound lends itself very well to concrete activities, with many possibilities for discovery/inquiry. No attempt is made to introduce the physiology of the ear, although you may choose to teach it in relation to this area.

A study of sound can be greatly expanded in the Language Arts to develop and enrich listening skills. Music can be integrated through discussion of musical terms found within this section. Activities on inventing and playing musical instruments could lead to additional study of ancient methods and modern electronic methods of producing music.

Throughout the study, children should be encouraged to bring and demonstrate their own musical instruments. If there is a high school or university nearby, the music director may be willing to cooperate in providing musicians and instruments. Most communities have choral groups that might be willing to perform. A note to parents asking for the names of family members or neighbors who play unusual musical instruments could produce interesting and entertaining results.

As the importance of sound is discussed, the value of being able to hear and speak clearly should be emphasized. Children should know that people of all ages suffer from hearing loss, and that almost everyone develops some degree of impairment as he or she grows older.

Sometime near the beginning of the study, the class should discuss, and perhaps list, ways sound can help us; for example, communication, warning, entertainment, aesthetics, and protection. Sound can also be harmful. Loud noise can injure the ears. Sound can be pleasing and soothing to an individual, but it can also be disturbing and irritating. The loudness of sound is measured in decibels. For public protection, many communities have laws restricting the decibel levels that can be produced by any means. With electronic sound equipment being so common, children should understand reasons for attempts to control noise levels.

In discussing pitch, or the frequency of vibrations, children should be aware that the human ear cannot detect the frequency of very high (fast) and very low (slow) vibrations. Dog whistles are too high pitched to be heard by people, but they can be heard by dogs and some other animals.

Resource people can be involved frequently in this study. These might include individuals of all ages who have hearing handicaps, a nurse, a doctor, an audiologist, an acoustics specialist, a music store owner, a musician, someone who makes or plays unusual musical instruments, or any others you may find helpful.

This is an area rich in "take home and do with family and friends" activities. Taking home concrete objects to show and talk about will help children develop increased language ability and be a source of strong motivation in science.

Regarding the Early Grades

With verbal instructions and slight modifications, many of these activities can be used with kindergarten, first-grade, and second-grade students. In some activities, steps that involve procedures that go beyond the level of the child can simply be omitted and yet offer the child an experience that plants the seed for a concept that will germinate and grow later on.

Teachers of the early grades will probably choose to bypass many of the "For Problem Solvers" sections. That's okay. These sections are provided for those who are especially motivated and want to go beyond the investigation provided by the activity outlined. Use the outlined activities and enjoy worthwhile learning experiences together with your young students. Also consider, however, that many of the "For Problem Solvers" sections can be used appropriately with young children as group activities or as demonstrations, still giving students the advantage of an exposure to the experience and laying groundwork for connections that will be made later on.

Activity 4.1
WHAT IS SOUND?

 Take home and do with family and friends.

Materials Needed

- Paper and pencil

Procedure

You have been in this room many times before. Maybe there are things about it you haven't noticed. Try this:

1. Close your eyes and be very quiet for three minutes. Listen carefully. Do you hear anything? Describe on a piece of paper what you hear.

2. If you heard new sounds, what were they, and why do you think you haven't heard them before?

3. How did the quiet make you feel?

For Problem Solvers: Try the same activity with your family at home. Everyone will probably be surprised at the sounds he or she doesn't usually notice.

Teacher Information

Many people are not aware of background sounds in their environment. Students may remark that it has never been this quiet before. Others may realize that they heard new sounds because they had really never listened for them before. This is an opportunity to talk about developing listening skills through paying attention or concentrating. Specialists in sound control (acoustics) can design nearly soundproof rooms where even voices at a normal conversational level cannot be heard. Usually people become accustomed to background noise of a low decibel level and ignore it.

A discussion of "how quiet makes me feel" could lead to an art, poetry (Haiku is an excellent approach for this type of creative poetry with older children), or creative-language experience ("What are some quiet words?").

An architect or sound-control specialist could be used as a resource person.

INTEGRATING: Language arts

SKILLS: Observing, inferring, communicating, using space-time relationships

Activity 4.2
WHAT SOUNDS CAN YOU IDENTIFY?

Materials Needed

- Cassette player or phonograph
- Tape of common sounds
- Pencil and paper

Procedure

1. Play the tape and listen to the sounds.
2. Describe or name as many sounds as you can.
3. What can you say about sounds in your life?

For Problem Solvers: If you have a tape recorder at home, record some sounds that you hear at home. Then take your tape to school and see if your classmates can identify the sources of the sounds you recorded.

Teacher Information

Many teachers enjoy preparing tapes of different sounds. You may want to prepare one on everyday sounds, such as a phone ringing, water running, dog barking, bird chirping, car starting, animal noises (sound toys available for young children are good sources), automobile horns, musical instruments, jet airplane taking off. Many schools have sound records for use with kindergarten and primary grades. Check your media center or library.

Take a sound field trip. Take several tape recorders on a field trip and try to collect as many sounds as you can.

Encourage children to do the "For Problem Solvers" activity and see if they can stump their classmates with sounds they hear at home.

Play soft classical music and loud rock music. Have children make a painting or color a picture showing how each makes them feel.

Classify sounds into categories; for example, warning sounds: siren, bell, honking horn, growling dog, screeching brakes. (Mothers' voices as they continue to call children often change in interesting ways.)

Have a class discussion of how sounds help us and occasionally harm us (too loud may damage ears or make us nervous).

INTEGRATING: Language arts, art, music

SKILLS: Observing, inferring, classifying, communicating, using space-time relationships

Activity 4.3
HOW WELL CAN YOU MATCH SOUNDS?

 Take home and do with family and friends.

Materials Needed

- Set of film canisters, each containing different small objects
- Masking tape

Procedure

1. Shake the canisters and listen to the noise they make.
2. Can you hear the different sounds they make?
3. Do two or more of the canisters make the same sound?
4. If you find canisters that sound alike, put them next to each other.
5. Have a friend listen to the canisters and see if he or she agrees.
6. You may want to make more canisters with different sounds to see how well your friends can detect the differences in the sounds.

For Problem Solvers: Make your own set of rattle cans. Put small things in them. You can use any containers that have lids and that you can't see through. Make two cans with each item. See if your brothers and sisters and friends can match them up in pairs. Then see if they can guess what's in the cans.

Teacher Information

Prepare the film canisters ahead of time. Place small objects in identical pairs of canisters. Seal the canisters with tape. Prepare a set of at least six pairs.

This is a preschool or early-grade activity. Older children may be interested in constructing the "shakers" for younger groups. Materials used in the film canisters to make noise could include: dried rice, beans, or peas; marbles; BBs; gravel; sand; bits of plastic foam; puffed rice; any other small objects found around the home. Be sure the canisters are prepared in pairs with approximately the same amount of material in each set of canisters. Any small, opaque containers with lids can be substituted for the film canisters, of course. The containers need to be the same size and made of the same material.

INTEGRATING: Music

SKILLS: Observing, inferring, classifying, communicating, comparing and contrasting, identifying and controlling variables

Activity 4.4
WHAT SOUNDS CAN YOU MAKE WITH A SHOE BOX?

 Take home and do with family and friends.

Materials Needed

- Shoe box with lid
- Rubber bands of various lengths and thicknesses

Procedure

1. Stretch four or five rubber bands of different thicknesses and lengths around a shoe box with the lid removed.
2. Pluck the rubber bands with your finger. What do you see? What do you hear?
3. Try different lengths and thicknesses. Look and listen.
4. What happened? What can you say about this?
5. Put the lid on the shoe box and repeat the activity. What happened? What do you think made the difference?

For Problem Solvers: Try making several of the same musical instrument, using boxes that are different sizes and that are made of different materials—cardboard, metal, plastic. Use rubber bands of any size you can find that will fit the boxes. Try string or fishline in the place of the rubber bands. Can you play a tune?

Teacher Information

The main purpose of this activity is to reinforce the idea that sound is produced by vibration. In addition, this activity introduces the idea of pitch (high and low sounds) in relation to the rate of vibration (the faster the vibration, the higher the pitch).

Resonance is introduced when the lid is put on the shoe box.

Older children may have had some experience with these concepts; however, this activity is intended to create awareness of pitch and resonance only. Later experiences should help children gain understanding as they are presented in different ways.

INTEGRATING: Music

SKILLS: Observing, classifying, measuring, predicting, communicating, comparing and contrasting, identifying and controlling variables, experimenting

Activity 4.5
HOW CAN YOU MAKE MUSIC WITH FISH LINE?

 Take home and do with family and friends.

Materials Needed

- 50 cm (20 in.) of monofilament fish line with a wooden dowel 10 cm (4 in.) long attached to one end
- Additional dowel
- Shoe box with lid
- Toothpick
- Pencil

Procedure

1. Put the shoe box on the edge of a table or desk.
2. Remove the lid, make a hole in one end of the box with your pencil, thread the fish line through the hole, and secure it with the toothpick (Figure 4.5-1).

Figure 4.5-1

Open Shoe Box

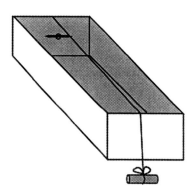

3. Put the lid on the box and stretch the fish line lengthwise across the top of the box. Put the additional dowel under the fish line near one end of the lid (Figure 4.5-2).

146

Figure 4.5-2

Box with Lid

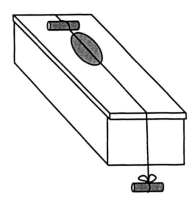

4. Slowly pull down on the dowel and pluck the fish line. What do you hear? What do you see?

5. As you pluck the line, pull down on the dowel to stretch it tighter. Watch and listen. What do you see? What do you hear? Try to play a simple tune. What might happen if you cut a hole in the lid of the shoe box? Try it.

For Problem Solvers: Experiment with different materials for the string on your homemade instrument. Try different types and weights of fish line, string, fine wire, or whatever is available. Which one can you get the highest notes with? Which one can you get the lowest notes with?

Teacher Information

This activity should help children discover the relationship between the rate (speed) of vibration and the pitch (high-low) of sound. You may want to relate this activity to the previous one with rubber bands. The hole cut in the lid will increase the resonance. Resonance is a way of increasing the intensity of a sound by causing one object (vibrating fish line) to create a sympathetic vibration of about the same frequency in another object (the walls of the shoe box).

The dowel on the top of the lid serves as a bridge to keep the string elevated enough to vibrate freely; stringed instruments use the same principles. A guitar, violin, cello, or viola could be used for comparison.

INTEGRATING: Music

SKILLS: Observing, classifying, measuring, predicting, communicating, comparing and contrasting, identifying and controlling variables, experimenting

Activity 4.6
HOW DO YOU MAKE SOUNDS WITH YOUR VOICE?

Materials Needed

- Prepared shoe box from Activity 4.5

Procedure

1. Hold your fingers on the front of your throat.

2. Hum and talk. Make high sounds and low sounds. Make soft sounds and loud sounds. What happened? Can you feel a difference?

3. Pluck the string stretched across the shoe box. Make it tighter as you continue to pluck. What happens?

4. Can you explain how your vocal cords work?

For Problem Solvers: Can you make a sound with your shoe-box guitar that is higher than your voice? Can you make a sound with your shoe-box guitar that sounds about the same pitch as your voice? Can you make the pitch of your voice higher? Can you make it lower?

What do you do with your shoe-box guitar to make the sound higher or lower? What do you think you do with your voice to make it higher or lower? Do something to find out—read from the encyclopedia or another book you can find. Ask someone who you think would know.

Teacher Information

Our vocal cords are caused to vibrate by air passing over them. Muscles in our throat tighten and loosen the cords to produce higher and lower sounds. The amount of air we pass by the cords determines loudness and softness. This is a reason proper breathing technique is so important to singers.

INTEGRATING: Music

SKILLS: Observing, inferring, classifying, measuring, predicting, communicating, comparing and contrasting, identifying and controlling variables, experimenting, researching

Activity 4.7
HOW MUCH NOISE CAN YOU MAKE WITH A PAPER CUP?

 Take home and do with family and friends.

Materials Needed

- Plastic cup (or paper)
- String, about 30 cm (12 in.) long
- Half of a toothpick

Procedure

1. Make a small hole in the bottom of the cup, at the center. You can use the toothpick or your pencil to make the hole.
2. Insert the end of the string through the hole in the cup.
3. Tie the string around the half-toothpick, so the toothpick will be on the outside of the cup.
4. Hold the cup in one hand. Squeeze the string with the thumb and index finger of the other hand, and pull, holding the string tight, but allowing it to slip through your fingers.
5. Did you hear anything? If not, squeeze a little tighter next time.
6. Wet the string with water and do it again.
7. What happened? Explain, and have fun!

For Problem Solvers: Experiment with different materials. The variables are the cup, the string, the water, and how tightly you held the string with your fingers. Change one variable at a time and see what differences you can make. Predict what difference each change will make before you try it.

If you can find a small feather or two and some rolly eyes, you could decorate this noisemaker and call it the yellow chicken, the red hen, or something like that. You decide. You could fashion a beak out of a clothespin or some other suitable object.

Why does this thing make sound? What is the role of the cup?

Teacher Information

This activity is very noisy, so you might want to save it for the end of the day (or perhaps just before your students go to another teacher!). You might even want to do it outdoors. Students will enjoy it, though, and they will learn as they try different variables to make their yellow chicken, or their red hen, or whatever they decide to call the noisy thing. The friction between string and fingers causes the string to vibrate, and the sound is amplified by the cup.

INTEGRATING: Music

SKILLS: Observing, classifying, measuring, predicting, communicating, comparing and contrasting, identifying and controlling variables, experimenting

Activity 4.8
HOW CAN SOUNDS BE SHAPED?

 Take home and do with family and friends.

Materials Needed

- Paper and pencils

Procedure

1. Take a deep breath and hum a note. Hold the note while you slowly open your mouth as wide as you can.

2. Hold your tongue and say some words.

3. Let go of your tongue and say the phrase "black bug's blood" rapidly several times.

4. List ways we change or "shape" the sounds our vocal cords make.

5. How many ways can you imitate how your parents call you to come home, or to get ready for school?

For Problem Solvers: In this activity you changed the sound of your voice by changing your mouth and by holding your tongue. Try to change the sound of your voice with your hands. Hold your hands over your mouth and make a long sound with your voice. Change the shape of your hands and see how much you can change your voice.

Speak into a box, into a garden hose, into other things. How many ways can you think of to change the sound of your voice?

Teacher Information

Our vocal cords produce pitch and loudness of sound, but we depend on our throat, mouth, tongue, and teeth to produce the phonetic "shaping" of the sounds. This ability to produce phonetic differences is one of the reasons we are able to develop the highly complex, inter-related process we call vocal communication.

For enrichment, introduce a unit on nonverbal communication in social studies or language arts.

INTEGRATING: Language arts, social studies, music, physical education

SKILLS: Observing, predicting, communicating, comparing and contrasting, identifying and controlling variables, experimenting

Activity 4.9
HOW CAN YOU MAKE BOTTLED MUSIC?

 Take home and do with family and friends.

Materials Needed

- Eight glass soda bottles of the same size and shape
- Water
- Paper slips numbered 1 to 8
- Pencil

Procedure

1. Pour water to different levels in the bottles.

2. Blow gently across the tops of the bottles until a sound is produced for each one. Arrange the bottles in a row according to the pitch of the sound from low to high.

3. You may want to add to or remove water from the bottles to make a musical scale. Under each bottle put a slip of paper numbered from one to eight.

4. Try to play a simple tune by blowing across the tops of the bottles. Can you decide what is vibrating to make the sound?

5. Use a pencil to tap the side of each bottle near the top. What happened? Check the numbers from low to high. What is vibrating to make the sound? What can you say about this?

For Problem Solvers: Try to tune the bottles to the piano. Can you make one of the bottles produce the same pitch as one of the piano keys? Can you match the piano with one full octave of sounds from the bottles? One octave is eight white keys in a row. If you are using bottles with lids, put the lids on overnight and see if the sounds still match the next morning.

Teacher Information

To do this activity, children may need to be reminded of the musical meaning of the term *pitch*.

In steps 1–4, blowing across the bottle causes the air to vibrate. This is the way pipe organs and musical wind instruments produce sound. A longer column of air will cause a slower vibration and a lower pitch. When the bottles are struck in step 5, it is the glass that vibrates to produce the sound. Water will slow the rate of vibration of the glass. Therefore, the greater the amount of water, the more slowly the glass vibrates, and the lower the pitch.

Remember, water expands and contracts according to its temperature. Water also evaporates. Both of these factors may make the bottles change pitch if they are kept for later use.

INTEGRATING: Music

SKILLS: Observing, classifying, measuring, predicting, communicating, comparing and contrasting, identifying and controlling variables, experimenting

Activity 4.10
WHAT KINDS OF SOUNDS CAN YOU MAKE WITH STICKS?

 Take home and do with family and friends.

Materials Needed

- Meter stick (or yardstick)
- Plastic and wood rulers
- One tongue depressor per student
- Pencil (optional)

Procedure

1. Place the meter stick on a table with one half extending over the edge. Hold one end of the stick firmly against the table. Push downward and release the other end. What happened? Move the stick so that different lengths extend over the edge. What is making the sound?

2. Try the rulers and tongue depressor. Learn to play a simple tune. You may want to mark the stick with a pencil to remind yourself of the position of each note.

3. Find a partner and see if you can learn to play a tune together.

For Problem Solvers: See how many different sounds you can make with all of the kinds of sticks you can find. Use popsicle sticks, tongue depressors, plastic rulers, wood rulers, meter sticks, blocks, boards, and whatever you can find. Pluck them, tap on them, and do whatever you can to make more new sounds. Share what you learn with the class.

Teacher Information

As the length of stick protruding from the table is increased, the speed of vibration will decrease and the pitch will go down. This is a "take home and do with family and friends" activity that can provide scientific understanding and oral language experience.

INTEGRATING: Music

SKILLS: Observing, classifying, measuring, predicting, communicating, comparing and contrasting, identifying and controlling variables, experimenting

Activity 4.11
HOW CAN YOU MAKE MUSIC WITH TUBES?

 Take home and do with family and friends.

Materials Needed

- Drinking straws
- Garden hose 1 m long
- Scissors
- Mouthpiece from a bugle, trumpet, or trombone

Procedure

1. Cut one end of a drinking straw to a point. Moisten the cut end and put it between your lips. Blow gently around the straw. Cut pieces from the end of the straw as it is being played. What happened? What can you say about this?

Figure 4.11-1

Drinking Straw with End Cut to a Point

2. Place a mouthpiece in a garden hose. Blow into the mouthpiece to see if you can make a sound. Change the shape of the hose. What happens to the pitch of the sound?
3. Try it without the mouthpiece. Can you make the same sounds?

For Problem Solvers: Making musical sounds with the soda straw and with the garden hose probably gave you lots of new ideas for making still more musical sounds. Try your ideas. Get several different kinds and sizes of soda straws and do whatever you can do with them to make new sounds.

Put a skinny straw into a fat straw and slide them in and out as you play notes. What happened?

Cut one or more holes along the top of a straw and make more new sounds. Can you play it like a flute?

Teacher Information

With practice, the students will be able to make the cut end of the straw vibrate to produce sound. This is similar to a clarinet or oboe. Paper straws work better than plastic because the plastic does not compress as easily to form a reed. Plastic straws are very usable for this activity, however.

When the group uses the garden hose, a child who plays the trumpet, trombone, or bugle may be able to demonstrate and help others learn to play. Changing the shape of the hose will not vary the pitch; however, cutting a length off either the straw or the hose will shorten the vibrating column of air and raise the pitch.

INTEGRATING: Music

SKILLS: Observing, classifying, measuring, predicting, communicating, comparing and contrasting, identifying and controlling variables, experimenting

Activity 4.12
HOW CAN YOU MAKE A KAZOO WITH A COMB?

 Take home and do with family and friends.

Materials Needed

- Combs of various sizes
- Kazoos
- Tissue paper 10 cm × 20 cm (4 in. × 8 in.)

Procedure

1. Fold the tissue paper over the comb, letting it hang down each side.
2. Hum into the paper-wrapped comb. What happened? What can you say about this?
3. Hum a tune on the kazoo. How does it make a sound?
4. Raise your head so you are looking at the ceiling of the room. Hold your fingers on the front of your neck. Hum a tune. What happened? What can you say about this?

Teacher Information

Sounds are produced by vibrations. With the tissue paper and comb, sound is produced by the vocal cords, which in turn cause the paper over the comb to vibrate and alter the sound. The same occurs when a kazoo is used.

This activity can provide a review of the way sound is produced through vibration and how sounds can be altered through the vibration of another object.

Kazoos may be purchased in novelty stores that carry party noisemakers. Some music stores also carry them.

INTEGRATING: Music

SKILLS: Observing, measuring, communicating, identifying and controlling variables, experimenting

Activity 4.13
WHAT IS A TRIPLE-T KAZOO?

 Take home and do with family and friends.

Materials Needed

- Toilet-tissue tube
- Waxed paper (about twice the diameter of the tube)
- Rubber band
- Paper punch

Procedure

1. Punch a hole in one end of the toilet-tissue tube. Reach as far into the tube as you can with the paper punch.
2. Wrap the waxed paper over the other end (opposite the punched hole) and secure the waxed paper with the rubber band.
3. Hum into the open end of the tube.
4. Make music with others who are making kazoos and with other instruments of all kinds that have been made by the class.
5. Color your kazoo. Be creative, and make it just the way you want it to be.
6. Why do we call it the "Triple-T" kazoo? When you think you know, tell your teacher, but keep it a secret from those who are still trying to decide.

Teacher Information

The sounds, and change in pitch, are produced by the voice, but the kazoo gives it an interesting sound. Children will enjoy adding the Triple-T kazoo to their collection of homemade musical instruments.

Why do we call it the Triple-T kazoo? Because it's made from a Toilet Tissue Tube, of course!

INTEGRATING: Music, art

SKILLS: Observing

Activity 4.14
HOW CAN YOU SEE SOUND?

Materials Needed

- Cardboard oatmeal drum or medium-sized tin can
- Salt, puffed wheat, or puffed rice
- Heavy rubber band (or string)
- Large balloon or sheet rubber

Procedure

1. Remove both ends from a can or cardboard container (be careful of sharp edges).
2. Stretch a balloon over one end of the can and secure it with the rubber band. You now have a simple drum.
3. Sprinkle salt on the drum head. Tap it and observe what happens. Hit it harder. What happened? What can you say about this?
4. Sprinkle salt or puffed rice or wheat on the drum head. Keep the drum level and shout into the other end. Have a friend observe the results, then trade places.
5. What happened? What can you say about this?

For Problem Solvers: Put some salt on the drum head. Hold it over the speaker of a stereo while you play music on the stereo. Turn the volume up and down. What is happening with the salt? Why? Do you see any difference when the volume changes? Do you see any difference with high notes and bass notes?

Teacher Information

When the drum head is tapped, the salt will form a pattern caused by the vibration. The pattern will change as the drum is hit harder.

Shouting into the can will cause the rubber diaphragm to vibrate (be sure it is tightly stretched). Pitch and loudness will change the pattern of the salt or puffed rice.

Loud musical instruments will also cause the patterns to change. Remember, for this to work, *the balloon must be stretched tightly across the can.*

INTEGRATING: Music

SKILLS: Observing, measuring, predicting, communicating, comparing and contrasting, identifying and controlling variables, experimenting

Activity 4.15
HOW CAN YOU SEE YOUR VOICE?

Materials Needed

- Prepared drum from Activity 4.14
- 2-cm × 2-cm (1-in. × 1-in.) mirror
- Glue
- Screen or white surface
- Flashlight

Procedure

1. Glue the mirror to the center of the drum head.
2. Darken the room and have a friend shine a flashlight on the mirror, so the light is reflected onto a screen or wall.
3. Speak in a loud voice into the can and observe the reflected light on the wall.
4. Make different sounds to see what happens.

For Problem Solvers: Hold the drum over the speaker of a stereo while you play music on the stereo and shine a flashlight onto the mirror. Turn the volume up and down. Watch the reflection on the wall. Do you see any difference when the volume changes? Do you see any difference with high notes and bass notes? Try a different musical selection. Try a different stereo if you have another one available. Is there any difference?

Can you think of any other ways to observe vibrations that are caused by sound waves?

Teacher Information

When the child shouts into the can, the drum head will vibrate, causing the reflected pattern on the wall to change shape. Different sounds will cause different shapes. This is a method of changing sound waves into light so they may be observed. It is a simple oscilloscope. This principle is used in many technical fields, such as medicine. Musical groups often use this principle to produce light shows to accompany their music. Your encyclopedia can provide additional information if children would care to explore this topic in greater depth.

INTEGRATING: Music

SKILLS: Observing, measuring, predicting, communicating, comparing and contrasting, identifying and controlling variables, experimenting

Activity 4.16
WHAT CAN WATER TELL US ABOUT SOUND?

Materials Needed

- Box of dominoes
- Pan of water
- Small rock
- Drawing paper
- Crayons

Procedure

1. Stand the dominoes on end on a solid surface approximately 3 cm (1 in.) apart.
2. Tip the first domino forward so it hits the one next to it. What happened?
3. Matter is made up of tiny particles called molecules that react very much as the dominoes did when the first one was disturbed. Energy in the form of vibration is transferred from one molecule to another.
4. Drop a small rock into a pan of water. Observe what happens to the water. When molecules bump against one another, they transfer energy to all the other molecules around them, causing vibrations to travel in all directions.
5. Can you draw a picture of the way you think sound travels in air? Try it, and show your picture to your teacher.

Teacher Information

The use of dominoes will help children see how energy is transferred from one object to another. The pan of water should show how the energy is transferred in all directions (in this case, in ripples). If a large pan is used, the children may observe that the ripples bounce off solid objects and reverse direction. Echoes are caused by sound waves traveling out and bouncing back in waves.

INTEGRATING: Music

SKILLS: Observing, measuring, predicting, communicating, identifying and controlling variables, experimenting

Activity 4.17
HOW CAN A THREAD HELP CARRY YOUR VOICE?

 Take home and do with family and friends.

Materials Needed

- Two paper cups
- Toothpick
- Cotton thread, about 4 m (4 yds.) long

Procedure

1. Use the toothpick or your pencil to punch a small hole in the center of the bottom of each cup.

2. Push one end of the thread through the hole of each cup.

3. Break the toothpick in half and tie each end of the thread to one piece of toothpick so the thread cannot pull out of the hole in the cup.

4. Keep the thread tight and be sure it doesn't touch anything.

5. Put the cup to your ear and have your friend talk into his or her cup. Now you talk and have your friend listen. Now whisper.

6. What happened? What happens when you touch the thread? Explain why you think this happens. Make a set of telephones at home and show them to your family.

For Problem Solvers: Make a "party line" by crossing the lines from two sets of telephones over each other. Three people can then listen while one person talks. See if you can include a third set of telephones.

Teacher Information

This is an inexpensive way to provide a telephone for each student in your class to take home and tell about. The telephone works in a very simple way. Sound waves cause the bottom of the first cup to vibrate. These vibrations, in turn, cause the thread to vibrate. The vibrating thread causes the bottom of the other cup and the air inside to vibrate. The sounds the students hear are a result of these vibrations; the air in the second cups strikes their eardrums in nearly the same way it struck the bottom of the first cups as their partners spoke into them.

Use heavy cotton thread. Polyester is easier to find, but it tangles easily. Dental floss is an excellent substitute, but more expensive.

Figure 4.17-1

Paper Cup with Toothpick and Thread

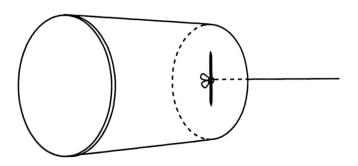

INTEGRATING: Music

SKILLS: Observing, measuring, predicting, communicating, identifying and controlling variables, experimenting

Activity 4.18
HOW WELL DOES SOUND TRAVEL THROUGH WOOD?

 Take home and do with family and friends.

Materials Needed

- Table (or desk)

Procedure

1. Have a partner tap an object on the table or desk loudly enough for you to hear.

2. Put your ear on the desk top and have your partner tap again.

3. What happened?

4. What can you say about this?

5. If anyone in the class has a ticking wristwatch, see if you can hear it through the table.

6. What can you say about sound traveling through solid objects? Can you think of a reason for this?

7. What does the statement "Keep your ear to the ground" mean? Where do you think it began?

Teacher Information

Sound travels better through solid objects because the molecules are more tightly packed and don't have to move a great distance to bump against one another and transmit the vibrations. Sound will travel a greater distance in solids for the same reason. The exception, of course, is specially designed acoustic materials that appear to be solid but are designed with many spaces to "trap" vibrations.

The tapping on the desk will be heard more clearly when the ear is against the desk.

Native Americans used this principle, literally keeping their ears to the ground, to hear sounds at great distances. Buffalo herds and horses' hooves could be heard before they were seen. "Keep your ear to the ground" has come to mean "listen carefully."

INTEGRATING: Social studies

SKILLS: Observing, predicting, communicating, identifying and controlling variables

Activity 4.19
HOW CAN YOU MAKE A COAT HANGER SING?

 Take home and do with family and friends.

Materials Needed

- Metal coat hanger
- Two heavy cotton strings 50 cm (20 in.) in length

Procedure

1. Tie the strings to the wide ends of the hanger.

Figure 4.19-1

Coat Hanger with Two Strings

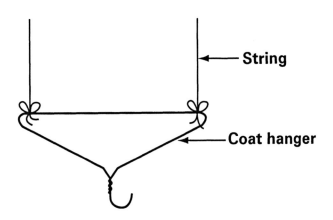

2. Hold the ends of the strings and hit the hanger against a solid object, such as your desk. Listen to the sound it makes.

3. Wrap the ends of the string around each of your index fingers. Put your fingers in your ears and tap the hanger on the solid object again.

5. Compare the first sound with the one you just heard.

4. What caused the sound? Discuss your ideas with your group.

For Problem Solvers: Were you surprised about the sound you heard from the coat hanger? Investigate this idea further. What variables could you change? Can you substitute something else for the coat hanger, such as a spoon, a piece of wire, another kind of coat hanger, or something else? Could you use a lighter or heavier string, or one of a different length, or a thin wire, or something else? Try tapping it against various objects and surfaces as well.

How does a doctor's stethoscope work? Do some research and find out. Do you see any relationship between the coat hanger activity and the stethoscope? Explain. Did you know that mechanics also use stethoscopes? The mechanic's stethoscope usually has a narrow probe sensor instead of a broad pad. Think of ways that you think a stethoscope might be helpful to a mechanic. Now back to the research—find out if you were right.

Teacher Information

When struck without the fingers in the ears, the hanger will sound flat and metallic. When the fingers are placed in the ears, the sound will be a loud gong because sound travels better through the relatively solid string than through the air.

INTEGRATING: Music

SKILLS: Observing, measuring, predicting, communicating, comparing and contrasting, identifying and controlling variables, experimenting

Activity 4.20
FROM HOW FAR AWAY CAN YOU HEAR A CLOCK TICK?

 Take home and do with family and friends.

Materials Needed

- Ticking clock
- Foot ruler
- Meter stick
- String
- Paper-cup telephone from Activity 4.17

Procedure

1. Listen to the clock tick. Move it as far from your ear as you can and still hear the ticking. Have a partner measure the distance.

2. Put one end of the foot ruler to your ear and the clock at the other end, touching the ruler. What happened?

3. Repeat step 2 using a meter stick. Substitute string for the meter stick. What happened?

4. Put the clock against one end of your paper-cup telephone and listen on the other end. What can you say about this? Can you see a relationship between this activity and the one with the hanger?

5. The sticks should not be held firmly or clutched in your hand. Why?

For Problem Solvers: Find a long board—preferably a 1″ × 2″ that is 8 feet long. Be sure you have your measurement recorded from #1 above, which indicates how far away you could hear the clock tick through the air. Put the board against your ear and have a friend put the clock against the board. Move the clock farther away until you can no longer hear it. Measure this distance and write it down. Could you hear the clock from any farther away through the board than you could through the air? Does sound travel better through air or through solids?

Teacher Information

Thin pieces of wood such as lathing of different lengths may be substituted for the foot ruler and meter sticks. The objects should not be held firmly, as the hand will absorb the vibrations and muffle the sound. The same phenomenon occurs when the thread on the paper-cup telephone is touched.

For your problem solvers, 1″ × 2″ lumber is called firring, and it is easy to find at all lumber stores or home improvement stores. Any long, thin board will do just fine.

INTEGRATING: Math

SKILLS: Observing, measuring, predicting, communicating, comparing and contrasting, identifying and controlling variables, experimenting

Activity 4.21
HOW FAST DOES SOUND TRAVEL?

Materials Needed

- Drum, cymbals, large metal lid or something else that will make a loud sound when visibly struck
- Stick to strike object

Procedure

1. Take your drum or other object out on the school grounds. Ask other members of the class to go with you.
2. Move about 100 meters (or about 100 yards) or more away from the other students.
3. Strike the object several times so the others can see the movement of your arm and hear the sound.
4. Remember, when you see an object move at a distance, you are seeing reflected light travel. When you hear the sound, you are hearing sound vibrations.
5. Tell what you observed. What can you say about the speed of light and the speed of sound?

For Problem Solvers: Using a stopwatch, have someone strike a metal post with a hammer from 100 meters away. Figure out a way to measure the distance. A greater distance (200 or 300 m) would be even better, but be sure you know how far it is. Start the stopwatch when you see the hammer strike the pole, and stop it when you hear the hammer strike the pole. Check the time several times for accuracy. Figure out how far sound travels in one second. How long does it take sound to travel one kilometer? Translate that to miles—how long does it take sound to travel one mile?

Teacher Information

Light travels very rapidly—over 186,000 miles a second. By comparison, sound is a slow-poke, moving at about 760 miles per hour at sea level. (Speed of sound is affected by temperature and density of the air. The speed range at sea level is about 740 to 780 as the temperature ranges from freezing to 75 degrees Fahrenheit.) Even at the short distance of 100 meters, it will be possible to see the child strike the drum before the sound is heard. Children who have been to athletic events in a large stadium may have noticed that movements that produce sounds on the playing field by athletes or bands are seen before the sounds are heard. Airplanes, especially fast jets, are sometimes difficult to locate in the sky by their sound because the sound is traveling so much more slowly that by the time it arrives, the plane has moved to a new position. Discuss these questions: (a) Would humidity affect the speed of sound? (b) Would sound travel faster through air or through water? (c) Would sound travel better on a cold day or on a hot day?

The speed of sound is not affected by loudness or frequency. Sound travels at about 330 meters per second in dry air at freezing point. Water vapor in the air increases the speed of sound slightly. However, sound travels faster in warm air than in cold air because air molecules are moving faster and therefore bump into one another more frequently. At room temperature, sound travels at about 340 meters per second, increasing about 0.6 meters per second for every degree rise in temperature above zero degrees Celsius. In water sound travels about four times as fast as it does in air, and in steel it travels about 15 times as fast as in air.

SKILLS: Observing, inferring, measuring, predicting, communicating, using space-time relationships, formulating hypotheses, identifying and controlling variables, experimenting

Activity 4.22
HOW CAN SOUND BE CONTROLLED?

Materials Needed

- Two identical shoe boxes
- Scissors
- Other materials or fabrics
- Foam rubber (1 inch thick)
- Glue (optional)
- Small paper cups (optional)

Procedure

1. Punch or cut a round hole approximately 2 cm (1 in.) in both ends of each shoe box. Try to make the holes nearly the same in both boxes.

2. Cut foam rubber to line the sides, top, and bottom of one shoe box. (Be sure to cut holes in the foam rubber to match the ones in the box.)

3. Measure and cut three pieces of foam rubber so they will fit from the bottom to the top of the shoe box and about halfway across, as shown in Figure 4.22-1.

Figure 4.22-1
Foam-lined Shoe Box with Foam Dividers

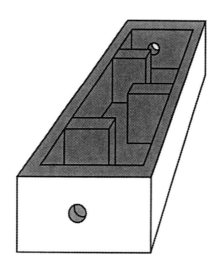

4. Put the lid on each shoe box and have a friend whisper something to you through each box. Then have your friend speak more loudly and make other kinds of sounds. Be sure your friend's mouth and your ear are against the box when the sounds are made. You may want to glue a small paper cup, with the bottom removed, over the holes in the ends. This will help collect the sound.

5. What happened? What can you say about this?

6. Try lining other shoe boxes with different materials.

Teacher Information

This activity will help children discover one way of deadening sound. Sound waves, traveling through the air, strike the many holes in the foam rubber. The sound is reflected in many directions by the distorted surface, and the result is a muffling of the sound. Sound traveling through the foam-lined box will be mostly absorbed, while it will transfer clearly through the empty box, or even be amplified by it.

INTEGRATING: Music

SKILLS: Observing, inferring, measuring, predicting, communicating, comparing and contrasting, identifying and controlling variables, experimenting

Activity 4.23
WHAT HAPPENS TO SOUND WHEN THERE ARE FEWER MOLECULES?

(Teacher-supervised activity)

Materials Needed

- 4- to 8-ounce glass jar with tight-sealing lid
- Thread or string
- Hot (not boiling) water
- Small bell
- Tape

Procedure

1. Use the string to suspend the bell in the jar by taping it to the inside of the lid. Be sure the bell does not touch the sides or bottom of the jar.

2. Gently shake the jar and listen to the bell.

3. Remove the lid with the bell attached and carefully pour about 2–3 cm (1 in.) of hot water into the jar.

4. Allow the jar to stand for about 30 seconds and then replace the lid. Be sure the bell does not touch the water.

5. Let the jar cool, then gently shake the jar again and listen to the bell.

6. What happened? What can you say about this?

Figure 4.23-1

Bell in Jar

170

For Problem Solvers: Find a junior high school science teacher or a high school physics teacher. Ask the teacher if he or she has a vacuum pump, and, if so, if he or she would show you the demonstration with the bell in a bell jar. The teacher will know what you mean. It will be similar to what you did for this activity, except that it uses an electric bell, and it's more effective because the vacuum pump removes more of the air. Perhaps you know a high school physics student who could arrange to borrow the equipment and demonstrate it for your class.

Teacher Information

Before hot water is poured into the jar, the children should be able to hear the bell clearly. Hot water in the jar will displace most of the air molecules with steam. With fewer air molecules in the bottle, sound vibrations will not travel as easily, so the bell will not sound as loud.

Discuss the problem of communication on the moon or any other place without air.

SKILLS: Observing, inferring, measuring, predicting, communicating, comparing and contrasting, identifying and controlling variables, experimenting

Activity 4.24
WHAT IS A TUNING FORK?

Materials Needed

- Tuning fork
- Small dish of water
- Soft rubber mallet or rubber heel from a shoe

Procedure

1. Hold the handle of the tuning fork in one hand and strike it with a rubber mallet or heel of a shoe. (CAUTION: You shouldn't hit the tuning fork with a hard object.)
2. Bring the double end near your ear. What happened?
3. Strike the tuning fork again. Touch the double end. What happened?
4. This time, after striking the tuning fork, lower it slowly into the dish of water. What happened?
5. Strike the tuning fork again. Gently touch the handle to a hard surface such as a table or desk.

For Problem Solvers: You noticed what happened when you touched the base of the tuning fork to the table. Experiment with the tuning fork to see if you can find other ways to make it louder. Try touching it to a box, the body of a guitar or violin, and other things. What materials and what shapes seem to have the greatest effect?

Teacher Information

Tuning forks may be obtained from music stores and science-supply houses. Children who play stringed musical instruments may have tuning forks for use in tuning their instruments. Specially designed tuning forks are often used by doctors for general hearing-screening tests. Each tuning fork is tuned to a certain pitch. The pitch depends on the thickness and length, and the material of which it is made.

Most tuning forks vibrate so rapidly that it is difficult to detect movement by looking at them. Your students will learn that when the tines of a vibrating fork are lowered slowly into a dish of water, the water will splash, demonstrating that vibration is occurring. When the handle of a vibrating fork is placed on a table or desk, the sound will be amplified. If the tuning fork is touched to a large paper cup, a shoe box, or the body of a stringed instrument, the sound will be amplified.

INTEGRATING: Music

SKILLS: Observing, inferring, predicting, communicating, comparing and contrasting, identifying and controlling variables, experimenting

Activity 4.25
HOW CAN YOU MAKE A GOBLET SING?

(Teacher demonstration)

Materials Needed

- Four to six good-quality glass goblets
- Water
- Vinegar

Procedure

1. Check the goblets carefully to be certain they have no cracked or chipped edges.
2. Add different amounts of water to each goblet (no more than half full). Put a few drops of vinegar in the water.
3. Firmly hold the goblet by the base with one hand. Moisten the fingers of your other hand with the vinegar water and rotate your fingers lightly around the rim of the goblet. What happened? Can you think why?
4. Try the other goblets. Can you describe what is happening?

For Problem Solvers: Take two goblets that are just alike. Be sure they are clean, dry, and that they have no chips or cracks around the rim. Place them about 30 cm (12 in.) apart. Hold one goblet steady while you moisten your finger with vinegar water and make this goblet sing. While it is producing a loud tone, grasp it firmly to stop the tone and immediately listen carefully to the other goblet. What do you hear? If you hear nothing from the other goblet, try it again.

Lift the lid of a piano and make a steady singing tone into the piano with your voice, while someone holds the sustain pedal down. Stop the tone and listen. What do you hear?

Place two guitars face to face, just a short distance apart. Be sure they have been tuned alike. Pluck one string of one guitar, then stop the vibration of that string by placing your hand over it and listen to the other guitar. What do you hear?

See what you can learn about *sympathetic vibrations.* Use your encyclopedias or other reference books.

Teacher Information

Great care should be exercised in performing this activity. The goblets must be of high quality and completely free of rough edges. When this activity is properly performed, the moist fingers will cause the glass to vibrate and produce a beautiful, clear tone. The combination of water and vinegar seems to produce just enough lubricant and friction to make the demonstration easier.

Your problem solvers will experiment with sympathetic vibrations. This means that the vibrations of one goblet will travel through the air and cause another glass to vibrate and produce the same tone. In order for this to occur, the condition of each glass must be almost exactly the same. Both should be dry, empty, and at the same temperature. Their physical appearance should be the same.

Sympathetic vibration may also be experienced by singing into a piano while holding the sustain pedal down. The vibrations of the voice will cause strings, tuned to the same pitch in the piano, to vibrate.

INTEGRATING: Music

SKILLS: Observing, inferring, classifying, predicting, communicating, formulating hypotheses, identifying and controlling variables, experimenting, researching

Activity 4.26
HOW CAN SOUNDS BE HEARD MORE CLEARLY?

 Take home and do with family and friends.

Materials Needed

- 4-ounce, 8-ounce, and 12-ounce paper (or plastic) cups
- Larger round tapered containers (such as popcorn drums)

Procedure

1. Remove the bottoms from the paper cups and other containers.
2. Choose two friends, select different-sized containers, and go outside.
3. Have your friends walk away from you in opposite directions for about 50 paces.
4. Take a small cup, point it between your friends and say "Hello" in a loud voice into the narrower end of the cup. Next, turn to face each friend and repeat the hello at about the same volume.
5. Now fit the three different-sized cups together as shown in the illustration and repeat step 4.

Figure 4.26-1

Paper Cups Nested to Form a Megaphone

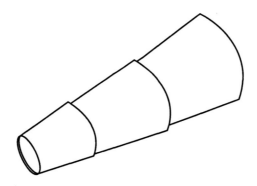

6. Trade places with your friends and repeat the activities. Discuss your findings. Can you explain what happened?

For Problem Solvers: Do some investigating to see how many applications you can find for the megaphone. Who uses it? When? Why? Notice the shape of the end of a trumpet, where the sound leaves the trumpet. Is it shaped like a megaphone? Why? What other musical instruments use that shape?

Teacher Information

This activity is related to the activity with the paper-cup telephone. The object the children have produced is a megaphone, which collects, concentrates, and directs sound waves. The children on the playground will discover that they can hear better when the paper-cup megaphone is pointed toward them. They should also observe that as the megaphone is lengthened and widened, the sound is clearer. We often cup our hands around our mouths when we shout, for the same reason. Many wind instruments have bell-shaped ends.

INTEGRATING: Music

SKILLS: Observing, inferring, classifying, measuring, predicting, communicating, comparing and contrasting, formulating hypotheses, identifying and controlling variables, experimenting, researching

176

Activity 4.27
HOW CAN YOU PLAY A RECORD WITH A SEWING NEEDLE?

(Teacher-assisted activity)

Materials Needed

- 8-ounce paper cup
- Thin sewing needles
- Thimble
- Masking tape
- Sheet of 12-in. × 18-in. construction paper
- Old phonograph records
- Record turntable

Procedure

1. Have you done the paper-cup telephone activity yet? If not, perhaps you will want to try it before you begin this exploration. Ask your teacher about Activity 4.17.

2. Thomas Edison, a famous inventor, invented a talking machine that he called a phonograph. At first, a wax cylinder was used. It was later improved by making a round, hard disk. You can make a simple phonograph to play sound.

3. Very carefully, push a sewing needle through the lower lip of a paper cup so that the needle touches the bottom of the cup (Figure 4.27-1).

Figure 4.27-1

Paper Cup with Needle

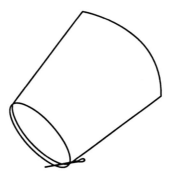

4. Put an old phonograph record (it might get damaged) on a revolving turntable and hold the cup by two fingers while lightly touching the point of the needle to the grooves in the record (Figure 4.27-2). What happened?

Figure 4.27-2

Paper Cup on Phonograph Record

5. Form a sheet of construction paper into a cone held together with masking tape. Insert a sewing needle through the narrow part of the cone (Figure 4.27-3).

Figure 4.27-3

Needle Inserted Through Cone

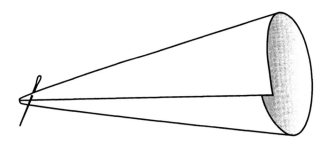

6. Lightly touch the needle to the grooves of the record spinning on the turntable. What happened? Can you explain why?

For Problem Solvers: Identify variables that you think might affect the production of sound in this activity and experiment with those variables. Try various needles or other objects that you think might substitute for the needle. You could try many different ideas in the place of this particular paper cup. Can you think of another way to turn the record, so you don't need the turntable? Explore, and have fun learning about sound.

Think about what sound is. If there is sound, something is vibrating. Examine the record carefully with a hand lens. Use a microscope also if you have one. Can you tell what causes the needle to vibrate? Can you see anything that would cause it to change its vibrating pattern to create different sounds? Does a needle work any better for this than a straight pin? Examine the points and examine the grooves again. Look at the points of each under the microscope or hand lens while they are resting in a groove of the record. Which would you expect to work best? Why?

Teacher Information

This activity should be done individually or in small groups. The paper-cup telephone in Activity 4.17 demonstrates sound traveling better through solids and amplifying sound through concentrating the vibrations in a confined area (the paper cup). This activity is similar to the paper-cup telephone in many ways. The grooves in the record cause the needle to vibrate, which transfers to the bottom of the paper cup. The shape of the cup concentrates and amplifies the sound, making it possible to hear the sound reproduced from the grooves of the record. The paper cone works in the same way, except the sound may be louder due to the size of the cone and the better vibration that is possible through thinner material.

CAUTION: **Young children will need help in inserting the needles and rolling the cones.**

INTEGRATING: Music

SKILLS: Observing, inferring, communicating, comparing and contrasting, formulating hypotheses, identifying and controlling variables, experimenting

Activity 4.28
CAN YOU THINK OF WORDS THAT SOUND LIKE THE OBJECT OR ACTION THEY DESCRIBE?

(Enrichment activity)

Materials Needed

- Paper and pencils

Procedure

1. Some words in our language seem to sound like the object or event they describe. Say "bark" loudly and sharply. It seems to make a sound similar to the sound a dog makes. Now try the word "wolf." Say it sharply in a deep voice. What do you hear? Words that imitate the natural sound of the object or action involved are called onomatopoeia.

2. Get together with several friends and, beginning with the list below, see how many words you can find that make a noise similar to the object or event:

bark	creak
wolf	knock
bear	peep
croak	puff

3. Take your list home and ask members of your family to help add to it.

4. Compare your list with those of other members of the class.

5. Write an exciting story using as many onomatopoeia words as you can.

Teacher Information

Fairy tales, children's stories, and poetry make liberal use of onomatopoeia. The huffing and puffing of the wolf in "Three Little Pigs" is an excellent example. If children are conscious of the words and how words make them feel, their writing skills can be improved through this technique.

INTEGRATING: Language arts

SKILLS: Classifying, communicating

Activity 4.29
CAN YOU INVENT OR MAKE A MUSICAL INSTRUMENT?

(Teacher-assisted activity)

Materials Needed

- A variety of tubes, cans, rubber bands, and so on, that will produce sounds (see Figures 4.29-1, 4.29-2, and 4.29-3)

Procedure

1. Throughout history people have made and played musical instruments. The only rule seems to have been that the sound an instrument made was pleasing to the person playing it. Hollow logs were probably the first drums; reeds, the first wind instruments; and tough stems or dried animal parts such as tendons or intestines, the first stringed instruments. Today, some of our music is produced by electronics or other synthetic means. But many of the old ways of producing music are still being used, and some old ways of producing music are being revived. Most of the instruments being used in symphony orchestras of today were invented hundreds and even thousands of years ago.

2. You can invent and play your own musical instrument. Look at the illustrations here. These ideas should help you begin. Your instrument does not have to be the same. Maybe you can invent a better one.

3. When you have finished making your musical instrument, find some others who have made instruments and see if you can learn to play a tune together.

Figure 4.29-1

Homemade Percussion Instruments

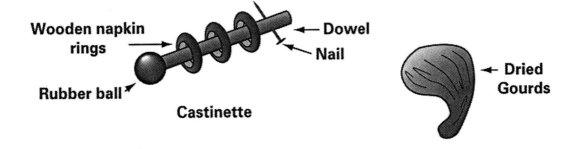

Figure 4.29-1
Homemade Percussion Instruments (continued)

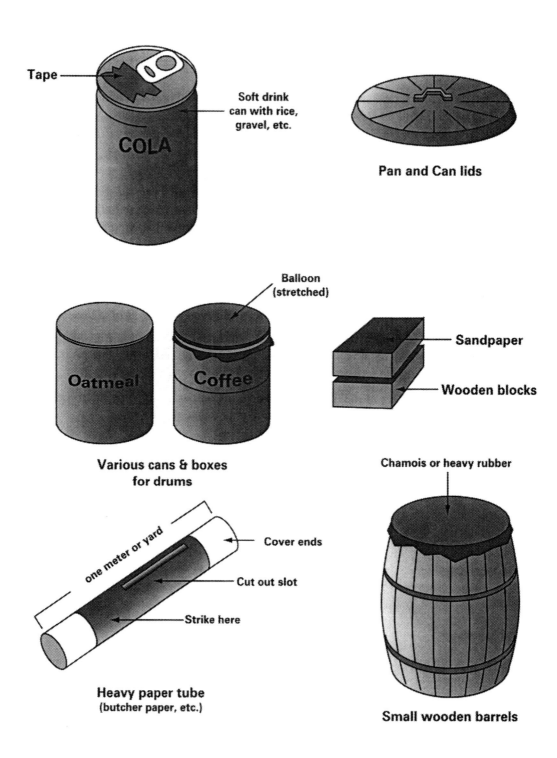

Tape

Soft drink can with rice, gravel, etc.

COLA

Pan and Can lids

Balloon (stretched)

Oatmeal

Coffee

Sandpaper

Wooden blocks

Various cans & boxes for drums

Chamois or heavy rubber

one meter or yard

Cover ends

Cut out slot

Strike here

Heavy paper tube
(butcher paper, etc.)

Small wooden barrels

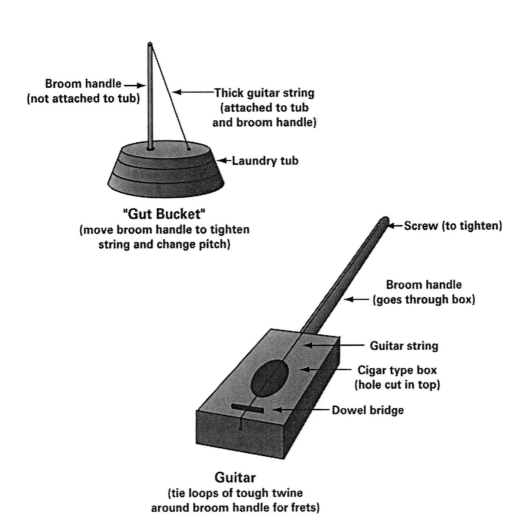

Figure 4.29-2

Homemade Stringed Instruments

Broom handle
(not attached to tub)

Thick guitar string
(attached to tub
and broom handle)

Laundry tub

"Gut Bucket"
(move broom handle to tighten
string and change pitch)

Screw (to tighten)

Broom handle
(goes through box)

Guitar string

Cigar type box
(hole cut in top)

Dowel bridge

Guitar
(tie loops of tough twine
around broom handle for frets)

Figure 4.29-3

Homemade Wind Instruments

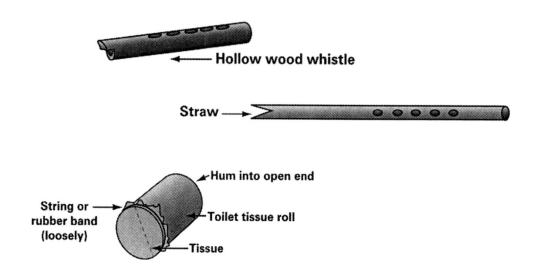

Teacher Information

This activity can be used in conjunction with an art class or a music class. Encourage students to be creative as they make their instruments.

INTEGRATING: Music, art

SKILLS: Observing, inferring, classifying, measuring, predicting, communicating, comparing and contrasting, using space-time relationships, formulating hypotheses, identifying and controlling variables, experimenting, researching

SIMPLE MACHINES

TO THE TEACHER

Acquiring an understanding of simple machines can help open our eyes to the world around us. All machines, regardless of complexity, are composed of various combinations of the six simple machines. These are often applied in unique and creative ways, but they are nonetheless the same six. After some exposure to these activities, students will enjoy applying their newly acquired awareness in identifying the simple machines in common appliances and equipment—the shovel, the egg beater, the bicycle, the automobile, and so forth.

This section lends itself especially well to the discovery of scientific principles. Most of the activities suggested are safe for students to perform independently.

For most of the lever activities, a 1-in. board, which is approximately 1 m (1 yd.) long and 10 cm (4 in.) wide, is adequate. Others call for a lighter material, such as 1/2-in. plywood.

It is recommended that you prepare your levers by marking positions 1, 2, 3, 4, and 5, measured at equal intervals as indicated in Figure A.

Figure A

Lever with Points Marked and Eye Hooks

Eye hooks mounted at each point provide for attaching the spring balance.

Fulcrums ranging in height from 5 cm (2 in.) to 10 cm (4 in.) should be adequate and can be made by cutting a wedge shape from 4-in. × 4-in. post material (Figure B). Scraps that are adequate can usually be acquired at a lumber store for little or no cost.

Figure B

4 in. × 4 in. Fulcrum

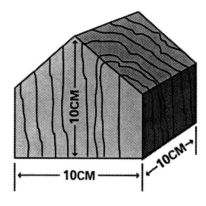

186

Regarding the Early Grades

Activities 5.1–5.6 can be easily adapted for younger children. Many of the later activities can be used by omitting the steps involving charting and mathematics. Young children can experience the concept "Machines make work easier" by feeling it and seeing it happen. These children can be encouraged to report in terms of "easier" and "harder" instead of by mathematical comparisons. For children who have experienced the teeter-totter and the wheelbarrow, these activities will help to clarify their earlier observations.

Activity 5.1
WHAT HAPPENS WHEN YOU RUB YOUR HANDS TOGETHER?

(Teacher-assisted activity)

 Take home and do with family and friends.

Materials Needed

- None

Procedure

1. Rub your hands briskly together for several **seconds.**
2. How do your hands feel?
3. Do it again, only faster. Then quickly hold your hands on your cheeks.
4. How do your hands feel to your cheeks?

Teacher Information

Whenever the surfaces of two objects rub together—the hands in this case—the resulting friction creates heat. In this simple activity, the heat is quickly noted and will vary according to the amount of moisture (perspiration and oil on the skin) that is present.

SKILLS: Observing, inferring, comparing and contrasting

Activity 5.2
HOW DO LUBRICANTS AFFECT FRICTION?

(Teacher-assisted activity)

 Take home and do with family and friends.

Materials Needed

- Pan of water or sink

Procedure

1. Rub your hands together briskly as you did for Activity 5.1.
2. How do your hands feel?
3. Next, dip your hands in the water.
4. While they're wet, rub them briskly again.
5. Do your hands feel any different? Can you explain this?

For Problem Solvers: Put a small amount of olive oil, cooking oil, or hand lotion between your hands, and then rub your hands together again. Is it any easier to rub your hands together? Is there any difference in the amount of heat produced?

Find a fairly large standard screwdriver. Hold it by the bit—the end that slants and fits the screw. Next, wet your fingers and hold it by the bit again. Is it just as easy to hold as before? Wipe the water off your fingers and the screwdriver, then put a little bit of cooking oil between your fingers and hold the screwdriver the same way. What difference do you find? Explain why.

Teacher Information

In addition to providing a cooling effect, the water also acts as a lubricant, reducing friction and thereby reducing the amount of heat produced by friction.

Your problem solvers will find that friction is greatly reduced by the use of a lubricant, such as cooking oil, olive oil, or hand lotion. If motor oil is available, let them try it with the screwdriver activity and compare with the other lubricants. If STP (trade name) is available, try that too.

Activity 5.3
HOW DO STARTING FRICTION AND SLIDING FRICTION COMPARE?

 Take home and do with family and friends.

Materials Needed

- Two or three large books
- String 2 m (2 yds.) long
- Spring balance

Procedure

1. Tie the books into a bundle, using the string.

2. Place the books on a table or on the floor. Attach one end of the spring balance to the string wrapped around the books.

Figure 5.3-1

Bundled Books with Spring Balance Attached

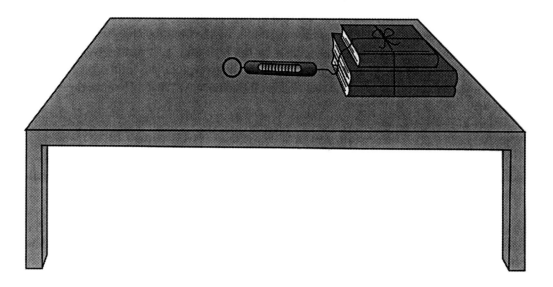

3. Holding the other end of the spring balance and watching the indicator needle carefully, pull the books 50 to 100 cm (1.5 to 3 ft.) across the table (or floor).

4. What was the reading on the spring balance when the books first began to move?

190

5. What was the reading on the spring balance as the books moved steadily across the table?

6. Repeat the activity, being sure to pull the books in a steady, not jerking, manner.

7. Is the amount of force required to start the books moving equal to the amount of force needed to keep them moving? If not, which is greater?

8. Repeat to verify your findings.

9. Discuss your findings with others.

For Problem Solvers: Do you think friction will be the same for a stack of books if a small book is at the bottom of the pile as it will be if a large book is at the bottom? If you don't think it will be the same, which do you think will have the least friction? Do some scientific investigation and find out. Think through your procedure and discuss it with your teacher or someone else before you begin. Test the question for both starting friction and sliding friction.

Continue your investigation to compare the friction of various surfaces rubbing against each other. What could you put under the stack of books that you think would allow the books to slide across the table with less friction? Try at least two or three different materials and remember to test both starting friction and sliding friction. Make a graph of your results.

Teacher Information

Starting friction is greater than *sliding friction*. More force is required to start an object than to keep it sliding. One factor is inertia—the tendency of an object at rest to remain at rest and of an object in motion to remain in motion.

Those who accept the "For Problem Solvers" challenge will practice their skills at designing a simple experiment, interpreting the data, and communicating their results in the form of a graph. They will also learn some useful information about friction and the difference that is made by the type of surfaces involved.

INTEGRATING: Math

SKILLS: Observing, inferring, measuring, predicting, communicating, comparing and contrasting, formulating hypotheses, identifying and controlling variables, experimenting

Activity 5.4
HOW DOES ROLLING FRICTION COMPARE WITH SLIDING FRICTION?

 Take home and do with family and friends.

Materials Needed

- Two or three large books
- String 2 m (2 yds.) long
- Spring balance
- At least six round pencils

Procedure

1. Tie the books into a bundle, using the string.

2. Place the bundle of books on a table or on the floor.

3. Attach one end of the spring balance to the string wrapped around the books.

4. While holding the other end of the spring balance and watching the indicator needle carefully, slide the books steadily 25 to 50 cm (10 to 20 in.) across the floor (or table).

5. Record the amount of force needed for both starting friction and sliding friction.

6. Next place the pencils side by side, about 5 to 8 cm (2 to 3 in.) apart.

7. Place the books on the pencils at one end of the row.

8. Pull the books again with the spring balance and record the amount of force required for starting friction and rolling friction.

9. Did the pencils change the force needed to drag the books across the table? If so, how much difference did they make?

For Problem Solvers: Add this data to the graph that you prepared from your investigations in Activity 5.3.

Predict whether the starting friction and rolling friction will be the same with the books on a skateboard as with the pencils. Place the same books on a skateboard and compare both starting friction and rolling friction with the results you got when using the pencils. Add your skateboard data to your graph.

Teacher Information

Rolling friction is less than sliding friction. This principle is used in wheels and bearings in a wide variety of applications, from wheels under a table to the workings of complex machinery. The Egyptians probably used wheels as rollers to move large stones when they built the pyramids.

INTEGRATING: Math

SKILLS: Observing, inferring, measuring, predicting, communicating, comparing and contrasting, formulating hypotheses, identifying and controlling variables, experimenting

Activity 5.5
WHAT IS THE ADVANTAGE OF A FIRST-CLASS LEVER?

(Teacher-supervised activity)

 Take home and do with family and friends.

Materials Needed

- Board 10 cm (4 in.) wide and 1 m (1 yd.) long (or other suitable lever)
- Fulcrum
- Book

Procedure

1. Place the fulcrum under the lever (board) at the middle (position 3 in the illustration).

Figure 5.5-1

**Lever on Fulcrum—Positions 1–5 Noted,
Book, and Arrow Marking the Effort Point**

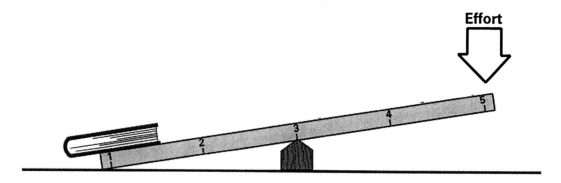

2. Place the book on the lever at position 1. Push down on the lever at position 5.
3. What happened to the book as you pushed down on the other end of the lever?
4. Repeat this procedure with the fulcrum at position 2 and again at position 4.
5. Is the same amount of effort required to raise the book regardless of the fulcrum position?
6. How does the required effort change as you move the fulcrum away from the book?

7. How does the required effort change as you move the fulcrum closer to the book?

8. Try to lift some other objects with your lever, such as a box of ditto paper. **Warning: *Do not* try to lift a piano or other objects that are heavy and tall, as they might tip over.**

9. To lift a heavy object, would you place the fulcrum near the object, away from the object, or does it matter?

For Problem Solvers: Look around you at school, at home, and everywhere else you go for the next several days. Find every example of levers that you can. Make a list of these. You will use your list as you do some of the next activities. Continue to add to your list as you go.

Teacher Information

The fulcrum divides a first-class lever into two parts, called the effort arm and the load arm. The load arm is the end upon which the load rests. The effort arm is the end we apply a force to in order to move the load.

With the fulcrum between the load arm and the effort arm, the first-class lever changes the direction of the load; that is, we move the load up by pressing down on the opposite end of the lever.

With a first-class lever, moving the fulcrum toward the load decreases the amount of force necessary to lift the load. When the fulcrum is closer to the load, we gain in force but lose speed and distance. When the fulcrum is closer to the effort, we gain in speed and distance but lose force.

Examples of first-class levers include scissors, pliers, and teeter-totters.

Warning: If a piano is used to verify responses to step 9, it should be closely supervised. Be sure to lift at the end of the piano rather than at the side. Use a heavy, thick board, a strong fulcrum, and plenty of *adult* help to steady the piano.

Integrating: Math

Skills: Observing, inferring, measuring, predicting, communicating, formulating hypotheses, identifying and controlling variables, experimenting

Activity 5.6
WHAT TYPE OF SIMPLE MACHINE IS THE TEETER-TOTTER?

 Take home and do with family and friends.

Materials Needed

- Teeter-totter

Procedure

1. Place the teeter-totter in such a position that it will balance with you on one end and a classmate on the other end.
2. Change the position of the teeter-totter on the fulcrum (bar in the middle) and try to balance with the same person.
3. What happened?
4. Now adjust the teeter-totter so you can balance with a different classmate.
5. What did you have to do? Why?

For Problem Solvers: You might have never thought of the teeter-totter as a machine until now, because teeter-totters are used for entertainment. Well, many toys and other things we use for entertainment are machines. The teeter-totter is a first-class lever. As a machine it allows a small person to lift a large person.

Place the teeter-totter in the middle, so it balances (or almost) by itself. Have two people get on it who are about the same size. Did it balance?

Find two people who are different sizes and who are willing to help you. They can be different ages. Predict where the teeter-totter needs to be placed on the bar in order for it to balance with these two people. Try it, and check your prediction. Do the same thing with several more pairs of people and try to improve your accuracy with each prediction.

Teacher Information

You might prefer to have students do this activity independently during their free time, but you, or a student who understands the principle of the first-class lever, should follow up to help assure correct learning.

The teeter-totter is a first-class lever. Either end could be called the effort arm or the load arm, but if you arbitrarily assign each end of the teeter-totter a name, the principles learned in Activity 5.5 will apply.

INTEGRATING: Math

SKILLS: Observing, inferring, measuring, predicting, communicating, comparing and contrasting, formulating hypotheses, identifying and controlling variables, experimenting

Activity 5.7
HOW CAN A LEVER BE USED TO LIFT HEAVY THINGS?

(Teacher demonstration)

Materials Needed

- Lever (2-in. plank)
- Fulcrum
- Automobile

Procedure

1. Place the plank on the ground and drive an automobile into such a position that one tire is on one end of the plank.
2. Set the parking brake.
3. Lift the end of the plank opposite the wheel and place the fulcrum under the plank near the wheel.
4. Push down on the effort arm of the lever.
5. What can you do with the lever that you couldn't do without it?

Teacher Information

This activity is suggested as a teacher demonstration because of the obvious potential risks involved. It demonstrates that levers can be used to lift very heavy loads with relatively little effort. Perhaps student assistants could be used safely for some tasks, but care should be taken to avoid unnecessary risks.

Consider having students try to lift one side of the automobile before using the lever. Be very careful because of possible back injuries. One student can lift a corner of the car using a lever, while several students could not do it without the lever.

INTEGRATING: Math

SKILLS: Observing, inferring, measuring, predicting, communicating, formulating hypotheses, identifying and controlling variables, experimenting

Activity 5.8
HOW CAN YOU PREDICT THE EFFORT REQUIRED TO LIFT A LOAD WITH A FIRST-CLASS LEVER?

Materials Needed

- Lever 1 m (1 yd.) long (preferably lightweight, such as 1/2-in. plywood)
- String
- Fulcrum 3–10 cm high (1–4 in.)
- Spring balance
- Two or three books
- "Record of Measurement I" chart
- Pencil

Procedure

1. Tie the books into a bundle. Place the fulcrum under position 3 as indicated in Figure 5.8-1.

Figure 5.8-1

Lever with Fulcrum at Position 3

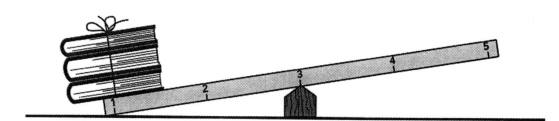

2. Place the books on the lever at position 1.

3. Use the "Record of Measurement I" chart for recording your measurements in this activity.

4. Attach the spring balance at position 5. Pull down and record the force required to lift the books.

5. Weigh the books and compare with the force required to lift them in step 4.

6. With the books on the lever at position 1 and the spring balance attached at position 5, move the fulcrum to position 4.

7. Pull down on the spring balance and record the force required to lift the books.

8. Repeat the above procedure with the fulcrum at position 2.

9. Compare your findings.

10. Estimate the force required to lift the books with the fulcrum halfway between positions 2 and 3. Record your estimate.

11. Try it. Record the actual force required. How close was your estimate?

12. Estimate the force necessary to lift the books with the fulcrum halfway between positions 3 and 4. Record your estimate.

13. Try it. Record your results. Was your estimate any closer this time?

Teacher Information

The effort required to lift an object with the first-class lever is proportionate to the relative lengths of the load arm and the effort arm. For example, with the fulcrum at position 3, the two arms are equal in length. If the load weighs 1 kg (or 1 lb.), the effort required to lift it should be 1 kg (or 1 lb.). (Note: 1 kg = 2.2 pounds, but load and effort are equal with fulcrum at position 3.)

With the fulcrum in position 4, the load arm is three times as long as the effort arm and the effort required to lift 1 kg (or 1 lb.) will be about 3 kg (or 3 lbs.).

With the fulcrum in position 2, the effort arm is three times as long as the load arm and the effort required to lift 1 kg (or 1 lb.) will be about 0.33 kg (or .33 lb.).

The degree of accuracy of the figures is affected by the degree of precision in positioning the load, fulcrum, and effort, and by the weight of the board itself. The results are therefore only approximate.

INTEGRATING: Math

SKILLS: Observing, inferring, measuring, predicting, communicating, comparing and contrasting, formulating hypotheses, identifying and controlling variables, experimenting

NAME _____ DATE _____

RECORD OF MEASUREMENT I

Actual weight of the load = _____ kg

Load Position	Effort Position	Fulcrum Position	Force
1	5	3	_____
1	5	4	_____
1	5	2	_____
1	5	between 2 and 3	Estimate: _____
			Actual: _____
1	5	between 3 and 4	Estimate: _____
			Actual: _____

Activity 5.9
WHAT DO WE LOSE AS WE GAIN FORCE WITH A LEVER?

Materials Needed

- Lever 1 m (1 yd.) long (preferably lightweight, such as 1/2 in. plywood)
- Pencil
- Spring balance
- Fulcrum at least 10 cm (4 in.) high
- Two or three books
- String
- "Record of Measurement II" chart
- Ruler

Procedure

1. Use the "Record of Measurement ll" chart for recording your measurements in this activity.

2. Tie the books into a bundle. Place the fulcrum under position 3 as indicated in Figure 5.9-1.

Figure 5.9-1

Lever with Fulcrum at Position 3

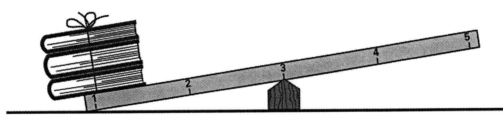

3. Review Activity 5.8 by doing the following. However, in addition to measuring the force required to lift the load for the various fulcrum positions, use the ruler to measure the distances traveled by the effort arm while the load arm travels the distances indicated on the chart.

   a. Place the books at position 1.

   b. Attach the spring balance at position 5, pull down, and record the force required to lift the books.

c. Weigh the books and compare with the force required above.

d. With the books on the lever at position 1 and the spring balance attached at position 5, move the fulcrum to position 4 (Figure 5.9-2).

e. Pull down on the spring balance and record the force required to lift the books.

f. Repeat the above procedure with the fulcrum at position 2.

g. Compare your findings.

4. With the last two fulcrum positions, estimate travel distances of the effort arm. Record your estimates.

Figure 5.9-2

Lever with Fulcrum at Position 4

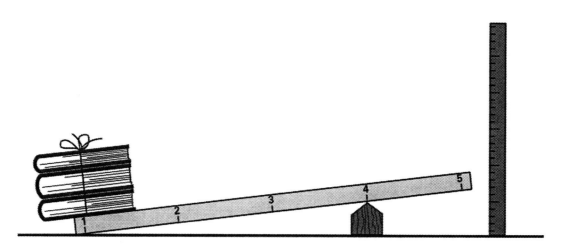

5. Try these and record the actual results.

6. As the force required at the effort arm decreases, does the distance the effort arm travels increase or decrease?

7. Write a statement about the force required to lift a load, the distance the load travels, and the distance the effort arm travels as the fulcrum is moved closer and closer to the load.

8. The lever you used here is called a first-class lever. Notice how it compares to the second-class lever and the third-class lever as you do other activities.

For Problem Solvers: Examine your list of levers and find all of them that are first-class levers. For each one, decide whether the advantage of using the lever in this application is to gain force or to gain distance and speed.

Continue to watch for more applications of the lever. Add them to your list as you find them.

Teacher Information

The total amount of work required to lift a load is neither increased nor decreased by the use of a lever. In using a first-class lever (as in this activity), we can decrease the amount of force required to lift a load by moving the fulcrum closer to the load. As the fulcrum moves closer to the load and the effort required to lift the load is decreased, the effort arm travels a greater distance and the load travels a lesser distance. We gain in terms of force required, but we sacrifice speed and distance.

The amount of force required to lift a given load using a first-class lever can be computed using the following formula:

$$load \times length\ of\ load\ arm = effort \times length\ of\ effort\ arm$$

For example, if we have a 200-kg load and we can apply only 50 kg of force to lift the load, the effort arm must be four times as long as the load arm. As the effort required to lift the load is divided by four, the speed and distance traveled by the load will also be divided by four.

In their list of first-class levers, your problem solvers should note that the advantage can go either way, depending on the position of the fulcrum. First-class levers can provide gain in force with a sacrifice of distance and speed, or a gain in distance and speed with a sacrifice of force. If the fulcrum is closer to the load, the gain is in force. If the fulcrum is closer to the effort position, the gain is in distance and speed. If the fulcrum is in the center of the lever, the only advantage is that it reverses the direction of the load. The first-class lever always reverses the direction of the load. For each example in their list, students should be able to easily determine the advantage by noting the position of the fulcrum.

INTEGRATING: Math

SKILLS: Observing, inferring, measuring, predicting, communicating, comparing and contrasting, formulating hypotheses, identifying and controlling variables, experimenting

RECORD OF MEASUREMENT II

Weight of the load = _____ kg

Load Position	Effort Position	Fulcrum Position	Force	TRAVEL DISTANCE Load Arm	Effort Arm
1	5	3	_____	10 cm	_____
1	5	4	_____	5 cm	_____
1	5	2	_____	5 cm	_____
1	5	Between 2 and 3	Estimate: _____ Actual: _____	5 cm	Estimate:_____ Actual: _____
1	5	Between 3 and 4	Estimate: _____ Actual: _____	10 cm	Estimate:_____ Actual: _____

Activity 5.10
HOW IS A SECOND-CLASS LEVER DIFFERENT FROM A FIRST-CLASS LEVER?

Materials Needed

- Lever
- Fulcrum
- Two or three books
- String

Procedure

1. Tie the books into a bundle.
2. Place the fulcrum at position 5 and hang the books, by their string, from position 4, as illustrated in Figure 5.10-1.

Figure 5.10-1

Lever, Books, and Fulcrum

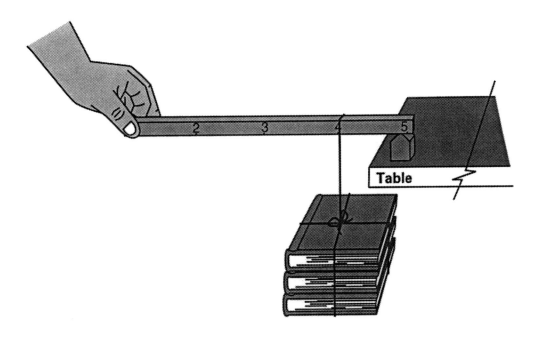

205

3. Holding the lever at position 1, lift the books.

4. Move the books to position 3, then 2, then 1, each time lifting from position 1.

5. Is it easier to lift when the load is closer to the fulcrum or farther from the fulcrum?

6. With the books at position 4, the fulcrum still at position 5, and the effort still applied at position 1, what is the length of the load arm? The effort arm?

7. This is a second-class lever. Notice the relative positions of the fulcrum, the load, and the effort for this second-class lever. How do these compare with the first-class lever you used in the previous activities?

Teacher Information

With the load placed between the fulcrum and the effort, we now have a second-class lever. The length of both arms is measured from the fulcrum, so with the load at position 3, the effort arm is twice the length of the load arm.

As with the first-class lever, the shorter the load arm and the longer the effort arm, the less effort required to lift the load. The effort arm travels farther and faster, however, than the load.

A major difference between the first-class lever and the second-class lever is that the second-class lever does not reverse the direction of the load; both effort and load travel in the same direction.

Examples of second-class levers include the paper cutter, the nutcracker, and the wheelbarrow.

INTEGRATING: Math

SKILLS: Observing, inferring, measuring, predicting, communicating, comparing and contrasting, formulating hypotheses, identifying and controlling variables, experimenting

Activity 5.11
WHAT DO YOU GAIN AND WHAT DO YOU LOSE BY USING A SECOND-CLASS LEVER?

Materials Needed

- Lever
- Fulcrum
- Two or three books
- String
- Pencil
- Spring balance
- Meter stick
- "Record of Measurement III" chart

Procedure

1. Use the "Record of Measurement III" chart for recording your measurements in this activity.
2. Tie the books into a bundle.
3. Weigh the books and record the results.
4. Place the fulcrum at position 5 and suspend the books, by the string, from position 1.

Figure 5.11-1

Lever with Books, Fulcrum, and Positions Noted

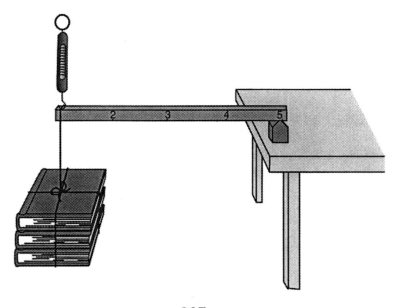

207

5. Record the amount of force required to lift the books, with the spring balance also at position 1, and compare this force to the weight of the books.

6. Measure the distance traveled by the spring balance (effort) as the books (load) travel 20 cm (8 in.).

7. Next, move the load to position 3 and record the force indicated on the spring balance. With the load between effort and fulcrum, you now have a second-class lever.

8. How does the amount of force required compare with the actual weight of the books?

9. Lift the load, measuring the distance traveled by the effort as the load is raised 10 cm (4 in.). Record the results.

10. How does the distance traveled by the load arm compare with the distance traveled by the effort arm?

11. If you were to move the load to position 4, how much force do you think would be required to lift the books? Record your estimate.

12. Try it and record the results. How close was your estimate?

13. With the load at position 2, how far do you think the load will travel as you lift the effort 20 cm (8 in.)? Record your estimate.

14. Try it and record the results. How close was your estimate?

For Problem Solvers: Examine your list of levers and find all of them that are second-class levers. For each one, decide whether the advantage of using the lever in this application is to gain force or to gain distance and speed.

Continue to watch for more applications of the lever. Add them to your list as you find them.

Teacher Information

The formula for computing effort and travel distance is the same for the second-class lever as for the first-class lever (see Activity 5.9). Remember to measure the length of each arm from the fulcrum.

All second-class levers provide gain in force with a sacrifice of distance and speed. In their list of second-class levers, your problem solvers should have included such things as the wheelbarrow, the nutcracker, and the paper cutter. The advantage of each one is in force.

INTEGRATING: Math

SKILLS: Observing, inferring, measuring, predicting, communicating, comparing and contrasting, formulating hypotheses, identifying and controlling variables, experimenting

NAME _____ DATE _____

RECORD OF MEASUREMENT III

Weight of the load = _____ kg

Load Position	Effort Position	Fulcrum Position	Force	TRAVEL DISTANCE Load Arm	Effort Arm
1	1	5	_____	20 cm	_____
3	1	5	_____	10 cm	_____
4	1	5	Estimate: _____ Actual: _____	Estimate: _____ Actual: _____	20 cm
2	1	5	Estimate: _____ Actual: _____	Estimate: _____ Actual: _____	20 cm

Activity 5.12

WHAT IS A THIRD-CLASS LEVER?

Materials Needed

- Lever
- Table
- Two or three books
- Strings

Procedure

1. Tie the books into a bundle and weigh them.
2. Use the edge of the table as a fulcrum. (You might need to have someone sit on the table to hold it down.)
3. Place the end of the lever under the edge of the table so your fulcrum (table's edge) is at position 5.
4. Suspend the books, by their string, at position 1.
5. Holding the lever at position 3, lift the books.
6. Is the effort required to lift the books greater or less than the actual weight of the books?
7. Move your hand to position 2 and lift the load.

Figure 5.12-1

Table, Lever, and Books Showing Effort Arm and Load Arm

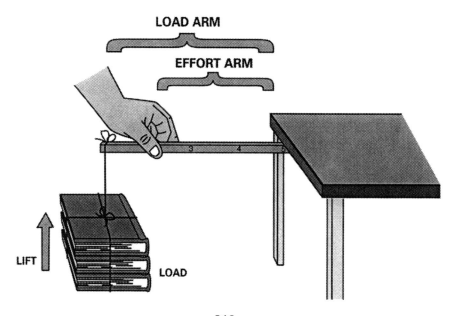

210

8. Lift the load from position 4.

9. Is it easier to lift the load as the effort (your hand) moves closer to the fulcrum (the table's edge)?

10. How is the third-class lever different from the first-class and second-class levers you have been using?

Teacher Information

As explained in earlier activities, second-class levers decrease the amount of effort required to lift a load, but in so doing they increase the distance the effort must travel to lift the load a given distance. The third-class lever reverses the advantage. With the effort now between the fulcrum and the load, the effort required to lift the load is greater than the actual weight of the load. The load, however, travels faster and farther than does the effort.

As with the other types of levers, the lengths of both the effort arm and the load arm are measured from the fulcrum. The load arm is always longer than the effort arm with a third-class lever.

The speed-and-distance advantage of the third-class lever is helpful in the use of such items as the fishing pole, ax, and broom. Our arms and legs are also third-class levers, with the joint as the fulcrum. The distance from joint to hand or foot is the load arm. The effort arm is from the joint to the point at which the tendons attach to anchor the muscle to the bone. These third-class levers offer advantages in speed and distance as a person swings a bat or a golf club, throws a baseball, or kicks a soccer ball.

INTEGRATING: Math

SKILLS: Observing, inferring, measuring, predicting, communicating, comparing and contrasting, formulating hypotheses, identifying and controlling variables, experimenting

Activity 5.13
WHAT IS GAINED AND WHAT IS LOST BY USING A THIRD-CLASS LEVER?

Materials Needed

- Lever
- Table
- Two or three books
- String
- Pencil
- Spring balance
- Meter stick
- "Record of Measurement IV" chart

Procedure

1. Use the "Record of Measurement IV" chart for recording your measurements in this activity.

2. Tie the books into a bundle.

3. Weigh the books and record the weight.

4. Use the edge of the table as a fulcrum. (You might need to have someone sit on the table to hold it down.)

5. Place the end of the lever under the edge of the table so your fulcrum (table's edge) is at position 5.

6. Suspend the books, by their string, at position 1.

7. Attach one end of the spring balance to the lever at position 3.

8. Holding the other end of the spring balance, lift with enough force to support the books. You are using a third-class lever.

9. Record the reading at the indicator and compare with the actual weight of the books.

10. Lift the load from position 3 and measure the travel distance of the load as the effort travels 10 cm.

11. Using your skills for predicting that you have learned in earlier activities, predict the force required to lift the load with the effort being shifted to position 2.

12. Try it, record the results, and compare with your prediction.

13. Leaving the effort at position 2, predict the travel distance of the load as the effort travels 10 cm.

14. Next, predict the outcomes with the effort being applied at position 4 and the effort traveling 5 cm, and record the results.

Figure 5.13-1

Third-Class Lever System with 10-lb Load and 20-lb Effort

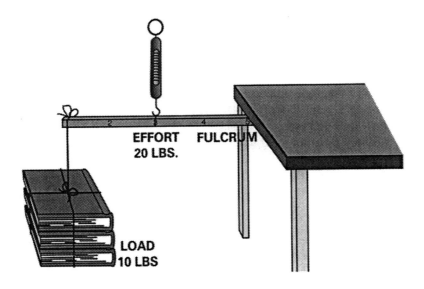

EFFORT 20 LBS.

FULCRUM

LOAD 10 LBS

15. Try it. Were your predictions close?

16. Select another point on the lever—somewhere between the numbers. Predict effort and distances and test your predictions.

For Problem Solvers: Examine your list of levers and find all of them that are third-class levers. For each one, decide whether the advantage of using the lever in this application is to gain force or to gain distance and speed.

Teacher Information

The formula for computing effort and travel distances for a third-class lever is the same as for first- and second-class levers. Remember to measure the lengths of the effort and load arms from the fulcrum.

With the system set up as indicated above, the effort required to lift a 10-lb. load would be 20 lbs., since the load arm is twice the length of the effort arm.

All third-class levers provide gain in distance and speed with a sacrifice of force. In their list of third-class levers, your problem solvers should have included such things as the fishing pole, the ball bat, ax, broom, golf club, and their own arms and legs. The advantage of each one is in distance and speed.

INTEGRATING: Math

SKILLS: Observing, inferring, measuring, predicting, communicating, comparing and contrasting, formulating hypotheses, identifying and controlling variables, experimenting

RECORD OF MEASUREMENT IV

Weight of the load = _____ kg

Load Position	Effort Position	Fulcrum Position	Force	TRAVEL DISTANCE Load Arm	Effort Arm
1	3	5	_____	_____	10 cm
1	2	5	Estimate: _____ Actual: _____	Estimate: _____ Actual: _____	10 cm
1	4	5	Estimate: _____ Actual: _____	Estimate: _____ Actual: _____	5 cm
1	?	1	Estimate: _____ Actual: _____	Estimate: _____ Actual: _____	5 cm

Activity 5.14

WHAT IS THE WHEEL AND AXLE?

Materials Needed

- Compass
- Stiff paper at least 10 cm (4 in.) square
- Pencil
- Scissors
- Tape measure

Procedure

1. Use the compass to make a circle on the paper.
2. Cut out the circle.
3. Insert the pencil through the center of the circle. You have made a wheel and axle.

Figure 5.14-1

Pencil and Paper Wheel on Table

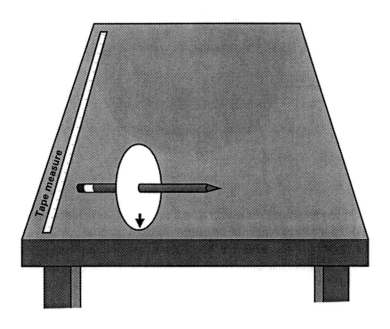

4. Roll your wheel and axle along the tabletop. How many times does the pencil rotate as the wheel rotates once?

5. Measure the distance the wheel traveled in one complete rotation.

6. Remove the pencil from the wheel, place the pencil on the table, and measure the distance it travels in one complete rotation.

7. How far would the pencil travel if rotated ten times?

8. Insert the pencil (axle) back into the wheel. How far does it travel now in ten rotations?

9. Name one advantage of the wheel and axle.

Teacher Information

The wheel and axle is a form of the lever. When the wheel or the axle turns, the other turns also. If the wheel turns around the axle, as on bearings, it is not a wheel and axle.

If the wheel is turning the axle, it is a form of second-class lever (Figure 5.14-2). The fulcrum is at the center of the axle. The radius of the wheel is the effort arm of the lever, and the radius of the axle is the load arm. There is increased force but less speed and distance.

Figure 5.14-2

Wheel and Axle Showing Load and Effort as Second-Class Lever

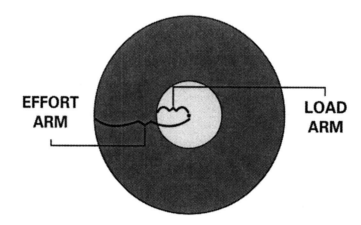

Examples of the wheel and axle acting as a second-class lever include the doorknob, the screwdriver, and the steering wheel of an automobile.

If the axle is turning the wheel, it becomes a form of third-class lever, with a gain in speed and distance but a decrease in force (Figure 5.14-3). The fulcrum is at the center of the axle. The radius of the wheel is the load arm and the radius of the axle is the effort arm.

Figure 5.14-3

Wheel and Axle Showing Load and Effort as Third-Class Lever

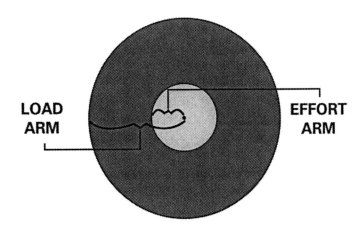

LOAD
ARM

EFFORT
ARM

Examples of the wheel and axle acting as a third-class lever include the drive wheels of an automobile and the rear wheel of a bicycle.

INTEGRATING: Math

SKILLS: Observing, inferring, measuring, predicting, communicating, comparing and contrasting, formulating hypotheses, identifying and controlling variables, experimenting

Activity 5.15
WHAT TYPE OF SIMPLE MACHINE IS THE PENCIL SHARPENER?

Materials Needed

- Pencil sharpener with suction mount
- String about 1 m long
- Book

Procedure

1. Clamp the pencil sharpener to the side of a file cabinet or other vertical surface and remove the cover.

2. Turn the handle of the pencil sharpener around, noting that it goes all the way around, just like a wheel.

3. Tie the book in such a way that a long string is left from which the book can be suspended.

4. Notice the amount of effort required to lift the book. Tie the end of the string firmly around the end of the pencil sharpener shaft. Use tape to keep it from slipping.

5. Allow the book to hang freely and support the pencil sharpener with your hands to keep it from pulling loose.

Figure 5.15-1

Pencil Sharpener on Vertical Surface, with Book Tied to It

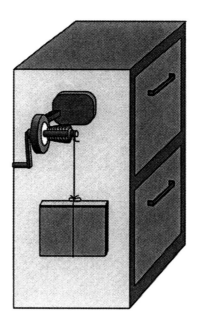

6. Turn the pencil sharpener handle around several times, making sure the string is winding around the shaft.

7. Is more or less force required to lift the book with this wheel and axle than to lift the books directly?

8. See if you can locate a picture of an old well with a windlass for raising a bucket full of water. What similarities do you see between the windlass and your pencil sharpener?

9. What type of machine is the pencil sharpener? The windlass?

Teacher Information

A wheel does not have to be a complete wheel in order to be considered a wheel and axle. It can be just a crank, as with the pencil sharpener used above or the water-well windlass referred to. The crank makes a complete circle when used, just as though it were a complete wheel. A type of windlass called a winch is often found on boat trailers and four-wheel-drive vehicles.

INTEGRATING: Math

SKILLS: Observing, inferring, measuring, predicting, communicating, comparing and contrasting, formulating hypotheses, identifying and controlling variables, experimenting

Activity 5.16
WHAT IS A FIXED PULLEY?

Materials Needed

- Single-wheel pulley
- Crossbar
- Spring balance
- Meter stick
- Cord or heavy string
- Pencil
- "Measuring with a Fixed Pulley" chart
- Bundle of books (or other heavy object)

Procedure

1. Use the "Measuring with a Fixed Pulley" chart for recording your measurements in this activity.

2. Weigh the books with the spring balance and record the results.

3. Arrange your pulley, crossbar, spring balance, cord, and bundle of books as shown in Figure 5.16-1, with the pulley attached to the crossbar.

4. Pull down on the spring balance to lift the books. Be sure to pull straight down and not to the side.

5. Pull down steadily on the spring far enough to lift the load 20 cm. Record the following information on your chart:

   a. Direction the load (books) moved as the effort (spring balance) moved downward.

   b. Distance moved by the effort as the load moved 20 cm.

   c. Amount of force required to lift the books.

6. Examine the information in your chart. Was lifting the books using the pulley different in any way from lifting the books without the pulley? Consider these questions:

   a. Did the pulley decrease the amount of force needed to lift the books?

   b. Did the pulley cause the books to move a greater or lesser distance than the effort moved?

   c. Did the pulley cause the books to move in the opposite direction from that of the effort?

7. With the pulley fastened to the crossbar, as it has been for this activity, it is called a fixed pulley. This simply means that the pulley does not move up or down, but remains in a fixed position as the load is moved.

8. What is accomplished by using a fixed pulley?

Figure 5.16-1

Pulley System with Books

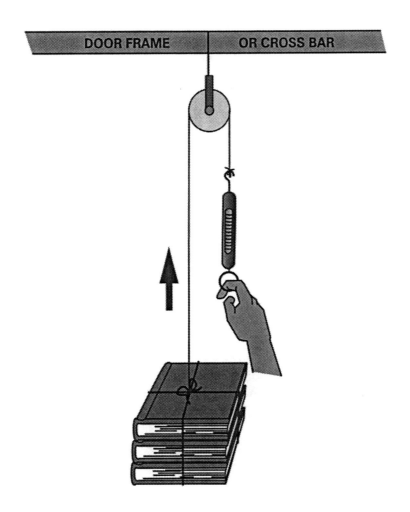

Teacher Information

When you use a fixed pulley, the load moves up or down but the pulley itself is fastened to a stationary object and therefore remains in a fixed position.

A fixed pulley does not alter the amount of force required to lift an object, but it reverses the direction of the force; that is, as the force is applied in a downward direction the load is lifted in an upward direction.

The fixed pulley is a form of turning first-class lever (see Figure 5.16-2). Think of the fulcrum as being at the center of the axle, the effort at one edge of the pulley wheel, and the load at the other edge. As with other first-class levers, the fulcrum is between the effort and the load. Curtains, drapes, and louvered blinds use fixed pulleys.

Figure 5.16-2

Fixed Pulley System Showing It As a First-Class Lever

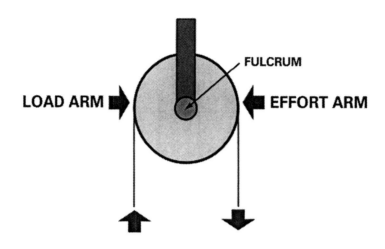

INTEGRATING: Math

SKILLS: Observing, inferring, measuring, predicting, communicating, comparing and contrasting, formulating hypotheses, identifying and controlling variables, experimenting

MEASURING WITH A FIXED PULLEY

Weight = _____ kg

a. TRAVEL DIRECTION

What direction does the load (books) move as the effort (spring balance) moves downward?

b. TRAVEL DISTANCE

How far does the effort move as the load moves 20 cm?

c. FORCE

How much force is required to lift the load?

Activity 5.17
WHAT IS A MOVABLE PULLEY?

Materials Needed

- Pulley
- Crossbar
- Spring balance
- Meter stick
- Cord or string
- Pencil
- "Measuring with a Movable Pulley" chart
- Bundle of books (or other heavy object)

Procedure

1. Use the "Measuring with a Movable Pulley" chart for recording your measurements in this activity.

2. Weigh the books with the spring balance and record the results.

3. Arrange your pulley, crossbar, spring balance, cord, and bundle of books as shown in Figure 5.17-1, with one end of the cord attached to the crossbar.

4. Lift the books by pulling up on the spring balance. Note the force indicated on the spring balance as you lift in a steady motion. Record this amount as the force required to lift the books using a movable pulley.

5. Compare the weight of the books with the amount of force required to lift the books using the movable pulley.

6. Measure and record the distance traveled by the effort (spring balance) as the load (books) travels 20 cm.

7. Estimate the distance the load will travel as the effort travels 30 cm.

8. Try it. Record the results and compare with your estimate.

9. Notice and record the direction traveled by load and effort as you lift the load.

10. Examine the information in your chart and consider these questions:

    a. Did the pulley decrease the amount of force needed to lift the books?

    b. Did the pulley cause the load to move a greater or lesser distance than the effort moved?

    c. Did the pulley cause the load to move in the opposite direction from that of the effort?

11. With the pulley fastened to the load, as it has been for this activity, and one end of the cord fastened to the crossbar, the pulley is called a movable pulley. The pulley itself moves up or down with the load.

Figure 5.17-1

Movable Pulley System

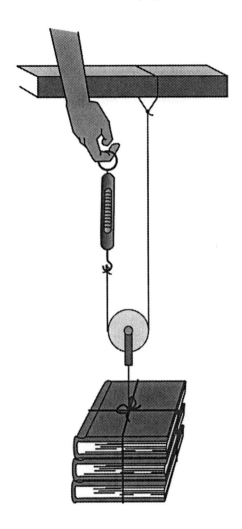

12. What effect does a movable pulley have on the force required to lift a load?

13. What effect does a movable pulley have on the distance a load travels compared with the distance traveled by the effort?

14. What effect does a movable pulley have on the direction of the load compared with the direction of the effort?

Teacher Information

A movable pulley is attached to the load and therefore moves up and down with the load.

When you use a movable pulley, the direction of travel does not change; the load travels in the same direction as the effort. However, the amount of force required to lift a load is less than the actual weight of the object. The travel distance of the load is less than that of the effort. Thus, the movable pulley offers an advantage as to force required, but it does so at the expense of travel distance and speed.

In computing the gain or loss from using a movable pulley, use the following as a guide:

a. The load will travel half the distance of the effort.

b. The force required to lift the load is half the actual weight of the object.

Note: The force required will be increased by whatever friction is involved as the pulley turns on the axle, the cord rubs against the sides of the groove in the pulley, and so forth.

INTEGRATING: Math

SKILLS: Observing, inferring, measuring, predicting, communicating, comparing and contrasting, formulating hypotheses, identifying and controlling variables, experimenting

MEASURING WITH A MOVABLE PULLEY

Weight of books = _____ kg

Force required to lift books = _____ kg

Travel Distance

What is the distance traveled by the effort (spring balance) as the load (books) moves 20 cm?

_____

What is estimated distance the load would travel as the effort moves 30 cm?

_____

What is the actual distance the load travels as the effort moves 30 cm?

_____

Travel Direction

What is the direction traveled by the load and effort as you lift the load?

Load _____

Effort _____

Activity 5.18
WHAT HAPPENS WHEN A SMALL PERSON TUGS ON A LARGE PERSON?

Materials Needed

- Pulley
- Rope
- Two chairs with sturdy legs

Procedure

1. Anchor the pulley to Chair A (see Figure 5.18-1).
2. Thread one end of the rope through the pulley and tie the end of the rope to Chair B.
3. Have a large person sit on Chair A and a small person on Chair B.
4. When you pull on the other end of the rope, which chair will move?
5. After you make your prediction, pull on the rope.
6. What happened? Why?
7. Discuss your ideas with your group.

Figure 5.18-1

Two Chairs Tied Together, with Pulley Attached to Chair A

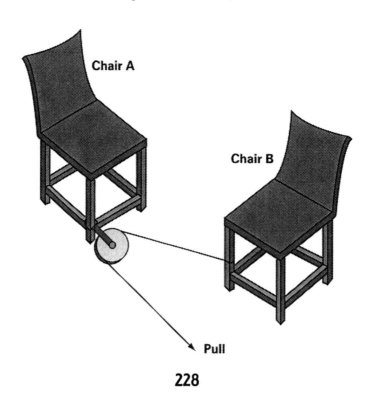

For Problem Solvers: Try to figure out a way to measure the force that is being exerted on each of the chairs. If you have more pulleys, figure out a way to make it still easier to pull the larger person sitting on a chair.

Teacher Information

Two ropes are pulling on Chair A, while only one rope is pulling on Chair B. The two ropes pulling on Chair A have equal tension. Twice as much force is exerted on Chair A as on Chair B.

INTEGRATING: Math, language arts

SKILLS: Observing, inferring, measuring, predicting, communicating, using space-time relationships, formulating hypotheses, identifying and controlling variables, experimenting

Activity 5.19
WHAT CAN BE GAINED BY COMBINING FIXED AND MOVABLE PULLEYS?

Materials Needed

- Two pulleys
- Crossbar
- Spring balance
- Meter stick
- Cord or heavy string
- Pencil
- "Measuring with a Combined Fixed and Movable Pulley" chart
- Bundle of books (or other heavy object)

Procedure

1. Use the "Measuring with a Combined Fixed and Movable Pulley" chart for recording your measurements in this activity.

2. Weigh the books and record the weight in Part One.

3. Arrange the pulleys, crossbar, spring balance, cord, and bundle of books as illustrated in Figure 5.19-1. Notice that one pulley and one end of the cord are attached to the crossbar.

4. You now have a pulley system that includes a fixed pulley and a movable pulley.

5. From your previous experience, see if you can predict the answers to the following questions. Record your predictions in Part One of the chart.

    a. Which direction will the load (books) move as you pull down at the effort position (spring balance)?

    b. Considering the actual weight of the books, how much force will be required to lift the load?

    c. How far will the load travel as the effort travels 40 cm?

6. After recording your predictions, test them by actual measurement. Record your measurements and compare them with your predictions.

7. Now record the following in Part Two:

    a. Change the number of books in your bundle, record the weight of your new load, and predict the amount of force necessary to lift it with the pulley system.

    b. Predict the travel distance of the effort as you lift the load 5 cm.

8. After recording your predictions, test them and record your actual measurements.

9. Were your predictions closer this time?

10. Can you think of any situation where it would be helpful to combine a fixed pulley with a movable pulley?

Figure 5.19-1

Pulley System with One Fixed Pulley and One Movable Pulley

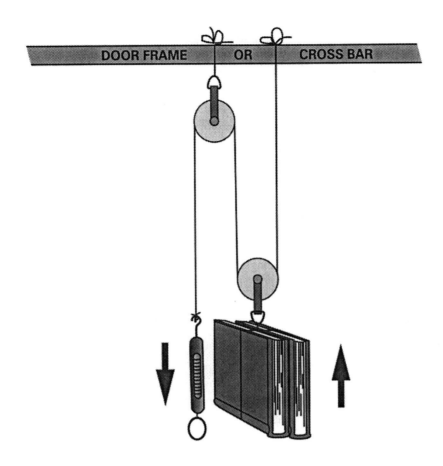

For Problem Solvers: Try to find an opportunity to visit a crane while it is working at a construction site. Find as many simple machines as you can, including all three types of levers, fixed pulleys, movable pulleys, and combined pulleys.

Teacher Information

A combination of a fixed pulley and a movable pulley offers the advantages of both. A load can be lifted with half as much force as would be expected by considering the actual weight of the objects (because of the movable pulley) and the load can be moved upward by pulling downward (because of the fixed pulley).

This system, including a fixed pulley combined with a movable pulley, is called a block and tackle. It is used for lifting automobile motors, for raising and lowering scaffolds for painters, and for many other purposes.

Enrichment

Allow students to experiment with various combinations of pulleys and test the mechanical advantage of their creations.

Combinations of more than one fixed pulley and an equal number of movable pulleys multiply the mechanical advantage of the movable pulley and decrease efficiency in terms of travel distance. For instance, in a system involving a double fixed pulley and a double movable pulley, a load of 4 lbs. would be lifted with approximately 1 lb. of force at the effort position, but the effort must travel 4 cm (or inches) for each cm (or inch) the load is to be lifted.

If a strong overhead beam (such as a tree branch) is available, students would enjoy experimenting with their pulleys in lifting heavier objects, such as each other, the teacher, or several students at a time. Such an activity should be closely supervised to assure safety. Beware of possible broken ropes and falls. Vertical distance lifted should be limited to minimize risk of injury.

INTEGRATING: Math, social studies

SKILLS: Observing, inferring, measuring, predicting, communicating, comparing and contrasting, formulating hypotheses, identifying and controlling variables, experimenting

MEASURING WITH A COMBINED FIXED
AND MOVABLE PULLEY

Part One

Weight _____ kg

	Predicted Results	**Measured Results**
Load direction	_____	_____
Force required	_____	_____
Load distance	_____	_____

Part Two

Weight _____ kg

	Predicted Results	**Measured Results**
Force required	_____	_____
Effort distance	_____	_____

Activity 5.20
WHAT IS AN INCLINED PLANE?

Materials Needed

- Board at least 1.5 m (4.5 ft.) long
- Roller skate (or toy truck or small wagon)
- Cord or heavy string
- Pencil
- "Measuring with an Inclined Plane" chart
- Spring balance
- Box of rocks (or books or other weights)

Procedure

1. Use the "Measuring with an Inclined Plane" chart for recording your measurements in this activity.
2. Using the string, attach the load to the roller skate.
3. Weigh the load, including the roller skate, and record its weight.
4. Place the board on a stairway, with one end at the bottom of the stairs and the other end resting on the fourth step.
5. Attach the spring balance to the skate and pull the load up the inclined plane (board). As you pull steadily, notice the force indicated by the needle and record the results.

Figure 5.20-1

Roller Skate with Load on Inclined Plane

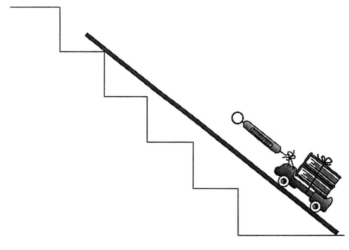

234

6. Compare the weight of the load with the force needed to pull the load up the inclined plane.

7. As you pulled the load up the inclined plane, was *more* force or *less* force required than the actual weight of the load? Record your answer.

8. Move the top of the board down to the first step (Figure 5.20-2).

Figure 5.20-2

System in New Position

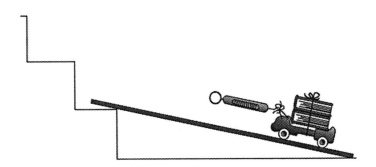

9. Judging from your first experience, how much force do you think will be required to pull the load up the slope? Record your prediction.

10. After recording your prediction, attach the spring balance to the load and try it.

11. Record the results. How close was your prediction?

12. Now predict the force required with the board on the second step. Try it after recording your prediction.

13. Was your prediction closer this time?

14. If your load weighed 100 lbs., how much force would you need to apply to push it up the inclined plane with the top of the inclined plane resting on the first step?

15. Think of some ways inclined planes would be useful. Write down two of them and show them to your teacher.

Teacher Information

An *inclined plane* is a slanting surface. It provides a mechanical advantage of force. We can move a load up an inclined plane with less force than would be indicated by the actual weight of the object (provided the friction isn't too great).

As with the use of any other machine, the total work required is not reduced but only redistributed. The advantage gained in force is sacrificed in distance and speed.

Mechanical advantage is computed by dividing the length of the inclined plane by the height, as in Figure 5.20-3.

Figure 5.20-3

Inclined Plane System

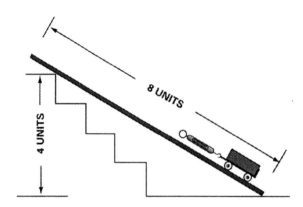

The weight of the object is twice the force required to move the object up the ramp (if friction could be eliminated), but we must move the object twice as far as if we lifted it straight up (eight units instead of four units).

Application of the inclined plane is illustrated as barrels of oil are rolled up a ramp, as a car drives up a mountain on a winding road, and as a person walks up a stairway or up the sloping floor of a theater.

Note: If it is inconvenient for students to use a stairway for their work with the inclined plane, have them support the end of their board on a stack of books or some other sturdy, adjustable support.

INTEGRATING: Math, social studies

SKILLS: Observing, inferring, measuring, predicting, communicating, comparing and contrasting, formulating hypotheses, identifying and controlling variables, experimenting

MEASURING WITH AN INCLINED PLANE

Weight- _____ kg

Position of Upper End	Position of Lower End	Force
4th step	bottom	more / less (circle one)
1st step	bottom	Prediction _____ Actual _____
2nd step	bottom	Prediction _____ Actual _____
1st step		Estimated force to move 100 pounds _____

Uses for inclined planes:

1. _____

2. _____

Activity 5.21
WHAT IS A WEDGE?

Materials Needed

- Wedge
- Stack of books
- Board

Procedure

1. Stack the books up on one end of the board.
2. Place your fingers under the end of the board near the books and lift it up about 3 to 8 cm. Notice the force required to lift the books.
3. Now place the tip of the wedge under the same end of the board (Figure 5.21-1).

Figure 5.21-1

Board, Books, and Wedge

4. Tap the wedge with your foot, forcing it under the end of the board.
5. What is happening to the load of books?
6. Can you tell whether the force required to drive the wedge under the board is greater or less than the force required to lift the load directly?
7. Why does the wedge so strongly resist being forced under the board?

For Problem Solvers: Make a list of all the examples of wedges that you can find.

Teacher Information

Two wedges can be made by sawing a block of wood in half diagonally (Figure 5.21-2). Note that each wedge looks like an inclined plane. It differs from the inclined plane only in its application. When it is used as an inclined plane, an object (load) moves up the incline. When it is used as a wedge, the inclined plane moves into, or under, the object.

Figure 5.21-2

Rectangular Block of Wood Showing Diagonal Cut

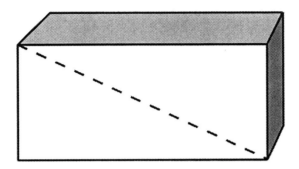

We gain in force and also change the direction of the force by using the wedge.

The longer or thinner the wedge, the greater the gain in force and the greater the loss in distance; that is, the farther the wedge must go under an object to lift it a given amount.

The maximum distance a load can be moved by a wedge is the thickness of the big end of the wedge.

The ideal mechanical advantage of the wedge can be computed by dividing the length of the wedge by the thickness of the big end. However, because of the great amount of friction that is usually involved, the actual mechanical advantage is almost always significantly less than the ideal. Friction, however, is often helpful when using a wedge because it keeps the wedge from slipping out.

Applications of the wedge are the ax, chisel, pin, nail, knife blade, woodsplitter's wedge, and so forth.

Enrichment

If a short log, a sledge hammer, and a woodsplitting wedge could be acquired, a demonstration of the use of the wedge in actually splitting the log would provide an excellent experience in seeing the usefulness of the wedge. **CAUTION: Splitting wood may splinter, so use care and be sure children stand back a safe distance.**

INTEGRATING: Math, social studies

SKILLS: Observing, inferring, measuring, predicting, communicating, comparing and contrasting, formulating hypotheses, identifying and controlling variables, experimenting

Activity 5.22
WHAT IS A SCREW?

Materials Needed

- Pencil
- Sheet of white paper
- Scissors
- Black marker
- Large wood screw
- Ruler

Procedure

1. Cut a triangle from a sheet of white paper by cutting diagonally, from corner to corner (Figure 5.22-1).

Figure 5.22-1

Rectangle Showing Diagonal Cut

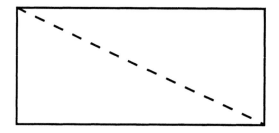

2. Using the marker, make a heavy black line along the hypotenuse (the longest side), as in Figure 5.22-2.

Figure 5.22-2

Triangle with Darkened Hypotenuse

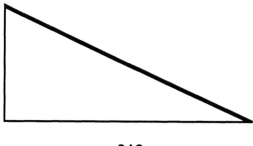

240

3. Hold the triangle upright on top of your table or desk. Which of the simple machines we have already studied does the triangle now look like?

4. Beginning with the short side, wrap the paper triangle around a pencil (Figure 5.22-3).

5. Hold the wrapped pencil side by side with the large wood screw.

6. Does the heavy line of the triangle resemble the threads of the screw?

7. How would you say the threads of a screw compare to an inclined plane? Think about how the triangle with its black edge looked before you wrapped it around the pencil.

Figure 5.22-3

Triangle Being Wrapped Around Pencil

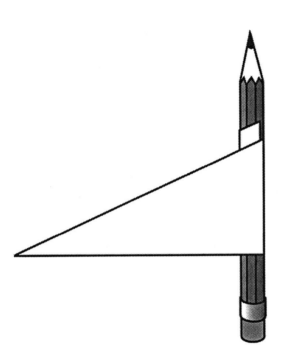

Teacher Information

The screw is a form of inclined plane that winds around in a spiral. The spiral-shaped ridge around the screw is called the *thread*.

INTEGRATING: Math, social studies

SKILLS: Observing, inferring, measuring, predicting, communicating, comparing and contrasting, formulating hypotheses, identifying and controlling variables, experimenting

Activity 5.23
WHAT KIND OF SIMPLE MACHINE IS THE SCREWDRIVER?

Materials Needed

- Wood screw
- Board (pine or other soft wood)
- Screwdriver

Procedure

1. Try to push the screw into the board with your fingers.
2. Place the tip of the screwdriver on the head of the screw and try to push the screw into the board without turning the screwdriver.
3. Did the screw go any farther than when you pushed with your hand?
4. Now turn the screwdriver as you press down hard with it on the head of the screw.
5. Can you get the screw into the board this time?
6. Notice how far the screwdriver handle travels as the screw turns around once.
7. How far does the screw move into the board as the screwdriver handle turns around?
8. What can you say about the gain or loss in force and in distance as you turn the screw into the board?
9. Make a list of ways people make use of the screw.
10. What kind of machine is the screwdriver?

Teacher Information

The screw offers a gain in force but at the expense of distance and speed. The handle of the screwdriver travels much faster and farther in a circular direction than the distance the screw moves into the board.

The screw also changes the direction of the effort from a turning motion to a pulling motion.

The ideal mechanical advantage of the screw is computed by dividing the circumference of the screwdriver handle (distance it travels in one complete turn) by the pitch (distance between two threads) of the screw. However, the actual mechanical advantage of the screw is greatly reduced by friction.

Friction helps by keeping the screw from turning backward or pulling out. The loss of force due to friction is made up by using another machine, the screwdriver. The screwdriver is a form of the wheel and axle.

The principle of the screw is applied in the use of the base of a light bulb, a bolt, a pipe wrench, caps on jars and bottles, and the piano stool.

INTEGRATING: Math, social studies

SKILLS: Observing, inferring, measuring, predicting, communicating, comparing and contrasting, formulating hypotheses, identifying and controlling variables, experimenting

Activity 5.24
WHAT KIND OF SIMPLE MACHINE IS THIS?

Materials Needed

Variety of simple and complex machines, as available, such as:

- Ball bat
- Bumper jack
- Egg beater
- Food grinder
- Pencil sharpener
- Rake
- Screw jack
- Tongs
- Fishing pole
- Broom
- Can opener (any kind available)
- Flour sifter
- Hand drill
- Pepper mill
- Scissors
- Shovel
- Tweezers
- Golf club

Procedure

1. Examine each of the devices. First, classify them into two groups—simple machines and complex machines.

2. Next, classify all of the simple machines according to the type of simple machines they are. Make a group of levers, wedges, etc. Then group the levers as first class, second class, and third class.

3. Now look at those you put in the group of complex machines. For each of these, make a list of the simple machines you see in them.

For Problem Solvers: Make a list of all the machines you have used today. For each one, name all the simple machines that are in it.

Examine a toy that has internal working parts. Think carefully about how it works and draw what you think is inside. What simple machines are there, according to your drawing? Do another one, and compare your ideas for each one with someone else who is doing the activity, or with your teacher or someone in your family.

Teacher Information

This activity will reveal what your students have really learned about simple machines. Try to allow them time to pursue the ideas suggested in "For Problem Solvers" as long as their interest lasts. Perhaps they can continue at home if necessary.

INTEGRATING: Math, social studies

SKILLS: Observing, inferring, measuring, predicting, communicating, comparing and contrasting, formulating hypotheses, identifying and controlling variables, experimenting

MAGNETISM

TO THE TEACHER

A study of magnetism is often a very helpful beginning point for introducing structured inquiry/discovery activities. Be certain to warn the children that magnets can break or lose their magnetism if dropped or hit together. In the case of U-shaped magnets, a piece of soft iron called a keeper should be placed across the ends.

This material is nongraded. However, some activities may seem more appropriate to certain age levels. Each teacher should feel free to reorganize and eliminate materials according to the needs of students, keeping in mind the level of psychological development that may influence the understanding of certain concepts. Inquiry and the use of concrete materials is a major purpose of this unit.

Many of the activities in this section seem to be most effective when presented to individuals, small groups, or teams. If your classroom organization permits, consider placing the materials in a science learning center, with time provided for children to move through the sequence at their own rate. Classroom discussions to reinforce the concepts should follow. If classroom demonstrations are used initially, children should perform the activities, and then the materials should be left on the science table for children to explore individually.

Many children are fascinated by magnets. They seem almost like magic. There is a natural desire on the part of many children to explore and share their discoveries with friends and others outside the classroom. Most magnets are fairly expensive, but many school supply outlets sell small magnets (for notices on bulletin boards, refrigerator doors, and so on) at a reasonable cost. If possible, try to get a number of these small magnets for out-of-school activities. Ideally, each child should have a pair of these small alnico (aluminum, nickel, cobalt) magnets.

One excellent source of magnets is audio speakers. Every speaker contains a magnet. They come in many different sizes and strengths and they are generally fairly easy to remove with a hammer and screwdriver. They are usually riveted in place; some are held with bolts and nuts. Check with a local shop that installs car stereos; they usually throw the old speakers away. Occasionally a speaker system in a school, or other large building, will be replaced and you might be able to get some dandies.

Bar magnets can be given new life by stroking them lengthwise several times across one pole of a powerful magnet. Stroke in one direction only. If poles are reversed, stroke in the opposite direction *or* use the other pole of the large magnet.

CAUTION: Audio tapes, video tapes, and computer disks are magnetic. If they come near a strong magnet, they may be erased. Spring-operated watch mechanisms may also become magnetized in a strong magnetic field.

Regarding the Early Grades

With verbal instructions and slight modifications, many of these activities can be used with kindergarten, first-grade, and second-grade students. In some activities, steps that involve procedures that go beyond the level of the child can simply be omitted and yet offer the child an experience that plants the seed for a concept that will germinate and grow later on.

Teachers of the early grades will probably choose to bypass many of the "For Problem Solvers" sections. That's okay. These sections are provided for those who are especially motivated and want to go beyond the investigation provided by the activity outlined. Use the outlined activities, and enjoy worthwhile learning experiences together with your young students. Also consider, however, that many of the "For Problem Solvers" sections can be used appropriately with young children as group activities or as demonstrations, still giving students the advantage of an exposure to the experience and laying groundwork for connections that will be made later on.

Activity 6.1
WHICH ROCK IS DIFFERENT?

Materials Needed

- Several similar rocks
- One lodestone
- Paper clip

Procedure

1. One of these rocks can do something the others cannot.
2. Can you find it?
3. What can you say about it?

For Problem Solvers: Look up the word *lodestone* in an encyclopedia or other reference book and learn all you can about this interesting rock. How is it different from other rocks? How is it different from other magnets?

Teacher Information

The children may choose a rock other than the magnetic lodestone. If this occurs and their reasons for the choice are logical, their answers should be accepted, as the process of inquiry is our objective. However, since it is assumed that most children have had some experience with magnets, a paper clip or other magnetic material on the table may assist in the discovery.

Lodestone is a particular type of iron ore that occurs naturally and has properties of magnets. Lodestones may be purchased from a science supply house at a nominal cost. Iron ore that is magnetic (attracted to a magnet) but does not behave as a magnet is called *magnetite*. Lodestone is magnetite that has polarity, or behaves as a magnet. Most people use the two terms interchangeably, in reference to the rock that behaves as a magnet.

INTEGRATING: Reading

SKILLS: Observing, inferring, comparing and contrasting, researching

Activity 6.2
WHAT DO MAGNETS LOOK LIKE?

Materials Needed

- A large collection of magnets of different sizes, shapes, materials, and colors
- Magnetic materials, such as paper clips, for testing

Procedure

1. What do magnets look like?
2. Use these materials to answer the question.

For Problem Solvers: Make a list, or make drawings, of all of the shapes of magnets you have in the classroom. Then explore elsewhere—at home, at your parents' work place if you can get permission, and wherever you can find magnets. Add to your list all that you find. Ask your friends if they know of still other types of magnets. Add these to your list, too.

Make another list of all the places and ways you can find that magnets are being used. Do you have any on your refrigerator? On your cupboard door latches? Where else can you find magnets being used? Ask your family and friends. Ask a mechanic if any magnets are used in automobiles or other equipment that he or she works with. Ask about electric motors. Do you have a metal salvage yard nearby? Ask about the use of magnets there.

If you have science books about magnets, you might find still more ideas there.

Teacher Information

The answer to the question is simple. The appearance of magnets varies a lot. You cannot tell if something is a magnet by its appearance. If possible obtain "cow magnets" from feed and grain stores. These magnets are put in the stomachs of cattle to collect bits of metal that have been eaten.

Children often have the idea that magnetism has something to do with the shape of the magnets, as magnets are most often shown in horseshoe or bar shapes. This activity will help children see that shape is not directly related to the property of magnetism.

Students might have unusual magnets of their own that they could bring to add variety to the shapes of magnets used.

INTEGRATING: Language arts, social studies

SKILLS: Observing, inferring, classifying, predicting, communicating, comparing and contrasting, researching

Activity 6.3
HOW DO MAGNETS GET THEIR NAMES?

Materials Needed

- The magnets used in Activity 6.2

Procedure

1. Magnets often get their names from their shapes or from what they do. See if you can find magnets that might have the following names:

   bar magnet

   cylindrical magnet

   disk (or disc) magnet

   U-shaped magnet

   horseshoe magnet

   cow magnet

2. Can you name any others?

Teacher Information

This activity may have some value in helping children learn new names for certain shapes. It will also provide a basic vocabulary for further study of magnets. Since magnets are so much a part of our everyday life, your children may bring in many new and unusual magnets to add to the collection.

INTEGRATING: Language arts

SKILLS: Observing, inferring, classifying, comparing and contrasting

Activity 6.4
WHERE DID THE FIRST METAL MAGNET COME FROM?

Materials Needed

- Nonmagnetized needle (with point broken off)
- Lodestone
- Paper clip

Procedure

1. Is the needle a magnet?
2. Test it by trying to pick up a paper clip or some other small object.
3. Rub it 20 times in the same direction with the magnetic rock.
4. Test your needle again. Is it a magnet?
5. What can you say about this?

For Problem Solvers: Check your reference books for the words magnet and magnetism. Try to find out who used magnets first, and what they used them for. What kind of magnets did they use? How did people make the first magnets that were made by people?

Teacher Information

Magnetism has been known for centuries. References to this "magical" property occur in Chinese and Greek mythology. This activity might provide opportunities for creative writing about the discovery of magnetism. Your encyclopedia can provide information about the history of lodestones.

The point of the needle can be easily broken off with a pair of pliers.

INTEGRATING: Reading, language arts, social studies

SKILLS: Observing, inferring, researching

Activity 6.5
WHAT MATERIALS WILL A MAGNET PICK UP?

 Take home and do with family and friends.

Materials Needed

- A tray of magnetic and nonmagnetic materials, such as a Canadian nickel, a United States nickel, and brass and steel safety pins (be sure to include gold-colored items, silver-colored items, and items of other colors)
- Magnet

Procedure

1. What are some things magnets can pick up or attract?
2. Make a list.
3. Make another list of things magnets will not attract.

For Problem Solvers: Now that you have tested several small items to find out if they are magnetic, take a magnet and test a lot of other things. Each time you think of a new material to check, make a prediction first, then check it out. Make a list of the materials that surprised you.

Classify your list of materials by making separate lists of things that are magnetic and things that are not magnetic.

Teacher Information

Children who have not yet acquired writing skills can make piles of magnetic and nonmagnetic materials. For older children, writing lists of their findings is a good exercise.

As students experiment with the materials, it is hoped that they will become motivated to seek the answer to the title question through the use of reference materials. An appropriate video tape, library book, encyclopedia, filmstrip, or textbook can provide an explanation.

Materials that magnets will pick up are generally those made of iron, nickel, steel, and cobalt. These are called the *strong magnetic materials.*

SKILLS: Observing, inferring, classifying, predicting, communicating, formulating hypotheses, researching

252

Activity 6.6
THROUGH WHAT SUBSTANCES CAN MAGNETISM PASS?

Materials Needed

- Paper clip suspended from a string toward a large mounted magnet
- Variety of magnetic and nonmagnetic materials, such as a piece of plastic, wood, aluminum foil, paper, iron lid

Procedure

1. What keeps the paper clip up?
2. Place different materials between the paper clip and the magnet.
3. What happened?
4. What can you say about this?

For Problem Solvers: Find other materials to test. Can you find any material that is not magnetic and that will block the magnetic force and cause the paper clip to fall?

Teacher Information

Use a string to suspend a strong magnet from a mount or ruler (Figure 6.6-1). Place a paper clip held by a thread below the magnet, leaving a space between the magnet and the clip. The string can be attached to the floor with tape, or can be anchored by a book.

Figure 6.6-1

Large Magnet Mounted, with Paper Clip Suspended

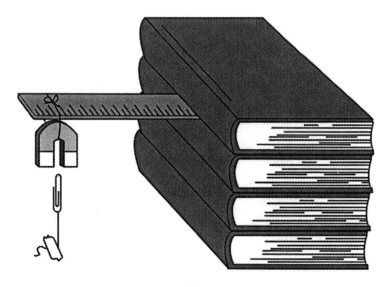

Nonmagnetic materials will pass between the clip and magnet without disturbing the magnetic field. When the iron lid comes near the gap, the magnet will be attracted to it and the clip will probably fall. In a later class discussion, it should be demonstrated that magnetic materials will disturb or cut a magnetic field. However, substances made of a magnetic material (iron, nickel, steel, or cobalt) may be made into temporary magnets and behave like a magnet while in the magnetic field. Thus the iron lid alone may not pick up paper clips, but when it comes near or touches a strong magnet, it will temporarily become a magnet through a process called *induction*. The extent of time the magnetic material retains its magnetic properties is often related to its hardness (how tightly the molecules are packed together). The steel needle used in Activity 6.4 will retain its magnetism for a long period. A soft iron lid or paper clip will lose its magnetism rapidly when removed from the magnetic field. Activity 6.14 develops this theory in depth with a somewhat different approach.

There is no insulator to magnetism, but students will enjoy trying to find one.

SKILLS: Observing, inferring, classifying, predicting, communicating, researching

Activity 6.7
WHICH MAGNET IS STRONGEST?

Materials Needed

- The magnets used in Activities 6.2 and 6.3
- Paper clip
- Ruler
- Spring scale

Procedure

1. Which magnet is the strongest?
2. Use these materials to answer the question.

For Problem Solvers: Find some information about new types of magnets. Find out if magnets have to be large in order to be strong.

Teacher Information

Often children will begin by putting two magnets together to see which one seems to "pull" harder. You may need to point out that this will not show which one is pulling harder. To help in the investigation, a spring scale, ruler, and paper clip are provided, but the children should not be given direction on how to use them. The purpose of the activity is to encourage creative inquiry. Success should be evaluated on the amount of creative exploration children undertake.

Younger children will often choose the largest magnet as the strongest. Teachers of young children should keep in mind the work of Piaget with preoperational thinking in utilizing this activity. It's very natural to assume that a larger magnet is stronger than a smaller magnet.

SKILLS: Observing, inferring, classifying, predicting, communicating, comparing and contrasting, researching

Activity 6.8
WHAT PART OF A MAGNET HAS THE STRONGEST PULL?

Materials Needed

- Bar magnet
- Paper clips

Procedure

1. See how many paper clips you can make stick to different parts of the magnet.
2. What happened?
3. Discuss your findings with your group.

Teacher Information

Many more paper clips will stick to the poles of the magnet. Few will cling to it between the poles. Magnets are strongest at the poles.

This activity will further illustrate the theory of induction. While the paper clips are touching the magnet, they temporarily become magnetized and several will "stick" to one another near the ends. When the clips are removed from the magnet, they rapidly lose their magnetic properties.

INTEGRATING: Math

SKILLS: Observing, inferring, measuring, predicting, communicating, formulating hypotheses, identifying and controlling variables, experimenting

Activity 6.9
WHAT IS A SPECIAL PROPERTY OF MAGNETISM?

 Take home and do with family and friends.

Materials Needed

- Two bar magnets
- Thread

Procedure

1. Tie the thread to the center of one bar magnet.
2. Hold the bar magnet in the air by the thread so it can turn freely.
3. Bring each end of another bar magnet near the one that is suspended from the thread.
4. What happened?
5. What can you say about this?

Figure 6.9-1

Bar Magnet Suspended from Thread

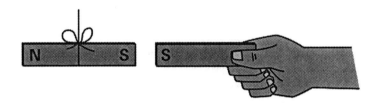

Teacher Information

Be sure the bars are correctly magnetized and that each has an "N" and an "S" marked on opposite ends. Like poles will push away. Unlike poles will attract one another. The poles of the bar magnet can be reversed by drawing the bar magnet several times across one of the poles of a powerful magnet. The direction in which the bar magnet is drawn across the pole of the larger magnet will determine the polarity of the bar magnet.

The ability to attract and repel each other is a special characteristic by which magnets can be identified.

SKILLS: Observing, inferring, predicting, communicating, experimenting

Activity 6.10
WHAT HAPPENS WHEN A MAGNET CAN TURN FREELY?

 Take home and do with family and friends.

Materials Needed

- Bar magnet
- Thread

Procedure

1. Hold the bar magnet by the thread.
2. If it spins, give it time to completely stop turning.
3. Observe the position in which it stops.
4. Do this several times.
5. What happened?
6. What can you say about this?

Figure 6.10-1

Bar Magnet Suspended from a Thread

Teacher Information

If the bar magnet is correctly magnetized, it should stop each time with the N end pointing toward magnetic north. Calling the N end of the magnet *north* has come about through common usage, as people knew about magnets and their behavior long before they understood them scientifically. Actually, since opposite poles attract, to be correct it should be called the *north-seeking* end.

INTEGRATING: Social studies

SKILLS: Observing, inferring, predicting, communicating

Activity 6.11
WHAT IS A COMPASS?

Materials Needed

- Sensitive compass
- Paper clip

Procedure

1. Bring the clip near the compass.

2. What happens to the compass needle?

3. What can you say about this?

Teacher Information

A compass is a freely suspended bar magnet. If a bar magnet is brought near, it will behave just as the suspended bar magnet did in Activity 6.9, showing that it has poles.

The children may also bring other known magnetic materials near the compass to further reinforce this idea. Understanding that a compass is a magnet is important for further investigations in this unit.

CAUTION: Very strong magnets may damage a compass by pulling the needle off its delicate support.

SKILLS: Observing, inferring, predicting, communicating

Activity 6.12
HOW CAN YOU MAKE A COMPASS?

Materials Needed

- Plastic, aluminum, or glass bowl
- Nonmagnetized needle
- Small piece of plastic foam
- Compass
- Water
- Bar magnet

Procedure

1. Is the needle a magnet? Don't guess. Devise a way to find out.
2. Rub the needle 30 times in the same direction with the bar magnet. Is the needle a magnet now?
3. Fill the bowl partly full of water.
4. Stick the needle through the plastic foam and float it in the pan of water.
5. Point the needle in different directions, then allow it to settle.

Figure 6.12-1

Needle in Floating Plastic Foam

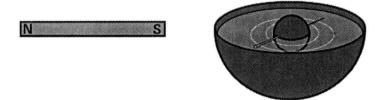

6. What happened?
7. Can you see a relationship to the compass?
8. What can you say about this?

For Problem Solvers: If you were lost in the woods and you didn't have a compass, but you had a small bar magnet or a magnetized needle, what would you do to find your directions? Would you like to create a story about that? Try it—it will be fun.

Teacher Information

The floating needle will behave like a compass, with one end always pointing to magnetic north. A story is told that this is the same type of compass used by Christopher Columbus. Since the metal needles of the time were poor, Columbus had a lodestone to remagnetize his floating needle. A bar magnet will affect the floating needle in the same way it did the compass. By moving the bar magnet under the dish, the children can discover that magnetism goes through water.

INTEGRATING: Social studies

SKILLS: Observing, inferring, predicting, communicating

Activity 6.13
WHAT ARE THE EARTH'S MAGNETIC POLES?

(Classroom demonstration and total group discussion)

Materials Needed

- 13-cm (6-in.) plastic foam ball cut in half
- Bar magnet
- Compasses
- Toothpicks
- Index card
- Iron filings

For Problem Solvers: Find one or more reference books and learn all you can about the earth's magnetic field. When did people first know about the earth's magnetic field? Was it useful information to them? In what ways? Do the earth's magnetic poles always stay at the same place, or do they wander around? Are true north and south and magnetic north and south the same? Do other planets have magnetic fields? Does the moon? What about the sun?

Teacher Information

This activity does not provide procedural steps for students. The concept of the earth's behaving as a large magnet with magnetic north and south poles is difficult to teach with simple inquiry/discovery activities alone. You might want to begin with a classroom discussion using one half of a plastic foam ball (or a grapefruit or large orange) with a bar magnet running through it and a tip sticking out of each end to represent the magnetic north and south poles. Toothpicks nearby could represent *true north* and *true south*, the axis (an imaginary line from true north to true south) on which the earth turns.

Figure 6.13-1

Ball, Bar Magnet, and Toothpicks

To further reinforce the idea, place an index card over the bar magnet with iron filings sprinkled on it. Scientists believe this pattern represents approximately the lines of force of the earth's magnetic field, with the strongest pull at the poles. With this basic idea in mind, a compass can be brought near the ball to show that it will point to the north and the south ends or poles.

See your encyclopedia for a discussion of northern and southern lights (aurora borealis and aurora australis). Scientists believe the stronger pull at the earth's poles attracts electrons given off from the sun. As they enter the earth's atmosphere they produce these unusual lights.

The earth's magnetic poles are offset somewhat from the true north and south poles. The difference between true north and magnetic north is called the *angle of declination*, and it varies according to your geographic location on Earth.

INTEGRATING: Reading, language arts, social studies

SKILLS: Observing, inferring, predicting, communicating, researching

Activity 6.14
HOW DO MATERIALS BECOME MAGNETIZED?

Materials Needed

- Plastic tube (toothbrush container or test tube) two thirds full of iron filings
- Strong magnet
- Compass

Procedure

1. Place the tube with the iron filings flat on a table.
2. Move the compass along the side of the tube. Observe the needle.
3. Rub the tube containing iron filings 30 times in the same direction across one pole of the strong magnet. Now move the compass along the side of the tube again. Observe the needle.
4. What happened?
5. Shake the tube several times. Move the compass along the side of the tube.
6. What do you think is happening?

For Problem Solvers: Find a screwdriver and try to pick up paper clips with it. If it will pick up one or more paper clips, the screwdriver is already a magnet. If it won't, stroke it the length of the shaft several times in the same direction with a good magnet. Then try to pick up some paper clips with the screwdriver.

What other tools or items do you think you can make into magnets? Wrenches? Scissors? Get permission before you try any of these things, unless they belong to you.

Teacher Information

This activity illustrates in concrete form one of the theories scientists use to explain what happens when an object becomes magnetized. In materials that can be magnetized are groups or *domains* of atoms that have north and south poles but are arranged randomly (Figure 6.14-1).

Figure 6.14-1

Domains Shown in Random Order

264

The iron filings in the plastic tube represent these domains. The compass will show that the tube does not have poles. When the *domains of atoms* come into the presence of a strong magnetic field, they line up, following the lines of force of the magnetic field (Figure 6.14-2).

Figure 6.14-2

Domains Shown in Uniform Arrangement

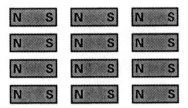

When the plastic tube is rubbed with a strong magnet, the iron filings line up inside and the compass test will show the tube has poles. Shaking the tube several times mixes the filings up and the compass test will show the tube no longer has poles.

The mixing up of the domains is one way of explaining how magnets may lose their magnetism. When an object is heated, the molecules move more rapidly and bounce against one another. Dropping or striking a magnet may jar the domains out of alignment. Magnets stored with *like* poles together seem to gradually shift the domains out of position.

As the domain theory is presented to children with the plastic tube model, it is important to remember that it is a simplified version. More complex concepts consistent with this model are studied in later years.

SKILLS: Observing, inferring, predicting, communicating

Activity 6.15
HOW CAN YOU FIND THE POLES OF A LODESTONE?

Materials Needed

- Lodestone
- Compass

Procedure

1. Bring the compass near different parts of the lodestone.
2. Observe the needle.
3. What happened?
4. What can you say about this?

For Problem Solvers: Try to identify all the poles that you can on your lodestone. Draw two outlines of the lodestone on paper and label one outline "Front" and the other "Back." Every place that one of the ends of the compass needle is attracted to is a pole. Label each one as S or N. Do the poles seem to be always at the points of the rock, or in the hollows, or both? Do they seem to be always in pairs? How many pairs of poles did you find?

Teacher Information

The compass will indicate that lodestones do have poles. Some lodestones may have several poles, but they should have equal numbers of north and south poles. Some scientists believe that lodestones are magnetized and aligned to the earth's magnetic poles as the iron ore from which they are formed cools.

Since ancient deposits of lodestone have poles pointing in directions different from the present north and south it is suggested that our present north and south poles may have switched several times over the years.

The different directions in which the poles of ancient deposits point are also studied as indicators of earth movement and the theory of *continental drift*.

SKILLS: Observing, inferring, predicting, communicating

Activity 6.16
HOW CAN YOU SEE A MAGNETIC FIELD?

Materials Needed

- Two thin books
- Shaker of iron filings
- Bar magnet
- Card

Procedure

1. Place the bar magnet between the two books.
2. Cover the magnet with the card.
3. Sprinkle iron filings on the card.
4. Tap the card gently several times.
5. What happened?
6. What can you say about this?

Figure 6.16-1

Books, Card, Magnet, and Iron Filings

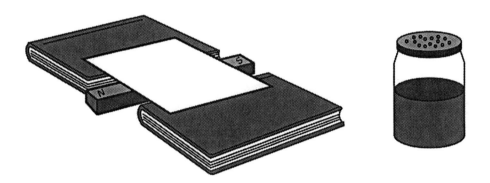

For Problem Solvers: Let's explore with magnetic fields. Put a second bar magnet end to end with the first one, with unlike poles together, and center them under the card. Sprinkle iron filings on the card and see what the magnetic field looks like now. Next, turn one of the bar magnets around, so the like poles are together, and again sprinkle the card with iron filings. Find other sizes and shapes of magnets and make pictures of their magnetic poles with the iron filings.

Teacher Information

You can demonstrate to the entire class at once by putting the magnets on an overhead projector, using a sheet of glass instead of a card, and shining the image on the screen.

The iron filings will be aligned with the magnetic field of the bar magnet, making it visible. Note that the filings in the middle will point to the poles, while the greater number of filings will cluster at the poles. Iron filings may be purchased from science supply houses. They also occur naturally in many types of sand and may be collected by running a strong magnet through a sand pile. Put the magnet in a baggy before dragging it through the sand, for easy cleanup.

Your problem solvers will experiment with magnets of different types and will compare the pattern of filings created by their magnetic fields.

SKILLS: Observing, inferring, predicting, communicating

Activity 6.17
HOW CAN YOU PRESERVE A MAGNETIC FIELD?

Materials Needed

- Two thin books
- Shaker of iron filings
- Bar magnet
- Card
- Spray paint
- Newsprint or other protective cover

Procedure

1. Do this activity outdoors. You need plenty of ventilation.
2. Place the bar magnet between the two books.
3. Cover the books and magnet with newspaper.
4. Cover the magnet with the card (see Figure 6.17-1).
5. What do you think the pattern of the magnetic field will be like for the magnet(s) you are using? Make your prediction before you sprinkle any iron filings.
6. Sprinkle iron filings on the card.
7. Tap the card gently several times.
8. When the magnetic field is formed, spray the card lightly with paint.
9. Allow the paint time to dry, then brush off the iron filings into a wastebasket.
10. Display your picture on a wall, along with those that are made by other students.

Figure 6.17-1

Newsprint, Card, and Magnet

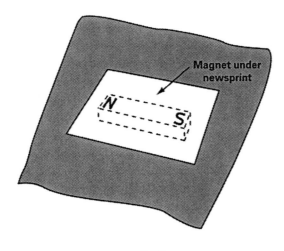

For Problem Solvers: Experiment with different magnets and combinations of magnets to create interesting patterns of magnetic lines of force, and paint them so the patterns can be preserved and displayed.

If you can get some spray adhesive, ask your teacher to help you repeat the same activity but using adhesive instead of paint. This time, don't brush off the iron filings when the design has dried. Don't move the card or the magnet until the adhesive is completely dry, which will likely take about 30 minutes. Be sure to do this activity outdoors.

You could also use light-sensitive paper in place of the card to make a permanent record. Even purple construction paper will fade if left by a window in the sunlight and will make a permanent print of the pattern of filings.

Teacher Information

This is a great way to permanently preserve patterns of magnetic fields for viewing and discussion. Some very interesting patterns will evolve as students get involved. You will get face patterns and many other creative designs.

If spray adhesive is available, help your problem solvers to try at least one of the patterns using adhesive instead of paint. They will be excited to see the iron filings preserved as a part of the pattern. Be sure to let the adhesive dry completely before moving the card or the magnets, and the iron filings that are near the poles will retain their standing position. These patterns will need gentle handling to avoid knocking the iron filings off.

INTEGRATING: Art

SKILLS: Observing, inferring, classifying, predicting, communicating, identifying and controlling variables

STATIC ELECTRICITY

TO THE TEACHER

The topic of static electricity has at least two things in common with magnetism: (1) the attraction and repulsion of one object for another, and (2) the attraction of all age groups to the topic. There is something, perhaps the element of mystery, that intrigues both young and old. Although our information about static electricity is still based largely on theory (another common thread with magnetism), much is known about its behavior. Through observation and experimentation, logical explanations of the phenomenon have developed.

This section is suitable for virtually every grade level, and most activities can be easily adapted for use where needed. Activity 7.1 is intended as a teacher demonstration and works well as an introduction to the unit. If used this way it will raise questions, not provide answers, which is exactly what it is intended to do. A better time to discuss concepts is after students have experimented, discovered, and formed general ideas about the way electrically charged objects seem to behave. Static electricity works best on a cool, clear day (moisture in the air tends to drain off the charge), but success with these activities is very high almost any time except, perhaps, on a hot, muggy day.

Static electricity is the object of curiosity, annoyance, and humor. During a severe electrical storm the emotion associated with it can be fear, in recognition of the all-too-real danger to life and property. The lightning bolt itself is current electricity because it is moving, but it results from the buildup of an electrostatic charge.

Many of the activities in this section involve objects receiving an electrostatic charge by induction. When two materials rub together, such as wool cloth and a balloon, electrons are transferred from one material to the other—from cloth to balloon, for instance. However, a neutral object can receive an *induced* charge simply by being near a charged object. If a neutral object is approached by a negatively charged object, the neutral object becomes positively charged. If the neutral object is approached by a positively charged object, the neutral object becomes negatively charged. The induced charge is always opposite that of the charged object. Thus, charged objects are attracted to neutral objects. A charged balloon will cling to a wall, a person, and so forth.

As you select materials to use with static electricity activities, avoid those that have been treated with antistatic chemicals. Such chemicals are often used in dishwashers (antispot substances), in clothes dryers (anticling products or fabric softeners), or on carpets and furniture (fabric protector). Sometimes these treatments can be washed out, and the materials can then be used for static electricity activities.

Although wool cloth is often suggested for use in static electricity activities because it gives up electrons readily to other materials rubbed by it, cotton cloth, flannel, and many other fabrics work well. Be sure the fabric is clean and is *not treated* by a fabric softener.

Regarding the Early Grades

With verbal instructions and slight modifications, many of these activities can be used with kindergarten, first-grade, and second-grade students. In some activities, steps that involve procedures that go beyond the level of the child can simply be omitted and yet offer the child an experience that plants the seed for a concept that will germinate and grow later on.

Teachers of the early grades will probably choose to bypass many of the "For Problem Solvers" sections. That's okay. These sections are provided for those who are especially motivated and want to go beyond the investigation provided by the activity outlined. Use the outlined activities and enjoy worthwhile learning experiences together with your young students. Also consider, however, that many of the "For Problem Solvers" sections can be used appropriately with young children as group activities or as demonstrations, still giving students the advantage of an exposure to the experience and laying groundwork for connections that will be made later on.

Activity 7.1
WHAT IS THE KISSING BALLOON?

(Teacher demonstration)

Materials Needed

- Balloon
- Wool cloth
- String
- Permanent marker
- Words to the story (given below)

Procedure (for teacher)

1. Inflate the balloon.
2. Draw a face on the balloon, using the marker.
3. With the string, suspend the balloon from the ceiling. Adjust the height so the balloon is at the level of your head when you're standing on the floor. Do this while students are out of the room.
4. With students still out of the room, rub the "nose" of the balloon with the wool cloth. If properly charged, the balloon will now face you any time you are reasonably near. If you walk around the balloon, it will follow.
5. You are now ready for your students to return to the classroom. They should take their seats without going near the balloon.
6. Without revealing scientific principles involved, tell the following story as an introduction to your study of static electricity. Following the study, the Kissing Balloon could be used again for review and/or evaluation. A suggestion for such an evaluation follows the story.

Story

"Students, I'd like you to meet a friend of mine. His name is George. George, meet the smartest fourth grade in the state." *At this point you are standing at least 2 m (2 yds.) from George.*

"There are a couple of things I think you should know about George, class. First, he's nearsighted, and second, he has an awful crush on me. He likes me so much that he just can't keep his eyes off me—when he can see me, that is." (*Walk over closer to George and he will turn to face you.*)

"You see? He just stares at me, and he keeps staring at me as long as I'm close enough for him to see me." (*Walk away.*) "When I walk away, he just looks all over, trying to find me again." (*Move closer again.*) "You'll be able to tell when I'm within his range of vision because he'll look right at me." (*Walk around George.*) "See, l told you he likes me. Now, if you'll promise not to tell anyone, I'll let George kiss me—just once, on the cheek." (*Lean over, where your cheek is very near George.*) "Aw, that's so nice."

"Now, for the next few days, we're going to do a few things that should give you some clues about George. We'll visit with him again on another day."

The story can be adjusted to let it be one of the students that George (or Sue, or whatever you want to call ol' Bubblehead) is attracted to. Fun will be had by all, and your students should be more highly motivated for their study of static electricity as a result of meeting George.

Evaluation

One idea for an evaluation following learning activities on static electricity is to repeat the kissing balloon activity, put the following terms on the chalkboard, and ask students to explain why George behaved the way he did. Instruct them to use some of the terms from the chalkboard in their explanation:

- Static electricity
- Attraction
- Repulsion
- Transfer of electrons
- Induction

Note: One of the properties of static electricity is that a charge can be held in a given location. When you rub George's nose with the wool cloth, the charge does not spread throughout the balloon, but remains localized. Otherwise, this activity would not be possible.

INTEGRATING: Language arts

SKILLS: Observing, inferring, predicting, communicating, formulating hypotheses

Activity 7.2
HOW DOES RUBBING WITH WOOL AFFECT PLASTIC STRIPS?

Materials Needed

- Two plastic strips
- Wool cloth
- Sheet of paper

Procedure

1. Hold the two plastic strips at one end and let them hang down, face to face. What did they do?
2. Place the two plastic strips on the table and rub them with wool, stroking in only one direction.
3. Carefully remove the strips, touching them only at one end.
4. Place them together and let them hang down again, face to face.
5. What happened? Why do you think they reacted this way?

For Problem Solvers: The variables in this activity are what is being rubbed, how you are rubbing, and what you are rubbing with. Experiment with the variables. Does it have to be these particular strips of plastic? Does it have to be plastic? Do you have to rub with wool cloth? Might cotton cloth work? See what you can learn through your investigation, and share your information with the class.

Teacher Information

At step 1 the plastic strips are both neutral and therefore neither attract nor repel each other. When rubbed with wool, which gives up electrons readily, the plastic strips take on a negative electrostatic charge; they gain an excess of electrons. Since the plastic strips are now charged alike, they will repel each other when they are held up.

SKILLS: Observing, inferring, classifying, predicting, communicating, formulating hypotheses, identifying and controlling variables, experimenting

Activity 7.3
WHAT CHANGES THE WAY BALLOONS REACT TO EACH OTHER?

 Take home and do with family and friends.

Materials Needed

- Two balloons of the same size
- Two pieces of string 60 cm (2 ft.) long
- Wool cloth

Procedure

1. Inflate the two balloons and tie the ends with string.
2. Hold up the two balloons by their strings so they hang about an inch or two apart. How do they respond to each other?
3. Rub one balloon with the cloth and repeat step 2. What happened?
4. Rub the other balloon with the cloth and repeat step 2. What happened this time?
5. Explain. Discuss your ideas with your group.

Teacher Information

At step 2, the balloons are neutral and do not react to each other. At step 3, the rubbed balloon has a negative charge and it induces a positive charge in the other balloon. Thus, the balloons attract each other. When the two balloons touch, electrons are transferred from the negatively charged balloon, giving the other one a negative charge, and the balloons repel each other. When both balloons have been rubbed with wool, at step 4, they have like charges (negative) and will repel one another.

SKILLS: Observing, inferring, predicting, communicating, comparing and contrasting, formulating hypotheses, identifying and controlling variables, experimenting

Activity 7.4
WHAT WILL A COMB DO TO PUFFED RICE?

 Take home and do with family and friends.

Materials Needed

- Comb
- Wool cloth
- Puffed rice (several kernels)

Procedure

1. Rub the back of the comb vigorously with the wool cloth.
2. Bring the rubbed part of the comb near the puffed rice. Hold the comb steady and observe until you see something different happen. It might take as long as a minute or two. Be patient.
3. Explain what happened and why.

Teacher Information

The comb, being rubbed with wool, takes on a negative charge. When it is held near the puffed rice, the rice becomes charged positively by induction and will leap and cling to the comb. Patience is needed at this point.

As the puffed rice remains in contact with the comb, some of the negative charge (electrons) will drain off the comb and onto the puffed rice. The puffed rice now has a negative charge—the same as the comb—and will leap from the comb. Notice that the puffed rice does not simply fall, but rather appears to be thrown from the comb by some force. The force is the repelling action of like electrostatic charges for each other.

As the puffed rice sits on the table, its excess electrons will probably drain off to the table and the cycle is sometimes repeated.

SKILLS: Observing, inferring, predicting, communicating, formulating hypotheses, identifying and controlling variables, experimenting

Activity 7.5
HOW CAN YOU MAKE PAPER DANCE UNDER GLASS?

Materials Needed

- Sheet of glass (or inverted shallow, clear bowl)
- Plastic bag (clean)
- Two books
- Small bits of paper

Procedure

1. Support the glass by placing a book under each end.
2. Place some small bits of paper under the glass.
3. Rub the top of the glass vigorously with the plastic.
4. Observe for a minute or two.
5. What happened?
6. Why do you suppose it behaves this way?

Figure 7.5-1

Glass Supported by Books

Teacher Information

Avoid paper that has been treated in any way (for example, to make erasing easy). Tissue paper works well and plastic foam is an excellent substitute. This activity is very similar to Activity 7.4. (See "Teacher Information" in Activity 7.4.) In this activity, the behavior appears the same but the charges have been reversed. The glass will give up electrons readily and become positively charged. In turn, it will induce a negative charge in the bits of paper. The paper will jump up to the glass, gradually give up some electrons and fall back to the table where the process of induction is repeated.

SKILLS: Observing, inferring, predicting, communicating, formulating hypotheses, identifying and controlling variables, experimenting

Activity 7.6
WHY DOES PAPER LEAP FOR A BALLOON?

 Take home and do with family and friends.

Materials Needed

- Balloon
- Wool cloth
- Bits of paper (only a few)

Procedure

1. Blow up the balloon and tie the end.
2. Rub the balloon with the wool cloth.
3. Hold the balloon about two inches (5 cm) from the bits of paper and observe for a minute or two. Hold the balloon steady as you observe the bits of paper.
4. What happened? Can you explain why?

For Problem Solvers: By now you know that like charges repel each other and opposite charges attract each other. For this activity you charged the balloon by rubbing it with the cloth. The paper was neutral. Why is the paper attracted to the balloon? Do some research about induction, with respect to electrostatic charges. What other activities in this series have materials receiving a charge by induction?

Teacher Information

Tissue paper, or most any regular writing paper, works very well for the bits of paper, and plastic foam is an excellent substitute.

As the negatively charged balloon approaches the bits of paper, the paper becomes charged positively by induction. The bits of paper are attracted to the balloon because of opposite charges. When the bits of paper come in contact with the balloon, some of the excess electrons on the surface of the balloon drain off into the bits of paper. The bits of paper now have the same charge (negative) as the balloon and they repel the balloon. As they drop onto the table top, the excess electrons drain from the bits of paper into the table top, and the process begins again.

Be sure students notice that as the bits of paper leave the balloon, they don't simply fall, but they are thrown from the balloon by the repelling force of like charges.

SKILLS: Observing, inferring, classifying, predicting, communicating, formulating hypotheses, identifying and controlling variables, experimenting

Activity 7.7
WHAT DOES PUFFED RICE RUN AWAY FROM?

Materials Needed

- Clear plastic box (shallow)
- Puffed rice or vermiculite
- Wool cloth

Procedure

1. Put a few pieces of vermiculite or puffed rice inside the plastic box.
2. Rub the top of the box with wool.
3. What happened?
4. Bring your finger near the top of the box.
5. What happened?
6. Can you explain your findings? Do you think the puffed rice is afraid of you?

Teacher Information

This activity involves an induced electrostatic charge beyond that of earlier activities. When your finger approaches the negatively charged plastic box, your finger becomes positively charged by induction, just as the puffed rice inside the box has been. Therefore, your finger and the puffed rice have like charges. Evidence of the resultant repelling effect is seen as the puffed rice is "chased" around the box by the finger.

SKILLS: Observing, inferring, classifying, predicting, communicating, formulating hypotheses, identifying and controlling variables, experimenting

Activity 7.8
HOW CAN YOU MAKE SALT AND PEPPER DANCE TOGETHER?

 Take home and do with family and friends.

Materials Needed

- Balloon
- Wool cloth
- Salt and pepper

Procedure

1. Inflate the balloon and tie the end.
2. Sprinkle a small amount of salt and pepper on a sheet of paper or on your desk top.
3. Rub the balloon with the cloth.
4. Bring the balloon within about an inch or two (2–5 cm) of the salt and pepper.
5. Observe for a minute or two.
6. Explain what is happening and why.

Teacher Information

In this activity you will see the salt and pepper do a "dance" because of the principles explained in "Teacher Information" for Activities 7.4 and 7.6. You will need to caution your students to watch very carefully. Otherwise they will probably not notice that the same grains of salt and pepper are attracted to the balloon, repelled, then attracted again over and over. Notice that they don't just fall from the balloon but are *thrown* by the electrostatic force.

SKILLS: Observing, inferring, classifying, predicting, communicating, formulating hypotheses, identifying and controlling variables, experimenting

Activity 7.9
HOW CAN YOU MAKE A STRING DANCE?

 Take home and do with family and friends.

Materials Needed

- Balloon
- String 30–45 cm (1 to 1.5 ft.) long
- Wool cloth

Procedure

1. Inflate the balloon and tie the end.
2. Charge the balloon by rubbing it with the cloth.
3. Lay the string on the table
4. Bring the balloon near one end of the string, but don't let it touch.
5. What happened?
6. Can you explain why?
7. With practice you might learn to be a snake charmer!

Teacher Information

The end of the string in this activity is charged by induction and attracted to the balloon. Students enjoy making the end of the string dance.

SKILLS: Observing, inferring, predicting, communicating, formulating hypotheses, identifying and controlling variables, experimenting

Activity 7.10
HOW CAN YOU FILL A STOCKING WITHOUT PUTTING A LEG INTO IT?

 Take home and do with family and friends.

Materials Needed

- Cool, dry day
- Sheer nylon stocking
- Clean lightweight plastic (such as a fresh vegetable bag from grocery store)
- Smooth wall, chalkboard, or cork board

Procedure

1. Holding it by the top, place the nylon stocking against the wall.
2. Use the plastic to rub and smooth the stocking against the wall. It is best to rub with long strokes in one direction from top to toe. Do this about 20 times.
3. Release your hold on the top of the stocking. What happened?
4. Keeping an arm's length away from the stocking, grasp at the top and slowly pull it away from the wall. Be sure nothing comes near it.
5. Still holding it at arm's length, do you observe any difference in the stocking?
6. Slowly bring the stocking toward you. What happened? Can you explain why this happened?

Teacher Information

This activity demonstrates induction and the attraction and repulsion of like and unlike static charges. Be sure the nylon you use has been washed thoroughly in clear water so any anti-cling treatment has been removed.

At first the nylon will hang limply against the wall. As the plastic is rubbed on the nylon it will remove electrons from the stocking, giving the stocking a positive charge. By the time the stocking has been stroked 20 times it should smooth out and cling to the wall without support. This is caused by a form of induction explained earlier in the section on static electricity.

When the stocking is pulled away from the wall and held at arm's length it will fill out in all directions as if an invisible leg were inside. This is because the entire stocking has a positive charge and like charges repel or push away from each other.

SKILLS: Observing, inferring, classifying, predicting, communicating, formulating hypotheses, identifying and controlling variables, experimenting

Activity 7.11
HOW CAN YOU BEND WATER?

 Take home and do with family and friends.

Materials Needed

- Sink
- Comb
- Wool cloth (or cotton)

Procedure

1. Turn on the water in the sink, just enough to get a very thin but steady stream.
2. Rub the comb vigorously with the cloth.
3. Bring the comb near the stream of water, being sure the comb does not touch the water.
4. What happened?
5. What do you think might have caused this? Discuss your ideas with your group.

Teacher Information

As has been the case with other activities, rubbing the comb with the cloth results in the comb taking on extra electrons and assuming a negative charge. Water molecules are polar, due to the way the two hydrogen atoms combine with an oxygen atom. This means the water molecule has a positive charge on one end and a negative charge on the other end. The negatively charged comb attracts the positive end of the water molecule, and the thin stream of water bends noticeably toward the comb.

SKILLS: Observing, inferring, communicating, formulating hypotheses

Activity 7.12
HOW CAN YOU MAKE A SPARK WITH YOUR FINGER?

 Take home and do with family and friends.

Materials Needed

- Darkened room with carpeted floor

Procedure

1. Turn the lights off and make the room as dark as possible.

2. Shuffle your feet across the carpet for a few steps.

3. Touch a doorknob or some other metal object. Watch carefully at your fingertip as you touch the doorknob.

4. What did you see? If you didn't see anything, try it again.

For Problem Solvers: What is the spark? Do some research on lightning and find out how the spark from your finger might be related to lightning. Is lightning static electricity? Don't jump to conclusions—study it out.

Find out about lightning safety. What things are important to do during a lightning storm and what things should you avoid doing?

Teacher Information

This activity is not dangerous, but it does tend to invite horseplay, so if a group of students is involved, close supervision might be needed. The objective of the activity is to see the spark that jumps between the finger and the doorknob after an electrostatic charge is built up from shuffling the feet across the room on the carpet. Students usually discover that a spark can also jump between their finger and another person's ear or nose. The spark will sometimes be felt and heard. If the room can be darkened, the spark can also be seen. If some students are frightened by the spark, they should not be required to participate.

The spark might be thought of as a miniature lightning bolt. Lightning is a huge spark of electric current that results from a buildup of static electricity in the atmosphere. When moisture in the air and other conditions are just right, in balance with the electrostatic charge, the charge will drain off due to the natural tendency to create electrically neutral conditions.

SKILLS: Observing, inferring, predicting, communicating, formulating hypotheses, identifying and controlling variables, experimenting

Activity 7.13
HOW CAN YOU MAKE AN ELECTROSCOPE?

(Upper grades)

Materials Needed

- Bottle with cork stopper
- Copper wire about 20 cm (8 in.) long
- Lightweight aluminum foil
- Nail
- Rubber comb
- Wool cloth
- Scissors
- Ruler

Procedure

1. Force the nail through the cork stopper to make a hole for the wire.
2. Remove the insulation from both ends of the wire.
3. Insert the copper wire through the cork stopper.
4. Bend the lower end of the wire (the end that will go inside the bottle) as illustrated in Figure 7.13-1.

Figure 7.13-1

Assembled Electroscope

5. Cut a strip of aluminum foil approximately 1/2 cm (1/4 in.) wide and 3 cm (1.25 in.) long.

6. Fold the aluminum foil in half and let it hang over the end of the wire, as illustrated. *Be sure all insulation is removed from the wire where the foil rests.*

7. Put the stopper on the bottle, being careful not to jar the strip of aluminum foil off the end of the wire.

8. Rub the comb with the wool cloth and bring the comb near the top end of the wire. As you do this, observe the foil strip carefully.

9. What happened? Can you explain why?

10. Try the same thing with other charged objects.

For Problem Solvers: Examine the electroscope and explain why it works the way it does. Share your explanation with at least one of your classmates. When you and your classmates can agree on the way the electroscope works, explain it to your teacher.

Try to make a new design of the electroscope. What are the critical parts? What purpose does the bottle serve? The stopper? The wire? The foil? Can you make something else work in place of any of these? Maybe some of these parts are not even needed at all. Test out your ideas.

Teacher Information

The electroscope is an easy-to-make device and should not be difficult to assemble for students who are motivated. They can use it to demonstrate the presence of an electrostatic charge in a comb, a balloon, or other charged object. As the charged object is brought near the upper end of the copper wire, the wire, being a conductor, becomes charged by induction and transfers the charge to the foil. The entire foil strip receives the same charge, and the two ends repel each other.

The very thin foil stripped from a gum wrapper works better for this activity than does heavier aluminum foil used in wrapping food.

SKILLS: Observing, inferring, classifying, predicting, communicating, comparing and contrasting, formulating hypotheses, identifying and controlling variables, experimenting

CURRENT ELECTRICITY

TO THE TEACHER

The study of this topic should follow the studies of magnetism and static electricity, as it requires background information from both. The activities are nongraded, but teachers of young children will need to adapt language and instruction.

The amount of electric current used in these activities (1.5 to 6 volts) is perfectly safe if you follow directions to avoid overheating of circuits. If your flashlight has two batteries it uses three volts of electricity. **Caution: Never use household current directly for these activities.** In many activities, a high-quality transformer could substitute for batteries. Before using a transformer, be sure you know exactly how much voltage it produces and that it is safe to use. Flashlight cells may be wrapped together securely with electrical tape, end to end, just as they fit in a flashlight.

The majority of these activities suggest using a lantern battery, while a few of them suggest flashlight batteries. The flashlight battery has the advantage of cost, while the advantages of the lantern battery are (1) it will last much longer, and (2) it has connectors, making it much easier to connect wires to the batteries. Battery holders with easy connectors can be purchased or made for flashlight batteries, eliminating that problem.

Be sure that your bulbs are compatible with the voltage of the batteries being used. A bulb designed for 1.5 volts will burn out if you attach it to a 6-volt lantern battery.

Technically a *battery* consists of two or more cells connected together, and the flashlight battery is not a battery at all, but is more properly called a *dry cell*. However, single dry cells are so commonly called batteries that to insist on technically proper use of the terms is futile. The popular square 6-volt lantern battery is a true battery, containing four cells of 1.5 volts each (voltage of the four cells is added because they are connected in series within the battery). The rectangular 9-volt lantern battery contains six cells of 1.5 volts each.

Materials such as light sockets, bulbs, and insulated copper wire can be purchased at a hardware or electronics store. An inexpensive wire cutter and stripper (to remove insulation) is a necessary item.

Most activities are designed for individuals or small groups. Costs can be reduced by setting up a learning center and rotating groups through it.

Before you begin this section it would be helpful to read all activities. Some of the same materials are used several times in different ways.

Many schools have magnets that have become weak. You can rejuvenate magnets by wrapping a coil of wire around them and sending an electric current through the wire (see activities on electromagnets in the Current Electricity section). If you recharge bar magnets, be sure the current flows through the wire in the proper direction to produce the correct poles as marked (use a compass to check). A simple device for making bar magnets stronger can be made from a toilet tissue tube with a coil of wire wrapped in one direction around it. Simply insert a bar magnet in the tube and turn on the current for a few seconds. If the poles are reversed, repeat the process but turn the bar magnet around or switch the wires on the battery terminals to send the current in the opposite direction through the coil. Bar magnets can also be given new life by stroking them lengthwise several times across one pole of a powerful magnet. Stroke in one direction only. If poles are reversed, stroke in the opposite direction *or* use the other pole of the large magnet.

Enrichment activities for this unit could focus on new ways to produce electric current.

Evaluation should use concrete materials, not just pencil and paper.

Regarding the Early Grades

With verbal instructions and slight modifications, many of these activities can be used with kindergarten, first-grade, and second-grade students. In some activities, steps that involve procedures that go beyond the level of the child can simply be omitted and yet offer the child an experience that plants the seed for a concept that will germinate and grow later on.

Teachers of the early grades will probably choose to bypass many of the "For Problem Solvers" sections. That's okay. These sections are provided for those who are especially motivated and want to go beyond the investigation provided by the activity outlined. Use the outlined activities, and enjoy worthwhile learning experiences together with your young students. Also consider, however, that many of the "For Problem Solvers" sections can be used appropriately with young children as group activities or as demonstrations, still giving students the advantage of an exposure to the experience and laying groundwork for connections that will be made later on.

Activity 8.1
WHAT MATERIALS WILL CONDUCT ELECTRICITY?

Materials Needed

- Circuit as shown in Figure 8.1-1, consisting of a lantern battery, lengths of insulated copper wire of 20 or 22 gauge, and a small light socket with miniature bulb
- Small objects made of different materials, such as paper clips, nails, wire, wood, rubber bands, glass, plastic, coins, rocks

Procedure

1. Test your circuit by touching the bare wires together. The light should go on.
2. Choose objects from the pile on the table. Touch both bare wires to each object about 2 cm (1 in.) apart and observe the light. If the item conducts electricity, the light will turn on.
3. Explain what is happening the best you can.

For Problem Solvers: Now that you have tested several small items to find out if they conduct electricity, take your circuit and test a lot of other things. Each time you think of a new material to check, first make a prediction of whether the material will conduct electricity, then check it out.

Classify the materials you used by making separate lists of materials that conduct electricity, materials that do not conduct electricity, and materials that surprised you. If you found some items that conduct electricity but not very well (the light came on, but it was dim), put them in a separate list.

Teacher Information

This activity introduces the idea of conductors and nonconductors. Nonconductors are sometimes called insulators. Most metals are conductors to some degree, since electricity will move through them. Some materials, such as glass, rubber, and plastic, are insulators, and electricity does not flow through them.

Figure 8.1-1

Battery, Bulb, and Wires

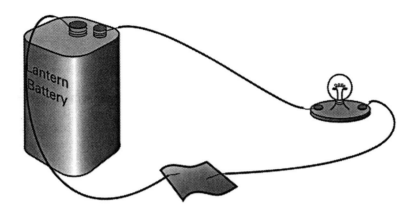

SKILLS: Observing, inferring, classifying, predicting, communicating, comparing and contrasting, formulating hypotheses, identifying and controlling variables, experimenting

Activity 8.2
WHAT IS A CIRCUIT?

 Take home and do with family and friends.

Materials Needed

- One 1.5-volt flashlight battery
- Two 25-cm (10 in.) lengths of single-strand insulated copper wire of 20 or 22 gauge
- Small light socket with flashlight bulb
- Small screwdriver

Procedure

1. In front of you are all the materials needed to make the light turn on. Can you connect them together so the bulb lights up? If you have trouble, read the following hints:

   a. Electricity will flow from the battery (power source) only if it has a complete path from one battery terminal (end) to the other.

   b. Electric current will go through the copper wire but not through the plastic or rubber insulation (covering).

   c. The bulb must be tight in its socket.

   d. The wires must be tightly connected.

2. What happens if the path from one battery terminal to the other is broken? Can you explain why?

3. When the light is on, this is called a complete circuit because it forms a complete path from the battery to the light and back to the battery.

For Problem Solvers: Remove the bulb from the socket and try to make the bulb light up without the socket. Use only the bulb, two wires, and the flashlight battery.

Make the bulb light by using only one wire.

Now that you know how to make a complete circuit, so the light comes on, try the activity with other people. You only need two wires, a flashlight battery, and a flashlight bulb. Give the materials to your dad, mom, brother, sister, a friend, or Great Uncle Newberry. See if they can make the light come on. Help them only if you have to, and don't be in too big a hurry to help—let them struggle for a while. Try it with several different people.

Teacher Information

One and one-half volts of electric current from a flashlight battery is perfectly safe for classroom use. This activity may be varied according to the age of the children. For younger children you may want to attach the wires to the socket and let them discover how to make it work by screwing the bulb in and touching the bare ends to the battery. Older children should be able to hook up the circuit by following the hints. You may need to help them clean off (strip) insulation from about 2 cm (1 in.) from each end of each wire. An inexpensive wire cutter and stripper obtainable from any hardware store is most helpful.

When completed, the circuit should look like the one shown in Figure 8.2-1.

Numbers indicating the gauge (thickness) of wire are in the reverse order of their thickness. For example, 20-gauge wire is heavier than 22-gauge. An ideal gauge for most of these activities is often called bell wire.

Figure 8.2-1

Battery and Bulb Connected in a Circuit

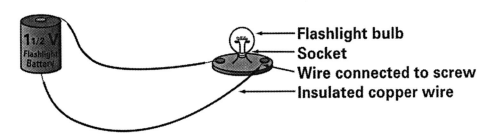

Your problem solvers will have an exciting time testing others on their newly learned skill. Your students will probably be surprised to learn that few adults can make the bulb light without a lot of struggle. They might even need help, which will do wonders for the self-confidence of the child. The real value will be that the child will learn how to make a complete circuit so well that he or she will probably never forget.

INTEGRATING: Language arts, social studies

SKILLS: Observing, inferring, classifying, predicting, communicating, comparing and contrasting, formulating hypotheses, identifying and controlling variables, experimenting, researching

Activity 8.3
HOW CAN WE MODEL A COMPLETE CIRCUIT?

(Group activity)

Materials Needed

- Group of students
- Labels "Battery" and "Light"
- Labels "Negative" and "Positive"

Procedure

1. Assign one person to be the battery and one person to be the light.

2. Put the labels on these two people.

3. Put the "Negative" label on the left arm of the "Battery" and the "Positive" label on the right arm of the "Battery." The arms now represent the negative and positive terminals of the battery.

4. Form a circle, with everyone holding hands.

5. Have the "Battery" squeeze the hand of the person on his or her left. That person should, in turn, squeeze with the left hand, and so goes the signal around the circle and back to the positive terminal of the "Battery."

6. This shows a complete circuit, with electricity flowing from the battery, all the way through the circuit, and back to the battery. The "Light" could smile brightly to show that the light turns on when the signal is received. This is called a *complete circuit*.

7. Have two people—any two—break the hand grip.

8. The "Battery" squeezes with the left hand again, but this time the signal stops where the break is, so it does not get back to the battery.

9. This time the "Light" does not smile, because electricity flows *only* if it has a complete circuit from the negative terminal of the battery all the way back to the positive terminal of the battery. This time it was an *incomplete circuit*.

10. Discuss this activity, sharing ideas about what happened and the difference between a complete circuit and an incomplete circuit.

11. Draw a complete circuit and an incomplete circuit, showing the battery, the bulb, and wire.

Teacher Information

It is hoped that this activity will help students begin to understand the difference between a complete circuit and an incomplete circuit and that electricity flows only if the circuit is complete.

In a good battery, chemicals react together in such a way that an abundance of electrons builds up at the negative terminal, with a shortage of electrons resulting at the positive terminal. That's why the terminals are called negative and positive. The natural tendency is toward neutrality, so when a conductor connects the negative terminal to the positive terminal, electrons flow through the conductor, from negative to positive, until the materials inside the battery are electrically neutral. Whether there is a light or other appliance in the circuit is immaterial to whether or not electrons will flow. We simply place an appliance in the circuit to take advantage of the fact that the battery will send electrons from the negative terminal to the positive terminal if the two terminals are connected.

If we remember that the reason electrons flow is to reduce the excess at the negative terminal and make up the shortage at the positive terminal, it's easy to understand why the circuit must be complete in order for electricity to flow. And incidentally, if the battery is still in good condition, the chemical reaction that caused the imbalance of electrons at the two terminals will continue and the battery will be ready to use again. It might take a few days for the battery to recharge itself, but if it isn't too old it will happen. This is not true of rechargeable batteries; these batteries use different chemicals and must be placed in a charger.

SKILLS: Observing, inferring, communicating, comparing and contrasting, using space-time relationships, formulating hypotheses

Activity 8.4
WHAT IS A SHORT CIRCUIT?

Materials Needed

- Complete circuit constructed in Activity 8.2
- One 25-cm (10-in.) length of copper wire, similar to that used in Activity 8.2, stripped on both ends

Procedure

1. Connect your circuit so there is a complete path and the light turns on.
2. Strip (clean off) the insulation from 1 cm (1/2 in.) in the center of each wire. Does the light still go on?
3. Put the bare ends of the extra piece of wire across the bare sections of your circuit wires. Does the light go on?
4. What do you think has happened? Why?
5. Feel the ends where the bare ends are touching. Do you notice anything?
6. You have made a short circuit. Discuss with your teacher and the other class members what that means.

Figure 8.4-1

Battery and Bulb, Short-circuited

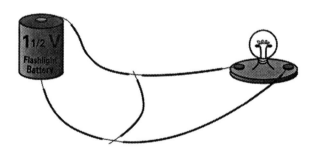

Teacher Information

When the additional wire is placed across the circuit, the light goes out. A general rule in electrical circuits is that electricity will follow the path of least resistance. This means it will follow the shortest, easiest path back to its source (battery). In this example you have made the path shorter and avoided a resistor (the light bulb). If you permit current to flow through the short circuit for more than a few seconds, the wire will begin to heat up. This is caused by providing an easy path for electricity to flow. The amount of electricity going through the wire increases beyond its normal capacity.

Caution: Do not leave the circuit connected this way for more than a few seconds. If the battery is strong the wire might become hot enough to burn fingers, though it will still not cause an electrical shock. It will also run the battery down very rapidly.

SKILLS: Observing, inferring, predicting, communicating, comparing and contrasting, formulating hypotheses, identifying and controlling variables, experimenting

Activity 8.5
HOW CAN YOU MAKE A SWITCH?

(Teacher-supervised activity)

Materials Needed

- Complete circuit used in Activity 8.2
- Metal strip 10 cm (4 in.) long by 2 cm (1 in.) wide
- Strip of wood (lath) 15 cm (6 in.) long
- Two small wood screws
- Hammer and nail
- Screwdriver

Procedure

1. Use the hammer and nail to punch a hole near one end of the metal strip.
2. Use a screw to attach the metal strip near one end of the piece of wood (if you punch a small nail hole in the wood, the screw will go in more easily).
3. Install the other screw in the wood so that the loose end of the metal strip touches but is not attached to it. Bend the metal strip up about 2 cm (1 in.).
4. Cut one of your circuit wires in the middle of the bare place you made when you were constructing a short circuit.
5. Attach one end of the bare wire to each screw.
6. When you finish, your circuit should look like Figure 8.5-1.
7. Can you use the switch to make the light turn on and off?
8. Discuss what the switch does.

Figure 8.5-1

Battery and Bulb with Switch in Circuit

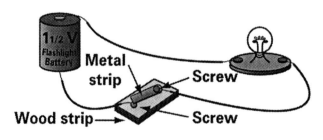

302

For Problem Solvers: In this activity you made a switch. An electrical switch is a device that allows you to easily turn electricity on and off. There are many ways you can make a switch. What other ways can you think of to make a switch? Can you make a switch out of a paper clip? Make several different kinds and test them in your circuit.

Teacher Information

If available, sheet copper should be used because it is easier to cut than sheet metal, and there is less chance of injury from sharp edges and corners. For best results, the wires should be under the screws when they are tightened down.

This circuit has the following parts:

a. A power source (battery).

b. A path through which the current can flow (wire).

c. An appliance (light) to use current.

d. A switch to turn it on and off.

SKILLS: Observing, inferring, measuring, predicting, communicating, identifying and controlling variables, experimenting

Activity 8.6
HOW CAN YOU MAKE A SERIES CIRCUIT?

Materials Needed

- Lantern battery
- Circuit from previous activity, including switch
- Two additional small light sockets with flashlight bulbs
- Two pieces of insulated single-strand copper wire 10 cm (4 in.) long
- Small screwdriver

Procedure

1. For this and some of the following activities, we will use a lantern battery instead of a flashlight battery. It is easier to use and will last longer.
2. In this activity, we will add two lights to our circuit.
3. Test to be certain your circuit will light the bulb.
4. Disconnect one wire from your light socket and connect it to one terminal of another socket with one 10-cm length of wire. Use another 10-cm length of wire to connect the other terminal of your second socket to the third socket. Connect the long wire from the battery to the third socket. When you finish, your circuit should look like Figure 8.6-1.
5. Now close the switch. Do the lights come on? Unscrew one bulb. What happened? Can you explain why?

Figure 8.6-1

Battery, Switch, and Three Bulbs Wired in Series

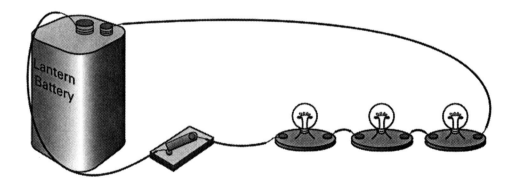

304

Teacher Information

Before letting the children use the lantern batteries, you may want to remove the screw caps on the terminals to remind the children not to leave the wires connected when they are not in use. Lantern batteries have the advantage over flashlight batteries of being easier to handle and simpler to hook up. There is no danger of electrical shock from these batteries.

Be certain the two 10-cm lengths of wire are stripped on both ends. The circuit the students have constructed is called a series circuit because the electric current travels through the wire in one path and the resistors (lights) and switch are all part of that single path. If one portion of a series circuit is missing, the current will not flow, because it must have a complete path *from* the power source *to* the power source. If a light bulb is removed, the path is broken and all the lights go out.

INTEGRATING: Math

SKILLS: Observing, inferring, measuring, predicting, communicating, comparing and contrasting, formulating hypotheses, identifying and controlling variables, experimenting

Activity 8.7
HOW CAN YOU MAKE A PARALLEL CIRCUIT?

Materials Needed

- Series circuit from Activity 8.6
- Screwdriver
- Wire stripper
- Two additional pieces of insulated single-strand copper wire 10 cm (4 in.) long

Procedure

1. Use the additional pieces of wire to change your circuit so it looks like the one in Figure 8.7-1.

Figure 8.7-1

Battery, Switch, and Three Bulbs in Parallel

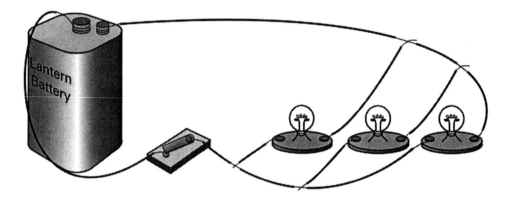

2. Close the switch so all bulbs are lit. Unscrew one bulb. What happened? Unscrew two bulbs.

3. Can you explain how this circuit is different from the one in Activity 8.6?

For Problem Solvers: In this activity and in Activity 8.6 you have learned about series and parallel circuits. You learned that an important difference is that if lights are wired in series, they all go out if one goes out. If they are wired in parallel, one light can go out and the rest of them stay on. Most sets of Christmas lights are wired in series. When one bulb burns out it's very difficult to tell which one is bad. Why do you think manufacturers make them that way? Talk to your family about it. Discuss it with your class. When Christmas season comes along, see how many light sets you can find that are wired in series and how many you can find that are wired in parallel. Which will you buy?

Teacher Information

A parallel circuit provides an independent path for the electric current to travel to each light and back to the power source. The lights will burn brighter because the current does not have to travel through a series of resistors (the other lights). And guess what—when one light goes out, the rest of the lights stay on.

The best living example of series versus parallel wiring comes to us each year at Christmas time. Thousands of perfectly good sets of Christmas lights are replaced each year because they are wired in series. One light goes out on the set and the entire set turns off. It simply isn't worth it to us to replace all of the bulbs one at a time in an effort to determine which bulb really is burned out. We trash the entire set and buy a new set. Manufacturers know that's what we'll do, so they keep making light sets in series. A very simple twist in the manufacturing process would wire the lights in parallel and we could easily replace one burned-out bulb, but we would then use the same set of lights for years and years. That would not sell lights! Search for the box that says something like "When one light goes out, the rest remain lighted." That set is worth much more than the one that invites you to replace the lights one at a time until the set comes on again. Think about that before you buy your next set of Christmas lights.

INTEGRATING: Reading, language arts, math, social studies

SKILLS: Observing, inferring, classifying, predicting, communicating, comparing and contrasting, formulating hypotheses, identifying and controlling variables, experimenting, researching

Activity 8.8
WHAT IS RESISTANCE?

Materials Needed

- Circuit used in Activity 8.1
- Large writing pencil with about 8 cm (3 in.) of wood removed on one half to expose the graphite core

Procedure

1. Touch the ends of the bare wire to the graphite ("lead") core of the pencil, as far apart as possible.
2. Slowly slide the bare wires closer together along the graphite and observe the light.
3. Can you use the information you have learned about conductors to explain this?
4. Have you seen anything like this principle used in a home or an automobile?

Figure 8.8-1

Battery, Bulb, and Lead Pencil

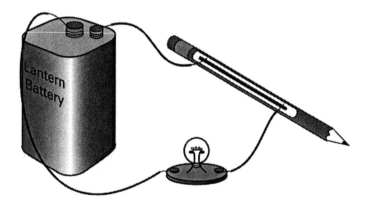

For Problem Solvers: If you have a switch at home that dims the lights, it works in about the same way as the pencil lead you used for this activity. A resistor switch is called a rheostat. This device makes it possible to change the amount of current going to an appliance (light, heater, etc.). Make a list of all the things you can think of that use resistor switches. Think about the kitchen. Think about the car. Share your list with others who are doing this activity and with your teacher.

Teacher Information

This is a demonstration of variable resistance. The core of a lead pencil isn't lead at all, but graphite. Graphite will conduct electric current, but not nearly as well as copper. Because it resists the flow of current, it is an example of one kind of resistor. As the bare copper wires are moved closer together, the resistance is gradually reduced and the light gradually becomes brighter. This is the principle of the rheostat used to dim automobile dash lights and some lights in homes, theaters, and public buildings.

INTEGRATING: Language arts, social studies

SKILLS: Observing, inferring, classifying, predicting, communicating, comparing and contrasting, formulating hypotheses, identifying and controlling variables, experimenting, researching

Activity 8.9
HOW DOES ELECTRIC CURRENT AFFECT A COMPASS?

Materials Needed

- Insulated 22-gauge copper wire, 50 cm (20 in.) long, stripped on each end
- Lantern battery
- Compass

Procedure

1. From your study of magnetism, do you remember that a compass is a magnet suspended so it can turn freely? The magnetic field of the earth causes it to point north unless another magnet or magnetic material comes near it.
2. Put your compass flat on the table and notice in which direction it is pointing.
3. Connect one end of the wire to a terminal of the battery and place the wire across the top of the compass.
4. Touch the other end of the wire to the second terminal of the battery (don't connect it).
5. Move the wire to different positions on top of the compass and observe the needle as you send current through the wire.
6. What is happening? Discuss this with the class.

Figure 8.9-1

Battery, Wire, and Compass

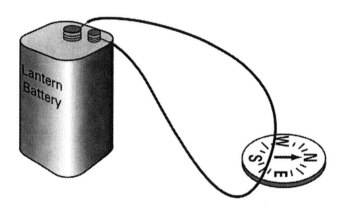

Teacher Information

When an electric current flows through a wire, a magnetic field is formed around the wire. Through this activity, students may decide that electricity is in some way related to magnetism. The next activity will help them visualize what is really happening.

CAUTION: When the copper wire is connected, it creates a short circuit. The wire should be connected only momentarily; otherwise, it will get very hot and the electricity will drain rapidly. Many fires are started by short circuits.

SKILLS: Observing, inferring, predicting, communicating, formulating hypotheses, identifying and controlling variables, experimenting

Activity 8.10
WHAT HAPPENS WHEN ELECTRIC CURRENT FLOWS THROUGH A WIRE?

Materials Needed

- Circuit used in Activity 8.9
- Iron filings
- 5 × 7 inch card

Procedure

1. Connect one end of the wire to a terminal of the battery.
2. Place the card flat and level over the middle part of the wire.
3. Connect the other end of the wire to the battery and quickly sprinkle iron filings on the card.
4. Disconnect the wire and observe the card. *Do not* leave the wire connected to the battery for more than a few seconds at a time.
5. Have you seen something like this before? Look carefully at the filings.
6. What conclusions can you make? Discuss this with the class.

Figure 8.10-1

Battery, Wire, Card, and Iron Filings

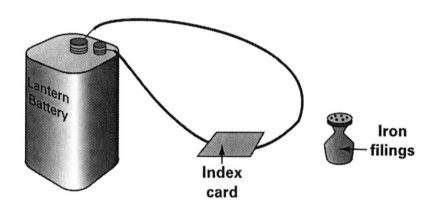

Teacher Information

When current flows through the wire, the iron filings will line up along the path of the wire because of the magnetic field created around it. Note that iron filings do not line up with the wire, but perpendicular to it instead. This indicates that the lines of force of the magnetic field are perpendicular to the direction of the flow of current.

SKILLS: Observing, inferring, predicting, communicating, formulating hypotheses, identifying and controlling variables, experimenting

Activity 8.11
WHAT IS AN ELECTROMAGNET?

Materials Needed

- 1 m (1 yd.) of 22-gauge insulated copper wire stripped on both ends
- Lantern battery
- Large iron nail no longer than 10 cm (4 in.)
- Paper clips

Procedure

1. In Activities 8.9 and 8.10, we learned that when an electric current flows through a wire, a magnetic field is formed around the wire.

2. Coil the wire ten times around the nail. Bring the nail near some paper clips. What happened?

3. Attach one end of the wire to a terminal of the battery. Bring the nail near some paper clips. Touch the other end of the wire to the other terminal of the battery. What happened?

4. Hold the nail above the table and disconnect the wire from one terminal of the battery.

5. What happened?

6. Explain why you think this happened.

Figure 8.11-1

Electromagnet with Paper Clips

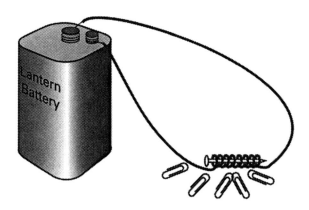

Teacher Information

The nail will not pick up paper clips until current flows through the coil of wire. When current flows through the coil of wire, a magnetic field is created around the coil and causes the soft iron nail to become a temporary magnet and attract the paper clips. When the electric current is cut off, the nail will lose its magnetism and the clips will fall off.

The nail you use should be no longer than about 10 cm (4 in.). Very large, thick nails will sometimes retain their magnetic properties for a longer period of time and will not release the paper clips readily when the current is turned off.

INTEGRATING: Math

SKILLS: Observing, inferring, comparing and contrasting, identifying and controlling variables, experimenting

Activity 8.12
WHAT IS A WAY TO CHANGE THE STRENGTH OF AN ELECTROMAGNET?

Materials Needed

- Same as for Activity 8.11

Procedure

1. As you perform the activities with electromagnets, remember not to leave the electro-magnets connected to the battery for more than a few seconds at a time.

2. Use your electromagnet with 10 coils to pick up as many paper clips as you can at one time. Record the number of clips it picked up.

3. Wrap 10 more coils of wire around the nail, connect it to the battery, and see how many clips you can pick up at one time. Record the number.

4. What do you think would happen if you wrapped 10 more coils around your electro-magnet? Try it.

5. What can you say about this?

Teacher Information

Increasing the number of coils of wire will increase the strength of the magnetic field. This is one way to make an electromagnet stronger. Using a stronger electric current will also increase the force of an electromagnet.

INTEGRATING: Math

SKILLS: Observing, inferring, measuring, predicting, communicating, comparing and contrasting, formulating hypotheses, identifying and controlling variables, experimenting

Activity 8.13
WHAT IS ANOTHER WAY TO CHANGE THE STRENGTH OF AN ELECTROMAGNET?

Materials Needed

- Two lantern batteries
- 1 m of insulated copper wire
- One 10-cm (4-in.) length of insulated copper wire stripped at both ends
- One large nail
- Box of paper clips
- Paper and pencil

Procedure

1. Make an electromagnet with ten coils of wire wrapped around the nail.

2. Use one battery with your electromagnet and see how many clips you can pick up at one time. Record the results.

3. Observe your lantern battery. Notice it has a terminal (connector) in the center and one near the outside edge. Unless otherwise marked, the center terminal is called positive (+) and the outer terminal is called negative (–).

4. Use the 10-cm wire to connect a second battery in series (connect the wire from the negative terminal of one battery to the positive terminal of the other battery). This increases the voltage to the sum total of the voltage of both batteries.

5. Connect your electromagnet as shown in Figure 8.13-1 and pick up as many clips as you can. Record the number of clips.

6. What do you think would happen if you used two batteries and 20 coils of wire? Try it.

Figure 8.13-1

Electromagnet with Two Batteries and Paper Clips

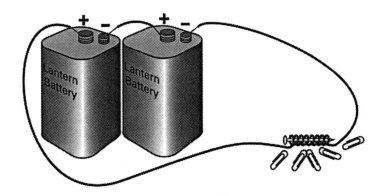

For Problem Solvers: In this activity and Activity 8.12, you learned two ways to change the strength of an electromagnet. Earlier you learned how to make a switch. Build an electromagnet with a switch in the circuit, so it's easy to turn the magnet on and off. Try different sizes and types of nails and bolts as the core. See if you can find a brass bolt to try as the core. Find a steel bolt to use instead of iron. Find out what works best and what doesn't work so well.

Use the shaft of a screwdriver as the core of an electromagnet. How does it work differently from the nail or bolt? Does it release all the paper clips when you turn off the power? Oops.

Do some research about electromagnets. Make a list of some ways they are used.

Teacher Information

Series wiring is commonly used to increase the voltage of dry-cell batteries. Six- and nine-volt batteries contain four and six cells. Each cell produces 1.5 volts, and when they are connected in series the voltage is added. More about batteries and how they work is developed later in this section.

INTEGRATING: Math

SKILLS: Observing, inferring, measuring, predicting, communicating, comparing and contrasting, formulating hypotheses, identifying and controlling variables, experimenting

Activity 8.14
WHAT HAPPENS WHEN CURRENT FLOWING THROUGH A WIRE CHANGES DIRECTION?

Materials Needed

- 50-cm (20 in.) length of insulated single-strand copper wire stripped at both ends
- Lantern battery
- Compass

Procedure

1. Place the center of the wire over the compass as you did in Activity 8.9. Touch the ends of the wire to the terminals of the battery and watch the needle.

2. Now touch the ends of the wire to the opposite terminals of the battery. Since electricity flows *from* the negative (–) terminal *to* the positive (+), you have reversed the flow of current through the wire.

3. Switch the ends of the wires several times. What happens to the compass needle?

4. Discuss your observations with your group.

Figure 8.14-1

**Compasses Near Wires
with Current Flowing in Opposite Directions**

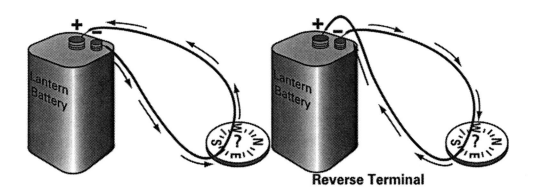

Reverse Terminal

319

Teacher Information

The direction of flow of electric current has not been a factor until now. At this point you should emphasize that electricity that is produced by a battery flows in one direction through the wire. It flows from the negative terminal of the battery to the positive terminal when a path is provided. We will discover later that some current moves back and forth, or *alternates*, within a wire.

Each time the direction of the flow of current changes in this activity, the compass needle will reverse, indicating that the poles of the electromagnetic field reverse when the direction of the flow of current is reversed.

SKILLS: Observing, inferring, communicating, comparing and contrasting, formulating hypotheses, identifying and controlling variables, experimenting

Activity 8.15
HOW DOES THE DIRECTION OF THE FLOW OF CURRENT AFFECT AN ELECTROMAGNET?

Materials Needed

- Electromagnet used in Activity 8.13
- Lantern battery
- Compass
- Two bar magnets
- String 20 cm (8 in.) long

Procedure

1. **Important: Throughout this activity, disconnect one wire from the battery except for the moment that you are using the electromagnet.**

2. Place the compass flat on the table. Connect your electromagnet to the battery and bring one point of it near the compass. Observe which end of the needle points to the electromagnet.

3. Switch the ends of the wires leading to the battery terminals. What happens to the compass needle?

4. Suspend one bar magnet from the piece of string. Bring each end of the other bar magnet near the N end of the suspended magnet. What happened? This should help you remember a characteristic of magnets that you learned when you were studying magnetism.

5. Bring your nail and coil of wire near both ends of the suspended bar magnet (don't connect it to the battery yet). What happened?

6. Connect the wires to the battery and bring the pointed end of the nail near the N end of the suspended bar magnet.

7. Now turn your electromagnet around so the flat end of the nail comes near the N end of the suspended bar magnet. What happened?

8. Keep the flat end near the suspended bar magnet and reverse the flow of current through your electromagnet by switching the wires on the battery terminals. Do this several times and observe the behavior of the bar magnet (don't move the electromagnet).

9. Describe your observations. What can you say about this characteristic of an electromagnet?

Figure 8.15-1

Electromagnet, Compass, and Suspended Magnet

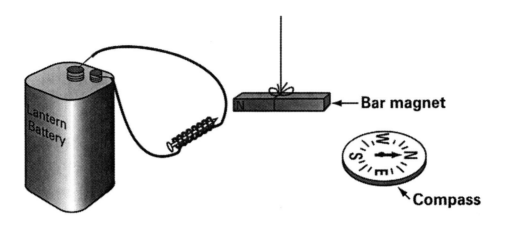

For Problem Solvers: You have discovered a very important relationship between magnetism and electricity. All electric motors work on two principles that you have learned—first, that a flow of electricity through a wire creates a magnetic field around the wire, and second, changing the direction of the current reverses the poles of an electromagnet.

Now do some research and see how much you can learn about electric motors and how they work on these principles of magnetism and electricity. You might want to even try building a simple electric motor that actually runs.

Teacher Information

Like permanent magnets, electromagnets have poles. When the direction of the flow of current is reversed (in this case by switching wires on the terminals), the poles of the electromagnet reverse. This characteristic of electromagnets gives them an advantage over permanent magnets in some applications. Because of this phenomenon, electric motors are possible. To demonstrate this try the following:

Have one student hold the electromagnet near the suspended bar magnet. Have another student touch the wires to the battery. As soon as the poles of the two magnets come close to each other, switch the wires on the terminals of the battery. The pole of the electromagnet, which was attracting a pole of the bar magnet, will reverse and repel the same pole of the bar magnet (remember opposites attract, likes repel). With practice, the students can make the bar magnet spin around by reversing the poles of the electromagnet. Now all that is needed is a device to switch the direction of current automatically and you have a simple electric motor.

SKILLS: Observing, inferring, communicating, comparing and contrasting, formulating hypotheses, identifying and controlling variables, experimenting

Activity 8.16
HOW CAN YOU TELL IF ELECTRIC CURRENT IS FLOWING THROUGH A WIRE?

Materials Needed

- 10 m (11 yds.) of 24-gauge insulated copper wire stripped at both ends
- Three 10-cm (4-in.) lengths of wire
- One 30-cm (12-in.) length of wire
- Sewing needle
- One 20-cm (8-in.) strip of wood lath
- Lantern battery
- Thread
- Paper clip
- Bar magnet

Procedure

1. Make a coil with your long piece of wire by winding it around a lantern battery or small fruit jar. Leave about 50 cm (20 in.) of wire at each end.

2. Remove the coil from the battery and use the 10-cm (4-in.) pieces of wire to hold the coil together in three places.

3. Use the 30-cm (12-in.) wire to secure the coil in an upright position on the lath.

4. Magnetize the needle by rubbing it 30 times in the same direction with a bar magnet. It should now pick up a paper clip.

5. Use thread to hang the needle balanced in the middle of the coil. Compare your finished product with Figure 8.16-1.

6. We have learned that electric current flowing through a wire creates a magnetic field around the wire. We found that when the wire is coiled, the magnetic field is stronger. The needle is a magnet. If an electric current flows through the coil of wire, what do you predict will happen to the needle?

7. Touch the bare ends of your coil of wire to the dry cell. Was your prediction correct?

8. This is a simple galvanometer used to detect the direction and flow of electric current. Touch the wires to a battery and notice the direction the needle points. Now, switch the wires on the terminals of the battery and notice the direction the needle points. This device can be used to detect the flow of even small amounts of electric current.

Figure 8.16-1

Coil of Wire with Suspended Needle

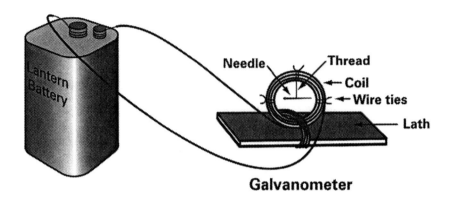

For Problem Solvers: In this activity you made a galvanometer. Design your own galvanometer. Try more windings in the coil. Try fewer windings in the coil. Try placing a directional compass within the coil instead of a suspended needle on a thread. What other variables can you think of to change it and perhaps make it better or easier to use?

Teacher Information

Ideally, each child should construct a galvanometer. Groups of three or four students working on one galvanometer should be maximum. If a student is able to construct, explain, and predict the behavior of a galvanometer, it will indicate that he or she understands some of the important ideas about magnetism and electricity.

Your problem solvers will substitute a directional compass for the suspended needle.

Very thin insulated wire is best for this activity in order to provide many windings without excessive bulk. The more windings the galvanometer has, the more sensitive it will be to small amounts of current electricity.

SKILLS: Observing, inferring, communicating, comparing and contrasting, formulating hypotheses, identifying and controlling variables, experimenting

Activity 8.17
HOW IS ELECTRICITY PRODUCED BY CHEMICALS?

Materials Needed

- Wide-mouthed glass cup or jar
- 8-cm (3-in.) zinc strip
- 8-cm (3-in.) copper strip
- Salt
- Lemon juice
- Water
- Galvanometer

Procedure

1. Pour water into the jar or cup until it is three fourths full.
2. Dissolve two teaspoons of salt in the water.
3. Tightly connect one end of your galvanometer to the copper strip and put it in the glass. Bend the zinc strip into a hook on one end and hang it inside the glass.
4. Wait a few seconds. Then observe the needle of your galvanometer as you firmly touch the other wire to the zinc strip.
5. What happened? Wait a few seconds, then touch the wire to the zinc again.
6. Discuss your observations with your group.

Figure 8.17-1

Homemade Cell and Galvanometer

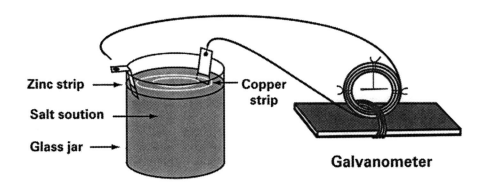

Zinc strip

Salt soution

Glass jar

Copper strip

Galvanometer

For Problem Solvers: Try vinegar as the electrolyte instead of saltwater, and do the activity again. (Be sure to rinse the jar thoroughly whenever you change the electrolyte.) Try lemon juice. Replace the copper strip with the carbon rod. Try a penny in the place of the copper strip, and a silver dime instead of the zinc (you'll have to find a dime that's several years old in order to get silver).

Teacher Information

When placed in an acid or base (alkaline) solution, some materials give up or take on electrons readily through a chemical process called ionization. Zinc metal builds up electrons and becomes the negative terminal. When a negative material (zinc) is connected to a positive material (copper or carbon) in the solution, electrons flow along the path from the zinc to the copper or carbon. In this circuit the galvanometer is in the path and detects the flow of current. You can explain this using the diagram in Figure 8.17-1 by adding plus (+) along the side of the copper or carbon rod and minus (–) along the zinc strip.

The reason the children are asked to wait a few seconds before touching the wire to the zinc is to allow time to build opposite charges on the copper and zinc strips.

Carbon rods and zinc strips may be obtained by dismantling old-style flashlight batteries. A carbon core runs through the center and the case is made of zinc. The newer long-life batteries are constructed differently, though the same basic principles apply as they develop an electrical charge. Six-volt lantern batteries contain four 1.5-volt cells.

SKILLS: Observing, inferring, communicating, comparing and contrasting, formulating hypotheses, identifying and controlling variables, experimenting

Activity 8.18
HOW DOES A LANTERN BATTERY
OR FLASHLIGHT BATTERY WORK?

(Teacher-supervised activity or teacher demonstration)

Materials Needed

- Flashlight battery (old style–lead-acid) cut in half
- Paper and pencil
- Figure 8.17 (for comparison)

Procedure

1. Compare the half battery with the materials you used in Activity 8.17.

2. Except for the galvanometer, all the types of materials used in Activity 8.17 can be identified in the battery. Can you find them?

3. Draw a picture of a battery cut in half. Label the parts. Compare your picture with those made by other members of the group. Explain how you think it works.

4. Have you ever seen a battery leak and damage a flashlight? Batteries contain a weak acid or alkaline solution, usually in a tightly packed absorbent material. Since your battery is old, this solution has probably dried up.

Figure 8.18-1

Cross Section of Lantern Battery

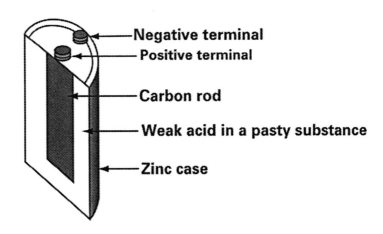

For Problem Solvers: With close supervision, dismantle a flashlight battery that is a newer, long-life variety. How is it different? Do some research and find out what materials are in this particular battery and how they react together to cause electrons to flow.

Teacher Information

By the end of this experience, students should be able to explain in general terms how electricity is produced by chemical means. Elementary-age students should simply understand that certain materials will develop a positive or negative charge in the presence of an acid or a base (salt), and that when these materials are connected by a conductor (wire), electricity flows through the conductor from negative to positive.

The battery shown in this activity is the lead-acid battery, which has been used for many years. Newer long-life batteries operate on the same principles, but they use different materials. You might choose to open both for comparison.

The old-style tall 1.5 volt lantern battery and the old-style lead-acid flashlight battery are constructed similar to the one shown. The six-volt lantern battery has four such cells connected in series. The nine-volt lantern battery has six such cells, again connected in series. Each cell produces one and one-half volts.

Technically the word battery implies a collection, so the four-cell and six-cell units are true batteries, while the single units are more properly called "cells." However, the single-cell unit is so commonly called a battery that to carefully distinguish between them is probably more confusing than helpful. Flashlight cells are even labeled as *batteries.*

Note: Batteries can be cut with a hacksaw.

CAUTION: This activity involves the use of cut-open flashlight cells, exposing acid substances. Close supervision is very important to keep the acid from getting in eyes or on skin, or on clothing or other materials that might be damaged by the acid. Wash hands thoroughly after handling the cells.

SKILLS: Observing, inferring, comparing and contrasting, formulating hypotheses

Activity 8.19
HOW CAN ELECTRICITY BE PRODUCED BY A LEMON?

(Close supervision is required)

Materials Needed

- Large, fresh lemon
- Zinc and copper strips
- Galvanometer
- Knife

Procedure

1. Just for fun, let's try to make a battery from a lemon.

2. Make two small slits in the lemon, close together, with the knife.

3. Attach the copper strip to one wire of the galvanometer and insert it into one of the slits in the lemon.

4. Push the zinc strip into the other slit. The zinc strip must not touch the copper strip.

5. Wait a few seconds, then observe the needle on the galvanometer as you firmly touch the wire to the zinc strip. What happened? Wait a few seconds more and try again.

6. Using information you learned in Activities 8.17 and 8.18, explain what is happening.

7. Could you use another fruit such as a grapefruit or a tomato? Try it.

Figure 8.19-1

Lemon Cell with Galvanometer

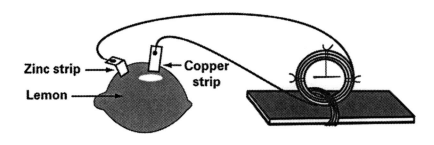

For Problem Solvers: There are many chemicals that can be used to create a flow of electrons. Try this activity with other citrus fruits. Try it with the juice in a cup instead of using the fruit itself. Try a penny in the place of the copper strip, and a silver dime (you'll have to find one that's several years old to get silver) instead of the zinc. Take it from there and continue your exploration. Be sure to write everything you use and what happened, so you will remember and be able to share your information.

Teacher Information

The lemon contains citric acid, which will cause the same reaction as other weak acids. Tomatoes and citrus fruits usually contain enough acid to affect the galvanometer.

SKILLS: Observing, inferring, communicating, comparing and contrasting, formulating hypotheses, identifying and controlling variables, experimenting

Activity 8.20
HOW CAN MECHANICAL ENERGY PRODUCE ELECTRICITY?

Materials Needed

- Galvanometer
- Galvanometer coil without needle
- Strong magnet

Procedure

1. Securely attach the wires from one coil to the other.
2. Hold the coil without the needle in one hand and with the other hand move the strong magnet back and forth through the center of the coil or around the coil.
3. Observe the needle on the galvanometer. Can you see a relationship in what is happening?
4. Think of some words to describe the behavior of the needle. Discuss this with your teacher and other students.

Figure 8.20-1

Coil of Wire, Galvanometer, and Two Magnets

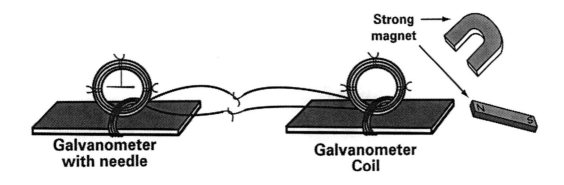

For Problem Solvers: Can you use the idea from this activity to design a generator? Figure out a way that you can spin a magnet within a coil of wire, or spin a coil of wire within a magnetic field. Try to design your generator with more than one coil or more than one magnet.

Teacher Information

When electric current flows through a coil of wire, a magnetic field is created around the wire. You will remember that from your experience in making electromagnets; that's why electromagnets work. In this activity the opposite is happening. Instead of producing a magnetic field around a coil of wire by sending an electric current through the wire, we are causing electrons to flow by moving a coil of wire within a magnetic field. Because of this phenomenon, the generator, which turns coils of wire through a magnetic field, has made electricity relatively inexpensive and plentiful.

Observe the needle closely as the magnet goes through the coil and you will notice that it reverses the direction in which it is pointing each time the magnet moves back and forth. This shows that as the magnetic field moves back and forth, the electrons move back and forth or *alternate* their direction within the wire. Electricity produced in this manner is called *alternating current.*

If you examine a small hand generator (crank type) you will notice it is nothing more than a coil of wire turned mechanically in a magnetic field. Commercial electricity is usually produced by water or steam. A turbine, which is an enclosed wheel with curved blades, spins rapidly when water or steam is directed into it under great pressure. This provides the mechanical energy to turn huge generators. Atomic energy is sometimes used to heat water and create steam to turn the turbines.

Many people think that hydroelectric plants somehow *extract* electricity from water as the water rushes through the dam. The dam is engineered to direct falling water through turbines, providing the power to spin coils of wire within magnetic fields, stimulating the flow of electrons through the wire. See your encyclopedia for further information.

Figure 8.20-2

Generator

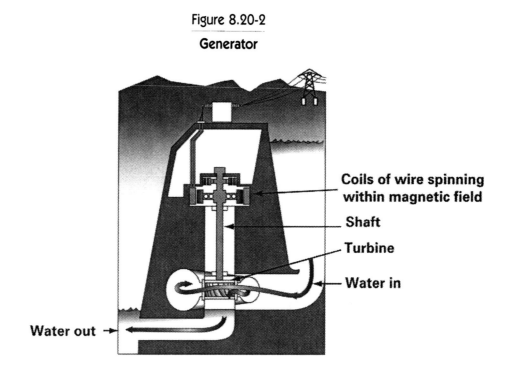

SKILLS: Observing, inferring, communicating, formulating hypotheses, identifying and controlling variables, experimenting

Activity 8.21
HOW CAN SUNLIGHT PRODUCE ELECTRICITY?

Materials Needed

- Solar cells
- Galvanometer
- Light source

Procedure

1. In recent years scientists have been trying to find new sources of electricity to replace our rapidly diminishing fossil fuel resources (coal and oil). A most promising source is solar (sun) energy. Look at your solar cell. When light strikes this cell, a very small amount of electrical energy is produced.

2. Connect your cell to the galvanometer and shine a bright light on it. As you turn the light on and off, observe the needle on the galvanometer. What happens to the needle?

Figure 8.21-1

Solar Cell in Galvanometer Circuit, with Light Source

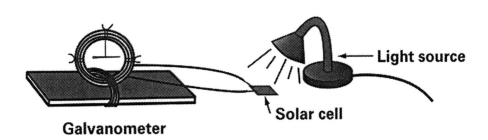

Galvanometer   Solar cell   Light source

For Problem Solvers: If you can get some solar cells, learn how to connect them to operate a small light bulb. Perhaps you can find some discarded calculators and use the solar cells from them.

Do some research and see what you can learn about solar energy as a source of electricity. Make a list of all of the things you can find that are powered by solar energy. Will it likely ever be a major source of electricity for our homes and factories?

Can solar energy be used as a power source for electric cars? Write to General Motors (ask about their Sun Racer) and to Ford Motor Company and ask for information about their research on solar batteries and solar-powered cars.

Teacher Information

Solar energy is becoming increasingly important and common in our lives. Most children have seen solar cells used in calculators, cameras, and other devices that require small amounts of electricity.

The space program has rapidly expanded the development of this energy source. Satellites use electricity produced in this manner to recharge the batteries that provide electrical power.

A major obstacle to wide use of solar power is the limited amount of electric current each cell can produce. Huge areas of solar cells are required to produce significant amounts of electrical energy. The current produced flows in one direction, just as in flashlight batteries. Also, on the earth, solar cells as primary producers of electrical energy are limited to daylight hours and further inhibited by cloudy days.

Solar cells (often in clusters connected in series) can be obtained from many electronic supply stores.

INTEGRATING: Social studies

SKILLS: Observing, inferring, classifying, communicating, comparing and contrasting, formulating hypotheses, researching

Activity 8.22
HOW CAN ELECTRICITY HELP US COMMUNICATE?

Materials Needed

- Two small light sockets with bulbs
- Two switches
- Lantern battery
- Six 1-m (1-yd.) lengths of insulated copper wire

Procedure

1. Use your materials to construct a circuit like the one in Figure 8.22-1.
2. Press one switch. What happened?
3. Release the first switch and press the second one. What happened?
4. Press both switches at once.
5. Can you think of some use for a device like this?
6. If it is available, you could splice more wire into the circuit and take one switch and light into another room.

Figure 8.22-1

Two Telegraphs Wired to One Battery

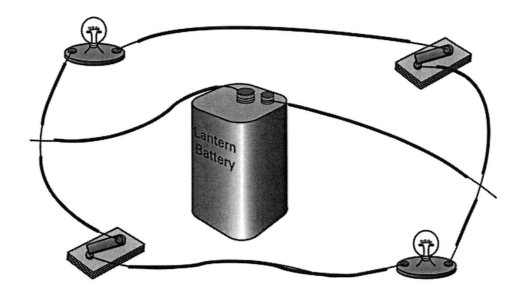

For Problem Solvers: Look up the Morse Code in an encyclopedia. If you and a friend would care to learn the Morse Code, you could have a lot of fun sending messages to each other. Or you might prefer to create your own code. Set up your telegraph sets so that you can be in separate rooms, or in separate parts of the room, and make each other's light blink with your switch.

Teacher Information

This is a variation of the telegraph. There are several ways to wire the circuit. This one is parallel. The original telegraph sets were wired in series so all keys but one had to be closed and all messages went through all the *sounders* in the circuit. Telegraph offices often followed the railroads and needed only one wire on the poles. The iron rails were used as the second or *ground* wire. The original telegraph, patented by Morse, used an electromagnet to attract a magnetic material (soft iron) and make a loud clicking sound. Telegraphers were trained to hear combinations of long and short "dots and dashes" to represent letters of the alphabet. This is called the Morse Code.

The completion of the transcontinental telegraph near the end of the Civil War was extremely significant. For the first time, a message could travel across the nation in seconds rather than in weeks. The circuit above uses the electric light, which was not invented until much later.

In addition to the activity suggested in the "For Problem Solvers" section, your motivated students might enjoy designing and constructing a telegraph using electromagnets.

INTEGRATING: Social studies

SKILLS: Communicating, comparing and contrasting, identifying and controlling variables

BIBLIOGRAPHY

Selected Professional Texts

Carin, Arthur A., *Teaching Science Through Discovery* (7th ed.). New York: Macmillan Publishing Co., 1993.

Esler, William K., and Mary K. Esler, *Teaching Elementary Science* (6th ed.). Belmont, CA: Wadsworth Publishing Co., 1993.

Gega, Peter C., *Science in Elementary Education* (7th ed.). New York: Macmillan Publishing Co., 1994.

Tolman, Marvin N., and Garry R. Hardy, *Discovering Elementary Science: Method, Content, and Problem-Solving Activities*. Needham Heights, MA: Allyn & Bacon, 1995.

Victor, Edward, and Richard D. Kellough, *Science for the Elementary School* (7th ed.). New York: Macmillan Publishing Company, 1993.

Periodicals for Teachers and Children

Astronomy. Astro Media Corp., 625 E. St. Paul Ave., Milwaukee, WI 53202.

Audubon. National Audubon Society, 950 Third Ave., New York, NY 10022

Cricket. Open Court Publishing Co., Box 100, LaSalle, IL 61301. Published monthly.

The Curious Naturalist. Massachusetts Audubon Society, South Lincoln, MA 01773. Nine issues per year.

Discover. Time Inc., 3435 Wilshire Blvd., Los Angeles, CA 90010

Ladybug. Carus Publishing Co., 315 Fifth St., Peru, IL 61354. Published monthly.

National Geographic. National Geographic Society, 17th and M Sts. NW, Washington, DC 20036

National Geographic School Bulletin. National Geographic Society, 17th and M Sts. NW, Washington, DC 20036. Published weekly during the regular school year.

National Geographic World. National Geographic Society, 17th and M Sts. NW, Washington, DC 20036.

Natural History. American Museum of Natural History, Central Park West at 79th St., New York, NY 10024

Odyssey. AstroMedia, 625 E. St. Paul Ave., Milwaukee, WI 53202. Published monthly.

Ranger Rick. 1412 16th St. NW, Washington, DC 20036. Eight issues per year.

Science. American Association for the Advancement of Science, 1515 Massachusetts Ave. N.W., Washington, DC 20005

Science and Children. National Science Teachers Association, 1840 Wilson Blvd., Arlington, VA 22201. Published monthly during the regular school year.

Science Digest. 3 Park Avenue, New York, NY 10016. Published monthly.

Science Scope. National Science Teachers Association, 1840 Wilson Blvd., Arlington, VA 22201. Published monthly during the regular school year.

Smithsonian. Smithsonian Associates, 900 Jefferson Dr., Washington, DC 20560

Super Science. Scholastic, Inc., 730 Broadway, New York, NY 10003-9538.

3–2–1 Contact. Children's Television Workshop, P.O. Box 2933, Boulder, CO 80322. Published monthly during the regular school year.

SELECTED SOURCES OF FREE AND INEXPENSIVE MATERIALS FOR ELEMENTARY SCIENCE

Note: Requests for free materials should be made in writing and on school or district letter-head. Only one letter per class should be sent to a given organization. It is a courtesy, when requesting free materials, to provide postage and a return envelope. It is most important to send a thank-you letter when free materials have been received.

The following list includes only those organizations and agencies who specifically approved their being included in the list.

American Gas Association
Education Programs
1515 Wilson Blvd.
Arlington, VA 22209

American Museum of Natural History
Education Dept.
Central Park W. at 79th St.
New York, NY 10024-5192

American Petroleum Institute
Public Relations Dept.
1220 L St. NW
Washington, DC 20005

American Water Works Association
Strudent Programs Manager
6666 W. Quincy Ave.
Denver, CO 80235

Animal Welfare Institute
P.O. Box 3650
Washington, DC 20007

Freebies: The Magazine with Something for Nothing
1145 Eugenia Place
Carpinteria, CA 93013

National Aeronautics & Space Administration
Education Services Branch FEE
Washington, DC 20546

National Cotton Council of America
Communications Services
P.O. Box 12285
Memphis, TN 38182-0285

National Geographic Society
1145 17th St. NW
Washington, DC 20036

National Institute of Dental Research
P.O. Box 547-93
Washington, DC 20032

Procter & Gamble
Educational Services
P.O. Box 599
Cincinnati, OH 45201-0599

For more comprehensive listings of sources of free and inexpensive materials, see the following sources. Annual editions are available for purchase from: Educators Progress Service, 214 Center St., Randolph, WI 53956.

Educators Guide to Free Audio and Visual Materials

Educators Guide to Free Films

Educators Guide to Free Filmstrips and Slides

Educators Guide to Free Science Materials

SELECTED SCIENCE SUPPLY HOUSES

American Science & Surplus/Jerryco
601 Linden Place
Evanston, IL 60202

Arbor Scientific
P.O. Box 2750
Ann Arbor, MI 48106-2750

Astronomical Society of the Pacific
390 Ashton Ave.
San Francisco, CA 94112

Baxter Diagnostics, Inc.
Scientific Products Division
1430 Waukegan Rd.
McGaw Park, IL 60085-6787

Brock Optical
P.O. Box 940831
Maitland, FL 32794

Carolina Biological Supply Co.
2700 York Rd.
Burlington, NC 27215

Celestial Products, Inc.
P.O. Box 801
Middleburg, VA 22117

Central Scientific Co. (CENCO)
11222 Melrose Ave.
Franklin Park, IL 60131

Chem Shop
1151 S. Redwood Rd.
Salt Lake City, UT 84104

Creative Teaching Associates
P.O. Box 7766
Fresno, CA 93747

Cuisenaire Co. of America, Inc.
P.O. Box 5026
White Plains, NY 10602-5026

Dale Seymour Publications
P.O. Box 10888
Palo Alto, CA 94303-0879

Delta Education
P.O. Box 915
Hudson, NH 03051-0915

Denoyer-Geppert Science Co.
5225 Ravenswood Ave.
Chicago, IL 60640-2028

Didax Educational Resources
One Centennial Dr.
Peabody, MA 01960

Discovery Corner
Lawrence Hall of Science
University of California
Berkeley, CA 94720

Edmund Scientific
101 E. Gloucester Pike
Barrington, NJ 08007-1380

Educational Rocks & Minerals
P.O. Box 574
Florence, MA 01060

Energy Sciences
16728 Oakmont Ave.
Gaithersburg, MD 20877

Estes Industries
1295 H St.
Penrose, CO 81240

Fisher Scientific
4901 W. LeMoyne St.
Chicago, IL 60651

Flinn Scientific, Inc.
131 Flinn St.
P.O. Box 219
Batavia, IL 60510

Forestry Suppliers, Inc.
P.O. Box 8397
Jackson, MS 39284-8397

Frey Scientific
905 Hickory Lane
P.O. Box 8101
Mansfield, OH 44901-8101

General Supply Corp.
303 Commerce Park Dr.
P.O. Box 9347
Jackson, MS 39286-9347

Grau-Hall Scientific
6501 Elvas Ave.
Sacramento, CA 95819

Hawks, Owls & Wildlife
R.D. 1, Box 293
Buskirk, NY 12028

Hubbard Scientific
3101 Iris Ave., Suite 215
Boulder, CO 80301

Idea Factory, Inc.
10710 Dixon Dr.
Riverview, FL 33569

Ideal School Supply Co.
11000 S. Lavergne Ave.
Oak Lawn, IL 60453

Insights Visual Productions
P.O. Box 230644
Encinitas, CA 92023-0644

Let's Get Growing
1900-B Commercial Way
Santa Cruz, CA 95065

Nasco
901 Janesville Ave.
Fort Atkinson, WI 53538-0901

National Geographic Society
1145 17th St. NW
Washington, DC 20036

National Wildlife Federation
1400 Sixteenth St. NW
Washington, DC 20036-2266

Radio Shack
Tandy Corp.
Fort Worth, TX 76102

Sargent-Welch Scientific Co.
911 Commerce Ct.
Buffalo Grove, IL 60089

Science Kit
777 E. Park Dr.
Tonawanda, NY 14150

The Science Man
P.O. Box 56036
Harwood Hts., IL 60656

Scott Resources
P.O. Box 2121F
Ft. Collins, CO 80522

Southwest Mineral Supply
P.O. Box 323
Santa Fe, NM 87504

Summit Learning
P.O. Box 493F
Ft. Collins, CO 80522

Tap Plastics
6475 Sierra Lane
Dublin, CA 94568

Teachers' Laboratory, Inc.
P.O. Box 6480
Brattleboro, VT 05302-6480

Tops Learning Systems
10970 S. Mulino Rd.
Canby, OR 97013

Uptown Sales, Inc.
33 N. Main St.
Chambersburg, PA 17201

SELECTED SUPPLIERS OF VIDEO TAPES, VIDEODISCS, AND CD-ROM FOR ELEMENTARY SCIENCE

Beacon Films
1560 Sherman Ave., Suite 100
Evanston, IL 60201

Carolina Biological Supply Co.
2700 York Road
Burlington, NC 27215

Churchill Media
12210 Nebraska Ave.
Los Angeles, CA 90025-3600

Elementary Specialties
917 Hickory Lane
Mansfield, OH 44901-8105

Emerging Technology Consultants, Inc.
P.O. Box 120444
St. Paul, MN 55112

Encyclopaedia Britannica Educational Corp.
310 S. Michigan Ave.
Chicago, IL 60604

Everyday Weather Project
State University of New York College at Brockport
Brockport, NY 14420

Hubbard Scientific, Inc.
1120 Halbleib Rd.
P.O. Box 760
Chippewa Falls, WI 54729

Insights Visual Productions, Inc.
P.O. Box 230644
Encinitas, CA 92023

Instructional Video
P.O. Box 21
Maumee, OH 43537

Kons Scientific Co., Inc.
P.O. Box 3
Germantown, WI 53022-0003

Miramar Productions
200 Second Ave., W.
Seattle, WA 98119-4204

Modern Talking Picture Service, Inc.
5000 Park St. N.
St. Petersburg, FL 33709

National Geographic Society
Educational Services
1145 17th St. NW
Washington, D.C. 20036-4688

Optical Data Corporation
30 Technology Drive
Warren, New Jersey 07059

Phoenix/BFA Films and Video, Inc.
2349 Chaffee Dr.
St. Louis, MO 63146

The Planetary Society, Education Div.
65 N. Catalina
Pasadena, CA 91106

Sargent-Welch Scientific Co.
911 Commerce Ct.
Buffalo Grove, IL 60089

Scholastic Software
730 Broadway
New York, NY 10003

Scott Resources
P.O. Box 2121F
Ft. Collins, CO 80522

Society for Visual Education
1345 Diversey Parkway
Chicago, IL 60614-1299

Tom Snyder Productions
80 Coolidge Hill Rd.
Watertown, MA 02172

Videodiscovery, Inc.
1700 Westlake Ave. N.
Suite 600
Seattle, WA 98109-3012

SELECTED SUPPLIERS OF COMPUTER SOFTWARE FOR ELEMENTARY SCIENCE

Apple Computer Co.
20525 Mariana Ave.
Cupertino, CA 95014

Carolina Biological Supply Co.
2700 York Rd.
Burlington, NC 27215

Denoyer-Geppert Science Co.
5225 Ravenswood Ave.
Chicago, IL 60640-2028

Emerging Technology Consultants, Inc.
P.O. Box 120444
St. Paul, MN 55112

Eureka!
Lawrence Hall of Science
University of California
Berkeley, CA 94720

MECC
6160 Summit Dr. North
Minneapolis, MN 55430-4003

Milliken Pub. Co.
P.O. Box 21579
St. Louis, MO 63132-0579

Optical Data Corp.
30 Technology Dr.
Warren, NJ 07059

Scholastic Software
730 Broadway
New York, NY 10003

Society for Visual Education
1345 Diversey Parkway
Chicago, IL 60614-1299

Special Times, Special Education Software
Cambridge Development Laboratory, Inc.
214 Third Ave.
Waltham, MA 02154

Wings for Learning/Sunburst
1600 Green Hills Rd.
P.O. Box 660002
Scotts Valley, CA 95067-9908

Videodiscovery, Inc.
1700 Westlake Ave. N., Suite 600
Seattle, WA 98109-3012

Printed in the United States
44606LVS00009B/1-2